JUDGES

Readings: A New Biblical Commentary

General Editor
John Jarick

JUDGES

Roger Ryan

SHEFFIELD PHOENIX PRESS

2007

Copyright © Sheffield Phoenix Press, 2007

Published by Sheffield Phoenix Press
Department of Biblical Studies, University of Sheffield
Sheffield S10 2TN

www.sheffieldphoenix.com

A CIP catalogue record for this book
is available from the British Library

Typeset by Vikatan Publishing Solutions, Chennai, India

Printed by Lightning Source

ISBN 978-1-906055-23-3 (hardback)
ISBN 978-1-906055-24-0 (paperback)

Contents

Preface

The 'reading' that follows is neither a revised nor an updated doctoral thesis written in university-speak. However, I hope it will be viewed as an accessible version—prepared for the general reader—of research on the book of Judges which was submitted to the University of Oxford for the degree of Doctor of Philosophy in 2005. In that work I attempt to give positive readings of the characters of judge-deliverers (chs. 3-16) against the consensus of scholars who generally understand them to be negative role models and anti-heroes. Even though my two manuscripts are different in style, purpose and presentation, both have a similar focus.

Although I am a Christian church minister, it is not my purpose to suggest how the Christian faith may be taught with reference to Judges by the hermeneutic principles of typology, analogy and parallels in order to illustrate the New Testament. Such a task may be attempted in a further study. It is my purpose to explain Judges in order to assist readers to understand the book in its historical and literary context.

I am grateful to have had the interest and support of a most considerate and encouraging supervisor in Dr John Jarick, tutor in Old Testament at St Stephen's House, Oxford, and for his kind invitation to contribute 'a reading' to the series from work which he has seen emerge during recent years. I am especially grateful to Professor John Barton of Oriel College, Oxford, who kindly read my research in essay form and made helpful suggestions. I wish to thank my examiners for giving their time to consider my work, to Dr Paul Joyce of St Peter's College, Oxford and Professor Gordon Wenham of the University of Gloucestershire. I have valued the helpful and generous comments of colleagues in Oxford in response to my seminar presentations. I also thank my friend and colleague, the Reverend Canon Dick Lewis, vicar of Christchurch and St Mark's, North Watford, for his support.

I am so very grateful to those who have shown generous interest in my work, read earlier drafts of the 'reading' and made helpful comments, to my wife Pauline and to the Ven. Christopher Skilton, the Archdeacon of Lambeth.

The reading is dedicated to Pauline, to our three daughters, Sarah, Vanessa and Zoe and to the members of my congregation at St Mary's Summerstown, in the Diocese of Southwark, who gave their long-term support to the project, winced through a Sunday morning expository sermon series and followed an imaginative retelling of Judges-stories for children.

Summerstown, London SW17

January 2007

Abbreviations

AB	Anchor Bible
AlEth	*Alcheringa Ethnopoetics*
BBC	Blackwell Bible Commentaries
BSac	*Bibliotheca Sacra*
BSC	Bible Student's Commentary
CBC	Cambridge Bible Commentary
CBQ	*Catholic Biblical Quarterly*
CBSC	Cambridge Bible for Schools and Colleges
DSBS	Daily Study Bible Series
ErIsr	*Eretz Israel*
ICC	International Critical Commentary
JBL	*Journal of Biblical Literature*
JNES	*Journal of Near Eastern Studies*
JSJSup	*Journal for the Study of Judaism*, Supplement Series
JSOT	*Journal for the Study of the Old Testament*
JSOTSup	*Journal for the Study of the Old Testament*, Supplement Series
JSS	*Journal of Semitic Studies*
Ko	*Koinionia*
ᴌxx	Alfred Rahlfs (ed.), *Septuaginta: id est Vetus Testamentum Graece Iuxta LXX Interpretes.* (Stuttgart: Privilegierte Württembergische Bibelanstalt, 1935)
ᴍᴛ	Masoretic Text
NAC	New American Commentary
NCB	New Century Bible
NCBC	New Cambridge Bible Commentary
ɴᴇʙ	*New English Bible*
NIB	Leander E. Keck *et al.* (eds.), *New Interpreter's Bible* (Nashville, TN: Abingdon, 1998)
NIBC	*New International Biblical Commentary*
NIVAC	New International Version Application Commentary
ɴʀsᴠ	New Revised Standard Version
OTG	Old Testament Guides
OTL	Old Testament Library
RTR	*Reformed Theological Review*
SBB	Soncino Books of the Bible

SBL	Society of Biblical Literature
Scr	*Scripture*
SJT	*Scottish Journal of Theology*
TynBul	*Tyndale Bulletin*

An Invitation

Come with me into the dangerous ancient world of biblical Israel inhabited by heroes, heroines, hissable villains, a chorus of naughty Israelites, countless silent victims and Yahweh the God of Israel who does whatever it takes to win his people back from the gods of Canaan to covenant loyalty.

- Read about Othniel who wins a bride as a reward for single-handedly taking a city in which Israel's warriors show no interest. Could this be the storyteller's brief outline of an ancient love story? Discover how Israel's war hero takes on and defeats a grisly world-class oppressor and brings peace to the land.
- Meet Ehud, Israel's civil servant, who makes a wooden dagger which he hides beneath his clothing. He gains access to an oppressive king's private apartment where he commits the perfect murder. Ehud makes his escape and, after calling out the Israelite army, slaughters the robust Moabite invaders who have oppressed Israel for eighteen years.
- Pause to take in the heroism of Shamgar who is not to be overlooked.
- Marvel over the courageous Barak who charges down a mountainside on foot as he leads his warriors to defeat an oppressor equipped with iron chariots and unknown numbers of infantry.
- Gasp as Jael, the woman who—when home-alone—deceives and slaughters an oppressor charioteer rapist by securing his head to the floor with a tent peg and hammer.
- Sing along with Deborah as she celebrates with glee the triumphs of Yahweh because her people are free at last from twenty years of oppression.
- Follow Gideon as he changes overnight from cynic to popular hero. He defeats vast numbers of invaders with a token force by simply standing still and making a lot of noise!

- Be horrified at Abimelech, a nasty man, a very nasty man indeed, who slaughters his rival half-brothers. Then beam with delight as the wheels of retribution turn in his direction.
- Be intrigued by the story of Jephthah who is first betrayed by his family, then head-hunted to be army commander and tribal leader. As the result of a vow made under duress, he is obliged to sacrifice his daughter. Be further intrigued when the identity of the story's prime-mover is revealed.
- Be amused at the stupidity of Philistines who take the baite and attempt to answer Samson's unanswerable riddle. Discover how Samson, armed only with a dog's dinner (a bone), is able to slaughter a thousand Philistines! Even though disabled and alone he is still able to kill even more Philistines and to demonstrate that their non-existent god is a creation of their own imaginations.
- Be aghast at the grim stories in the final chapters, weep with the victims and wonder how it is that anyone survives.
- Ponder the complex character of Israel's God (Yahweh) who manipulates nations and characters as he drives their stories forward. Yahweh uses any means available in order to secure the loyalty of wayward Israelites. When reason and argument fail, intimidation and violence are employed. When intimidation and violence fail, Yahweh only speaks when he is spoken to.
- Ask yourself: for what purpose did an ancient storyteller collect these violent claret-soaked stories in which mercy, compassion and forgiveness are lacking and retell them in bright, bold colours against the sweeping panoramas of the ancient world? Judges is fraught with shocking episodes of real violence which are presented raw on the page but are neither glorified nor trivialized.

The book of Judges was written by an ancient scribe who dared to be dark. Do not imagine that you know what is going to happen next or who will do what to whom or why in this intriguing unpredictable distant story-world in which characters take enormous risks with their lives and readers are treated like mature adults. The reading which follows allows an ancient text to breathe.

Introduction

Judges is Understood in this Reading as...

... a collection of stories from Israel's past arranged in a chronological scheme which tells how Israelites ignore their covenant with Yahweh (Josh. 24) in preference to the gods of the land. Israelites choose the easy option and live in peaceful co-existence with the inhabitants rather than engaging in battle for the exclusive rights to the sacred turf. The land is successively overrun by oppressive invaders. When Israelites cry out for help, heroic deliverers or judges bring peace to the land. In the concluding chapters Yahweh says little and does less; Israelites deal with their problems as best they can.

Who Wrote Judges?

In Jewish tradition it is thought that Samuel was the author. However, as no author is named in the text, Judges is assumed to be anonymous. Suggestions are proposed for possible authorship, for example: Huldah the prophetess (2 Kgs 22.14-20; 1 Chron. 34.22-28), Jeremiah and/or his scribe Baruch ben Neriah (Jer. 36.4). Scholars refer to 'the Deuteromomist' which is abbreviated to 'Dtr'. The author could be a historian, a theologian, a lawyer, an editor. My preference is to refer to the author as a 'storyteller' because what we are reading is a collection of stories.

When was Judges Written?

Probably in the sixth century BCE.

Target Audience

I propose that Judges was written for exiled Israelites in Assyria, Egypt and Babylon such as those who sit on river banks and cry for the restoration of their land and homes as they ask among themselves how they have arrived at such a desperate situation (Ps. 137).

Big Ideas and Take Home Messages

Israelites who listen as the text is read aloud are given four warnings. First, stay loyal to Yahweh. Second, do not lose your national and religious identity. Third, do not assimilate with the inhabitants of the land. Fourth, Yahweh will use any means to retain your covenant loyalty; he may summon oppressors and he may not answer when you call.

For a longer scholarly introduction to Judges see my 'Afterword' (pp. 169-212). But first, let's accept the invitation to read a reading.

Judges 1:
Prologue (Israel's Successes and Failures)

Israelites have arrived in the land and are spoiling for a fight. But they have a problem: they are leaderless. Joshua is dead and battle orders are required. So they ask Yahweh, the God of Israel, not to choose a leader, but to identify the tribe that will resume the conquest and dispossess the Canaanite inhabitants of their homes. Judah is nominated; the land is theirs for the taking.

Even though we are pulled into the story without preamble, the opening sentences present us with an unpleasant proposition. Israelites do not want to negotiate for a fair division of the land; they do not offer rent, make lease agreements or pay a deposit. Israelites do not request Yahweh's advice about peaceful co-existence in order to get along with their new neighbours. Israelites want to force the Canaanite inhabitants from their homes. Neither they nor Yahweh show any sensitivity to the local culture when hostilities are commenced. We may consider that an injustice is proposed but the storyteller is unconcerned. A story is to be told and Yahweh responds to Israel's request with a terse but affirming answer. Judah may go to war.

The prologue is a chronological and geographical account of Israel's attacks upon the Canaanite inhabitants. Initial success is followed by failure when Israelites settle for co-existence.

The background to Israel's request and to Yahweh's response may be explained by the following: Yahweh promises a specific area of land to Abraham and to his descendants (Gen. 12.1-3). In Moses' conquest instructions he says that Yahweh will defeat and subdue the inhabitants who will be dispossessed and destroyed. The gift of occupied land to Israel is explained as Yahweh's act of judgment upon the wickedness of the inhabitants (Deut. 9.1-5; cf. Lev. 18; Deut. 18.9-14; Wis. 12.3-11). Yahweh instructs Joshua in a war oracle to enter and take possession by force of arms (Josh. 1.1-9). Some nations, however, remain *in situ* in order to give Israel combat experience and to test Israel's loyalty to Yahweh (Judg. 3.1, 4).

So, Israelites have arrived from Egypt. No sympathy is expressed for the inhabitants who occupy the sacred turf. Canaanites have the status of mere trespassers. Any sympathy that we may have will be directed to the injustice which gives Judges its negative story structure: Israelites ignore Yahweh, the God who brought them out of Egypt, in favour of local gods. Our sympathies are directed to Yahweh, the God of Israel, rather than to the residents of the land. Judges is written from Yahweh's point of view and it is assumed that we will read the text uncritically and from Yahweh's point of view.

However, according to the prologue, Israel's so-called successful 'conquest' of the land is limited to the highlands. Either the tribes are not strong enough to carry out eviction or they lack the fighting spirit required for conquest.

Successes (vv. 1-20, 22-27)

The inquiry about the resumption of conflict with the Canaanites is the sort of request which is made to a priest. Such requests are generally about which of the tribes are to take the initiative in battle (1.1; 20.18) or which alternative option is to be taken, such as whether or not to embark on a course of action, whether to go to war or desist (18.5; 20.23, 27; cf. 1 Sam. 14.37). When the answer is perceived to be Judah, Simeon's support is enlisted, apparently because their allotted territory is within Judah's inheritance area (Josh. 19.9). Israel's attack is not a haphazard taking of any land but the seizure of what is called 'allotted territory' or 'inheritance' of occupied land as precisely apportioned by lot (Josh. 14-19).

The Judah–Simeon alliance makes a good start when Canaanite and Perizzite tribes are defeated and the local lord of Bezek flees the battlefield. The treatment of the Canaanite leader, when he is apprehended, may be considered extreme (Judg. 1.6), but it is Bezek himself who accepts the mutilation of his hands and feet as a just retribution from God because—following his own victories—it was also his custom to disable defeated enemy kings by butchering their hands and feet and enjoying their fumbling attempts to pick up food like dogs from beneath his table. The number of Bezek's 'seventy' defeated and mutilated kings may be a storyteller's synonym for 'many', such as Gideon's 'seventy' sons (8.30; 9.5). The storyteller will return to the retribution theme in the Abimelech story (ch. 9).

Hebron, which has the obscure local name *Kiriath-arba*, meaning 'city of four'—perhaps referring to four settlements in the Hebron area—is also taken. Caleb, who is a surviving respected and noble leader of the older Israelite generation that left Egypt, defeats and expels the three sons of Anak (v. 20; cf. Josh. 15.14) who may be the survivors of an earlier defeat by Joshua (Josh. 11.21-22). *Anak* means 'long-necked', which indicates tall men or giants in an episode that suggests Caleb's courageous attack upon those whom Israel fears in the report from his reconnoitre of the land (cf. Num. 13).

The next for seizure is Debir, which bears a name associated with a temple sanctuary or shrine. Debir has an obscure former name and is known among the locals as *Kiriath-sepher,* which may indicate a city associated with religious scrolls or the keeping of local livestock records. A related question needs to be addressed: why does Caleb offer his daughter Achsah as a matrimonial incentive to whoever captures this particular city? Maybe she is a desirable marriage prospect who has attracted the attention of suitors, and should one of them take Debir that would decide the matter for a harassed father? May Debir be a desirable acquisition that presents Caleb with the opportunity of marrying off a plain and portly daughter to a capable warrior? May Debir be strongly defended and its capture require the extra inducement of marriage into a prestigious family? Even though he has acquired honour as Israel's giant-killer, Caleb himself may be too old or too war-weary to participate in further conflict.

The reason for a daughter being offered as a prize is, however, more straightforward. Israel's warriors do not want to be troubled with a city inhabited by scribes in an age when few, if any, can use, or see any value in, the new technology of writing and reading. Neither will catch on! If Debir had contained desirable spoils such as precious metals or a valuable water supply, no further inducement would be required. Israelites need an incentive to leave their tents and engage in conflict for a city associated with scribes, records and scrolls.

We are not told how the city is defended, or how it is taken, if it is attacked by a frontal assault or if resistance is offered. We are simply informed that Othniel, who is either Caleb's younger brother or nephew, does the deed and wins a bride. Lack of information invites speculation. Is there a romantic story hidden in the shadows and gaps of selective storytelling? Could it be that Achsah and Othniel already know one another and are they sweethearts? Does the information that Othniel is related to Caleb—a detail that the storyteller intriguingly provides— somehow prevent them from making their love known until she is offered as a prize which accompanies a territorial conquest opportunity? May the full story be untold because romance is too soppy a digression to be included among robust accounts of conquest and heroism? Our storyteller has no time for romantic interludes.

Achsah, whose playful name means bangle or bracelet, does not fare as badly as we may anticipate. Although she is crudely offered as a human prize to any able warrior, she is given to a warrior who acquires honour. Othniel possesses the spoil of a Canaanite city by right of conquest and gains the reputation and status of Israel's war hero. Othniel's marriage—unlike marriages of other Israelite males (Judg. 3.6)—is within Israel. Moreover, the storyteller allows Achsah to make an entrance; she is more than someone's daughter or a trophy-wife. Achsah takes initiatives. Unusually for female characters in the Old Testament she is given character and speech as well as a name. She has been crudely used as a female prize in a male world of conflict; now she seizes the opportunity to present her own demands. Her language is robust; she is not hesitant, timid or in awe of her father or of her new heroic husband. It appears that Achsah has unfinished family business with her father and she uses her new status—not only as his daughter but as the bride of Israel's new champion—to enhance her inheritance.

Who is it that Achsah approaches with a request for watered land—Othniel or Caleb? Does she urge her new husband to ask her father for a dowry or does she urge her father directly to give her land when she arrives seated on a donkey? The Hebrew word which is translated 'urge' (Judg. 1.14, NRSV) is only used here by our storyteller but is used elsewhere when one character manipulates another to do something evil such as when Jezebel incites King Ahab (1 Kgs 21.25). However, it does not appear that Achsah has an unscrupulous end in view. Like other Hebrew women in Judges, she is clever and shrewd. Some may think she urges Othniel to act as an intermediary and make a request of her father, which is in the mutual interest of both herself and her new husband. What she does is to lay a family obligation directly upon her father. Achsah has been 'used' as a prize; now she takes the opportunity for advancement which is presented when she asks for a gift of choice watered land. There are no pleasantries and Caleb is denied a daughter's gracious greeting. She makes her demand, 'give me a present'.

The NEB translation is unfortunately misleading when it reads, 'as she [Achsah] sat on the ass, *she broke wind*, and Caleb said, "What do you mean by that?"' (Judg. 1.14). This exchange is corrected in more recent translations to read: 'As she *dismounted* from her donkey, Caleb said to her, "What do you want?"' (NRSV). What the storyteller says is that when she makes her entrance, she simply dismounts from a donkey. The reason why her father asks what she wants is not because her arrival is accompanied by an unladylike gesture of a personal nature, but because he is embarrassed—and so he should be—that he has just offered her as a public inducement to *anyone* who will capture a Canaanite city of limited value.

A daughter faces her father. She looks him in the eye. Her hands are on her hips. She frowns. She is focused. She says her piece and there is steel in her voice. She demands land with a water supply and she wants it now! But Achsah will not be fobbed off with any land. She is location specific. She already possesses land in the dry Negeb; now she demands the additional 'blessing' of a water supply, and *gullot mayim* (which appropriately means 'bowls of water', v. 15; Josh. 15.18-19) will do very nicely. Achsah, like other female characters in Judges, seizes the day; she lays a family obligation on her father which is in the mutual interest of herself and her new husband. Achsah has been used by her father; now her turn arrives. How can a father refuse? Caleb grants his daughter more than she demands; she is given two water supplies, the upper and the lower. There is more to Achsah than a trophy-trinket on offer as a matrimonial prize in a patriarchal world of conflict.

The local name 'city of palms' (Judg. 1.16) is thought to be Jericho (3.13; Deut. 34.3) from which Kenites, who are related to Moses, migrate south with the Judahites to Arad. Kenites may also live among nomadic Amalekites (cf. 1 Sam. 15.6). The storyteller will mention the Kenites and their settlements later when Israel is threatened by Sisera and his iron chariots (Judg. 4).

The storyteller's next conquest episode presents us with an abrupt ethical-alert! Not only is the city of Zephthah captured but the Canaanite inhabitants are 'devoted to destruction' (Judg.

1.17, NRSV) by the Judah–Simeon alliance. The Hebrew word *ḥērem*—which is sometimes misleadingly referred to as 'the ban'—is a code word for the separation, destruction and ritual sacrifice to Yahweh of those who inhabit the land. It is at Yahweh's command that Canaanites are to be utterly destroyed, including men, women, children and livestock with their goods, gods and religious infrastructure (cf. Deut. 7.1-2; 13.16; 20.17). However, there is no command from Yahweh to specifically destroy the inhabitants of Zephthah even though the alliance adopts the same conquest methods as Joshua at Jericho, Ai, Makkedh and other cities (Josh. 6.17-21; 8.26; 10.28-40). Moreover, the storyteller is unconcerned that the annihilation of a population will be unacceptable to later readers when Zephath is left in ruins and the site renamed *Hormāh* (or 'Cursed' in the Greek translation [LXX B]), a name which vividly keeps alive in local memory the fate of its former inhabitants.

This is not the place for an extended discussion about Yahweh's conquest commands for Israel to utterly destroy the Canaanites by the *ḥērem* war ritual. What can be said here is that ancient people were very different to us; they lived in a different world and held a different world-view. This is not to suggest we are superior to people of the past; rather, that which may trouble us did not trouble them. The reasons for such a brutal strategy in Israel's warfare—which was not unknown in the ancient Near East—is because the land is already occupied and Israelites are not to assimilate or to make covenants with the inhabitants. Canaanites are to be exterminated because they are in the wrong place; they occupy the land. They also pose a threat to Israel's religious identity which unbalances Israel's world. Israel's future is threatened by others and matters are to be corrected by the removal of that threat. The total destruction of a population was how things were done in the distant past; it was how settlers claimed new land, how battles were conducted, how wars were concluded. The elimination of the occupants by the *ḥērem* war ritual—a practice which is nowhere regretted in the Old Testament—enabled settlers to live in peace. The practice of taking no prisoners is to be understood as part of the struggle for land among the peoples of the ancient world which removed rivals and predators. We may consider such a prospect to be outrageous, particularly when we think of the horrific events of the modern world such as 'genocide' and 'ethnic cleansing' during this century and the last. What is also a matter of moral concern is that the extermination of a city's population is not perceived by the Judges storyteller to be an immoral act but a war ritual which is acceptable to Yahweh as a part of Israel's conquest of the land. A further episode of a population's 'consecration to destruction' is yet to be told (Judg. 21.10-11).

Judah's successful conquest seizures continue when taking the coastal cities in which the storyteller will later place the Philistines (chs. 14–16), Gaza, Ashkelon and Ekron. None of the cities are renamed and the inhabitants are not 'devoted' or annihilated.

A surveillance team is sent by the 'house' of Joseph to reconnoitre Bethel in order to identify the prospects for taking the city (1.23). The spies either threaten an inhabitant or make an offer which he is obliged to accept—he is to show them how they may enter his city in return for a safe passage for himself and his family. The inhabitants of Bethel are slaughtered but there is no mention of consecration to Yahweh or total destruction (*ḥērem*). A safe-passage story is also told when a similar 'kindness' is shown to Rahab who also betrays her neighbours to advancing Israelites (Josh. 2.12). The Bethel 'traitor' and his family escape to safety and he builds his own city in Hittite territory to which he nostalgically gives the name Luz, the former name of Bethel (Judg. 1.26). Bethel becomes an Israelite cultic site (2.1; 20.18, 26, 31; 21.2, 19) and the location for the ark of the covenant (20.27).

Failures (vv. 21, 27-36)

Judah's conquest successes are limited to the highlands. The tribe is unable to defeat the Canaanites who occupy the lowlands because they are equipped with iron chariots (*barzel*, 1.19) and possess strategic advantage over infantry. The storyteller will show in two accounts—preserved in narrative and verse (chs. 4 and 5)—that Sisera's 900 'iron' chariots give his army military advantage with the ability to oppress Israel for twenty years.

Other tribes also fail to evict the inhabitants: Benjamin (1.21), Manasseh (v. 27), Ephraim (v. 29) and Asher (vv. 31-32). It is unclear if Canaanite resistance is offered or if Israelites lose interest and opt for co-existence. When the remaining tribes take up residence in their allotted territory, they make no attempt to attack or expel the inhabitants. It appears they merely co-exist as Israel's neighbours. Israel does no more than hire the Canaanites as their labour force. Rather than going to the extremes of either annihilation or assimilation, when they are established in the land, Zebulun (v. 30) and Naphtali (v. 33) put the locals to work (v. 28). Israelites use Canaanites in much the same way as they were worked by the Egyptians. The nature of the work is not specified but it appears that Israel becomes economically dependent on the inhabitants as a subservient slave class.

Danites are restricted by the Amorites to the highlands and later migrate north (v. 34; cf. ch. 18).

To summarize, the prologue has a specific narrative function. Exilic listeners are to share a sense of shame when initial success is localized and unsustained. Three tribes are able to defeat the Canaanites with the assistance of Yahweh (vv. 4, 22). The fate of the inhabitants of one defeated city is uncertain and the inhabitants of two cities are unsparingly slaughtered. The lowlands are defended by Canaanites equipped with iron chariots. No attempt appears to be made by Israel's other tribes to dispossess the inhabitants. Israelites settle for co-existence and become economically dependent on the Canaanites who are made to be a servant class which represents the making of a covenant of sorts. No mention is made of any attempt to destroy the Canaanite religious system.

The storyteller also writes to impress exilic listeners with the courage and ability of selective individuals: Caleb is the giant-killer; Othniel—who will appear again as Yahweh's first judge-deliverer (3.9)—captures a city, wins a bride and makes a good marriage within Israel; Achsah acts in the economic interest of herself and her new heroic husband and is given a dowry of choice watered real-estate.

Israel's occupation of the land is patchy and localized, a combination of success and failure. Israelites have been warned not to assimilate with the inhabitants but they choose the softer option of peaceful co-existence. In the following chapter the storyteller wears a different hat when making theological comments about Israel's situation from Yahweh's point of view.

Judges 2:
Theological Perspective

Rebuke (vv. 1-5)

Yahweh's glum messenger arrives in Bochim from Gilgal and addresses Israel.

Gilgal is where Israel crossed the Jordan and the site of Joshua's camp and Israel's first home in the land which is marked with twelve stones, taken from the river bed, and set in a circle as a reminder to Israelites and a teaching aid for children that keeps the memory of their past alive (Josh. 4.19-24). The stones identify the place where Yahweh dried up the Jordan and Israel crossed into the land. The stone circle is a significant aid to memory about Israel's past. It is also the site where Joshua received Yahweh's instructions for a second circumcision of males, where the passover is celebrated in the land for the first time and where Israelites first ate a meal prepared from the produce of the land (Josh. 5.2, 10-11; cf. Deut. 8.7-9). The stones are placed at the site where Joshua met one who identified himself as the prince or commander of Yahweh's army and gave instructions for the Jericho campaign (Josh. 5.13ff). It is from this prestigious site—associated with the faithful fulfilment of all that Yahweh has promised—that his messenger arrives at Bochim with a grim message for 'all Israel'.

The messenger's speech is not one of welcome or commendation for Israel's successful land seizure. A dreadful reprimand is issued for the cultivation of co-existence with the Canaanite inhabitants. Yahweh's messenger first reminds 'all Israel' what Yahweh did for them in the past: they escaped Egyptian slavery and are now resident in the land which was promised to their ancestors. Yahweh has kept his promises; Israelites have not. Israel has been instructed not to make a covenant with the Canaanites but to destroy their religious infrastructure. Yahweh's instructions have been ignored. Israel is therefore to look at what Israel *has* done—at the catalogue of failure itemized above. For the future, Canaanites will remain as their adversaries in the land. They will be ensnared by the lure of their gods. The inhabitants will cause pain and distress, they will be as painful as thorns in their eyes and at their sides (cf. Num. 33.55; Josh. 23.12-13). Yahweh will do nothing to assist with their expulsion. The rebuke of Yahweh's messenger is similar to the rebuke of a prophet (Judg. 6.7) and to Yahweh's direct communication with Israel (10.10-16).

The location for the messenger's speech is given an appropriate name. Bochim suggests 'weeping', which describes 'all Israel's' emotional response to Yahweh's reprimand. The storyteller does not say whether Israel's tears are for what Israel has done or an acknowledgment for Israel's failures. The eyes of Israelites are not filled with tears of repentance. Moreover, there is no indication of the nature of Israel's 'sacrifice' (2.5). At Bochim, Israelites are merely sorry for themselves.

Israel's Apostasy

The storyteller's theological account of Israel's apostasy and the story cycle that follows is less than complementary. Israelites fail to keep their oaths of loyalty to Yahweh and to their covenant renewal (Josh. 24). Yahweh is abandoned in preference to the local gods of the land. When Israel 'serves' Canaanite deities in preference to Yahweh, the storyteller points our sympathy towards Israel's neglected and rejected deity. According to the storyteller's theological perspective, Israel's conduct is evaluated as 'evil'. Moreover, Yahweh is not an indifferent bystander. Yahweh observes everything, burns with anger and becomes threatening, intimidating and violent. It is not that powerful nations are merely 'allowed'—as in ancient people movements—to oppress an apostate Israel. Oppressive nations act as Yahweh's commissioned agents when he 'sells' and 'gives' Israel into the hands of others. Israel's oppression is Yahweh-sponsored. Israelites whinge and complain under the consequences of their own bad behaviour, that is, until Yahweh has a change of mind.

The theological explanation discloses the storyteller's disapproval of Israel's behaviour. Israel's past is not 'beefed-up' with imaginative stories of their courageously winning the land by overcoming overwhelming odds in order to impress us with happy endings. The theological account of Israel's apostasy is told *against* Israel and from Yahweh's point of view. Israelites are shown up as an apostate nation who turn against the God who delivered them from oppressive foreign slavery and brought them into a desirable land.

The storyteller's theological perspective as a whole begins with a brief narrative detail when Joshua sends the Israelites to claim their land inheritance (Judg. 2.6). The perspective concludes with apostate Israelites living in co-existence with the local inhabitants; they intermarry and serve Canaanite gods. Israel's disloyalty to Yahweh and threat of assimilation among the inhabitants become the central theological issues of Judges.

Yahweh has brought Israelites out of Egyptian slavery. They have been guided and protected as they moved from the wilderness into a choice land of prosperity and plenty. Yahweh has kept all his covenant promises (Exod. 34.10-11) and Israel is secure. Moreover, Yahweh has defeated all who offered resistance along the way. Joshua's call for Israel's wholehearted loyalty to Yahweh at the Shechem covenant renewal ceremony receives a positive response when Israelites make an unequivocal oath of loyalty:

> Far be it from us that we should forsake the Lord to serve other gods; for it is the Lord our God who brought us and our ancestors up from the land of Egypt, out of the house of slavery, and who did those great signs in our sight. He protected us along all the way that we went, and among all the peoples through whom we passed; and the Lord drove out before us all the peoples, the Amorites who lived in the land. Therefore we also will serve the Lord, for he is our God (Josh. 24.16-18, NRSV).

However, Israelites are only loyal to Yahweh during the remaining years of Joshua's life and the lives of the elders who were eyewitness to the great works that Yahweh did for Israel since leaving Egypt. Restraint is cast aside and Israelites give way to the attraction of the local gods. This act of apostasy comes about because parents fail to keep alive the imaginations of their children with the memory of Yahweh's saving acts. For example, Moses anticipated that families would continue with their unique way of life and religious practice which marks them out as the loyal people of Yahweh. When children ask their parents about the significance of the decrees, statutes and ordinances which they follow, parents are to take the opportunity to tell the stories about how Yahweh kept his promises by bringing them out of Egyptian slavery and how they are to live in the land (Exod.

13.11-16; cf. Deut. 6.20-25). However, parents neglect the moral and ceremonial regulations and the educational value of covenant ceremonies for their children who see nothing distinctive about how their parents conduct their lives. The children's questions, which Moses anticipated would be forthcoming, are unasked. Israel's shared memories and stories die with the wilderness generation (cf. Deut. 4.9-10; 6.6-9; 6.20; 11.19; 31.12-13; 32.46). When Yahweh's stories are forgotten, Yahweh is forgotten.

How is Israel's rising generation to serve Yahweh and obey his commandments if his commandments are not taught? After Joshua's death young Israelites have no interest in either Yahweh or in their past. Israelites are unaware of the necessity of keeping covenant loyalties. Their past is ignored because they are focused on the opportunities presented in the new land. Yahweh is yesterday's god.

The Attraction of 'New' Gods and Yahweh's Response to Israel's Disloyalty (vv. 11-23)

To 'serve' a god (v. 11) means to acknowledge the god as lord of every area of life and existence. Israel has been warned that such service is to be for Yahweh exclusively (Deut. 6.13; 10.12). The warning not to 'serve' other gods is one of the theological themes of the book of Deuteronomy (7.4, 16) and of Joshua's covenant renewal (Josh. 23.7). However, once in residence, Israelites make their own way in the land and co-exist among the Canaanites. Israel prefers local gods to the lordship of Yahweh. Inter-marriage follows (Judg. 3.6).

Two Canaanite deities specifically attract Israel's attention. The name *baal* can mean 'lord', 'owner' or even 'husband'. When the storyteller refers to 'the baals' (2.11; 3.7; 8.33; 10.6, 10) it is to local representations of the Canaanite storm and fertility god 'Baal' (2.13). The baals are installed as cultic lords or patrons of shrines at places or districts which bear a name such as Baal-hermon (3.3) and Baal-berith (8.33). Baal is the Canaanite weather god of storm and rain who in antiquity was identified as the 'lord of the earth' and 'the rider of the clouds' who opened windows in the heavens and dispensed dew, rain and snow. Asherah (2.13; 10.6) or Ashtoreth (3.7) is a Canaanite goddess who is represented in local wooden cultic poles or pillars (6.25-30) and known in antiquity as the patron of fertility. There is very little description in the Old Testament of how Baal and his female consorts are worshipped. The Elijah stories demonstrate that rain and the fertility of the soil does not depend on an inactive and nonexistent deity but on Yahweh (1 Kgs 18.38) who provides the 'dew of heaven' for the 'fatness of the earth' (Gen. 27.28).

The Canaanite gods of the land are fundamental for human existence because they are thought to be the providers of economic success and prosperity. Such a god is Baal who, accompanied by a goddess consort, is established as local god in residence. The evidence of Baal's work is evidently all around for newcomers to see in a prosperous land which 'flows with milk and honey' (Num. 13.27); moreover, the land possesses

> flowing streams, with springs and underground waters welling up in valleys and hills, a land of wheat and barley, of vines and fig trees and pomegranates, a land of olive trees and honey, a land where you may eat bread without scarcity, where you will lack nothing, a land whose stones are iron and from whose hills you may mine copper (Deut. 8.7-9, NRSV).

Young Israelites are impressed with the gods of the land who evidently make luxurious provision for their devotees. Yahweh is unacknowledged as the provider of the land's food and resources (Deut. 8.10). The emerging generation of Israelites use the methods of a more settled agricultural economy, which is dependent on rain for its fertility and produce. The gods who are credited with providing rainfall hold particular attraction.

Israel is focused on the future and interested in the gods who patronize the land *now*. Yesterday's god is redundant. Israel's expectations for the future are high. Israel has invested everything on residence in the land and a return to Egypt is no longer contemplated (Num. 11.5, 18). Yahweh is abandoned and forgotten.

However, Israel's God is not indifferent. The storyteller uses a quaint Hebrew metaphor for Yahweh's anger when we are informed that 'his nose becomes hot' (Judg. 2.14, 20). Yahweh does not respond with a fire or a plague, nor is the land blighted. Yahweh's method is to send plunderers; some demand tribute, others loot Israel's harvest. On each occasion Israel is overpowered and oppressed. Yahweh does not flinch from disposing of disloyal Israelites as he pleases when he 'gives' and 'sells' Israel to those whom Yahweh strengthens for the purpose (3.12). Israel's disloyalty is met with Yahweh's opposition (Deut. 28.25, 30-34, 48ff; Lev. 26.17, 36-39). When Israel attempts self-defence or attack, Yahweh does nothing and Israel is defeated (Judg. 2.15; cf. 20.19-21, 24-25).

Yahweh and Israel have mutually agreed to a covenant. When Israelites forget the covenant and abandon Yahweh in favour of local gods, Yahweh becomes angry and makes a conflict opportunity of Israel for powerful plundering nations. A scheme emerges. Yahweh's judgment on Israel is by invasion and oppression. When Israel cries out for deliverance Yahweh takes the initiative by providing the solution to Israel's oppression and raises up judges who deliver Israel from Yahweh's plunderers. While Israel welcomes deliverance, Israel pays no heed to the delivering judges and in time returns to the gods of the land. Even after being delivered, Israel continues to behave like an unfaithful marriage partner favouring the local baals in preference to Yahweh.

The storyteller explains that Yahweh's provision of judge-deliverers is due to a 'change of mind' when compassion replaces anger. When Yahweh hears Israel's groaning, he becomes sympathetic and regrets being the cause of Israel's distress (v. 18). Yahweh's change of mind is not a repentance issue. Yahweh simply makes a policy change from anger at Israel's apostasy to compassion about Israel's oppression. However, any loyalty that Israel shows to Yahweh is short-lived: once the delivering judge dies, Israelites return to Canaanite gods. Yahweh complains that Israelites are like untrainable oxen who wander away and become more stubborn than their ancestors (v. 19; cf. Exod. 32.9; 33.3; Deut. 9.6, 13; 10.6; 31.27).

Yahweh's scheme to restore a wayward Israel becomes a 'cycle' of repetition when the storyteller gives Yahweh speech. Israel is not owned as '*my* people' but referred to with contempt as '*this* people' because they have briskly walked away (Judg. 2.20) from a covenant which Israel has not only agreed but renewed. Again Yahweh changes his mind and this time goes to the extreme of deciding not to evict the remaining nations from the land. The continued presence of the inhabitants will test Israel's obedience in a public examination of their conduct (v. 22) in which both Israel and Yahweh, and anyone who is interested, will know Israel's worth in comparison with their ancestors (cf. Exod. 17.7).

Theological Summary

Some of the features from the storyteller's theological perspective will be repeated in the introduction and conclusion to the cycle of stories that follow:

- Yahweh and Israel make a covenant of mutual loyalty (Exod. 21-23) which both parties renew (Josh. 24).
- Israel abandons Yahweh in favour of local Canaanite deities (Judg. 2.11-12, 19; 3.6).
- Yahweh is angry at Israel's apostasy (2.12-13, 20).
- Yahweh sends oppressors and enemies (v. 14).
- Yahweh does not protect Israel (v. 15).
- Israelites groan due to their poor quality of life (v. 18).
- Yahweh changes his mind and has compassion for those he has oppressed (v. 18).
- Yahweh sends judges who deliver an oppressed Israel (vv. 16-18).
- Israelite do not listen to the judge-deliverers but behave worse than before by continuing to serve other gods and arranging marriages with Canaanite families (v. 19; 3.6).

Yahweh makes a permanent policy of not evicting the resident national groups who are left in the land, first, to test Israel (2.22; 3.1-4) and, second, to provide opportunities for young Israel to acquire skills in self-defence (3.1).

Ancient listeners and modern readers will be impressed by the performances of Israel's first three 'deliverers': Othniel, who is already established as Israel's war hero and defeats a world-class invader; Ehud, who single-handedly kills an oppressor king in occupied territory; and Shamgar (who is not to be overlooked), when he is outnumbered 600 to 1 and slaughters Philistines by improvising with a farming implement for prodding wayward cattle.

Judges 3:
Othniel, Ehud and Shamgar

Israel and the Nations (vv. 1-6)

Israel is in trouble. The storyteller begins with what looks like a title: 'these are the nations', which is the introduction to a list (cf. Gen. 10.1; Exod. 1.1; Num. 1.5). There follows two lists of those nations with whom Israelites will have to contend. The first is a list of three national groups that Yahweh leaves in the land to provide Israel with the opportunity of learning self-defence. First listed are the five unnamed leaders of the Philistine cities (Gaza, Ashdod, Ashkelon, Gath and Ekron, Josh. 13.3) who are among the 'sea people' who migrated from the Aegean. Following their defeat by the Egyptians they were settled along the south coast by Pharaoh Ramses III. Second, the Sidonians (or Phoenicians), whose area marks the northern extent of Canaanite territory (Gen. 10.19); these are not to be confused with the inhabitants of the un-war-like Laish who live peacefully and safely in a remote region (Judg. 18.7). The Sidonians are powerful enough to oppress an apostate Israel (10.12) although the storyteller does not include an account in a story cycle. A third group are the Hivites who live on Mount Lebanon.

Now that Israel has settled for peaceful co-existence alongside the inhabitants, they will be easy prey for migrating war-like nations. Israel is provided with the opportunity to practise conflict on three national groups should local disputes arise.

As well as keeping an apostate Israel on the defensive, others in the land also present Israel with a simple choice to remain loyal or be disloyal to Yahweh.

Also remaining undisturbed in the land are other Canaanite groups: Hittites, Amorites, Perizzites, Hivites (a second listing) and Jebusites with whom Israelites do what they are specifically commanded not to do when intermarrying with their families. None of the Canaanite religious furniture is pulled down, broken, cut, hewn or burnt (Deut. 7.5) and Yahweh is abandoned in favour of other deities. However, the storyteller does not present the God of Israel as an indifferent bystander. Yahweh becomes angry and acts in the character of a merchant who 'sells' Israel to a formidable new owner with a fearsome villainous name.

The storyteller clearly wants us to be impressed with the successful performances of Israel's first three deliverers who are able to defeat formidable oppressors. First, Cushan, who is a world-class oppressor with a long fearful name associated with Babylon and is able to travel from his distant homeland; second, an alliance of three armies with a portly king; and third, a regiment of Philistines.

The character of Othniel is the storyteller's first judge-deliverer. His story, which is told only in outline, is accompanied by an accumulation of introductory and closing phrases, some of which also occur at the beginning and conclusion of other judge-deliverer stories which follow:

- The evil that Israel does is specified as forgetting Yahweh and serving the resident gods of Canaan: the Baals and Asherahs.
- In response, Yahweh becomes angry.
- Yahweh 'sells' Israel in a change of 'ownership' which lasts for eight years.
- Israel 'cries out' to Yahweh.
- Yahweh raises up a deliverer.
- The spirit of Yahweh comes upon the deliverer.
- He judges Israel.
- He delivers Israel.
- Yahweh gives the king of the oppressors into the deliverer's hands.
- The land rests for forty years.
- The judge-deliverer dies.

Othniel vs. Cushan, King of the Land with Two Rivers, who is Twice as Wicked as Anyone Else (vv. 7-11)

We have met Othniel before. He is well connected as a member of Caleb's family and he already possesses honour as Israel's champion and war hero. He is the master of Debir (a city associated with scrolls and records, Judg. 1.11-13; Josh. 15.16-17) which is his spoil by right of conquest (Deut. 20.14). His prestige is reinforced by his marriage to Achsah, Caleb's daughter.

Such is the calibre of those who Yahweh raises up to deliver an oppressed Israel. Moreover, when Othniel is empowered by Yahweh's spirit, he is able to defeat one who is characterized as a formidable world-class oppressor. The storyteller is careful to display the status of Yahweh's first judge-deliverer not by presenting us with an ingenious account of a military campaign, but by the formidable characterization of Israel's first oppressor. Othniel's heroism is outstanding.

The storyteller beefs-up the invader's name into a foreboding characterization. Cushan is called 'Rishathaim', meaning 'double wicked', which implies that he is more wicked than the occupants of the land (cf. Deut. 9.4, 5). The name is also a contemptuous metaphor for Babylon, 'the land of double bitterness' (Jer. 50.21). Cushan is the king of 'Aram-naharaim' which is the 'Land with Two Rivers' and identified as Upper Mesopotamia and the Tigris and the Euphrates. The totality of Cushan's vivid pseudonym— '"king" of the Land with Two Rivers who is twice as wicked as anyone else'—is the storyteller's caricature used to impress upon us not only the dread of Israel's new owner, but also the heroic ability of Othniel by whom he is defeated. When equipped with Yahweh's spirit, Othniel is able to defeat none other than the 'Great Conqueror', an ambitious and formidable world-class potentate who is able to travel from his own land and whose fearsome name is carefully recorded four times, twice in Judg. 3.8 and twice in v. 10.

There are wide gaps in Othniel's story. We are not told how he delivers Israel; no details are provided about his preparation, his campaign or the battle. The only indication of Othniel's deliverance method is the phrase 'he went out to war', which means that he leads Israel's army in battle against the oppressor's army. Elsewhere in Judges the same phrase refers to two armies who face each other or to one army's preparation to face another (cf. 20.14, 18, 20, 23, 28). We are not told if Othniel accomplishes Israel's deliverance by acting alone like Ehud and Samson, with a few like Gideon or at the head of Israel's militia like Barak and Jephthah. Moreover, we are not to know if a more violent and bawdy account is omitted leaving the mere summary. It appears that the storyteller's interests lie elsewhere.

The story of Yahweh's first judge-deliverer is hardly a story at all but is told in sparse detail in order to emphasize extreme contrast. First, we are to be in no doubt about the tyrannical nature of Israel's first oppressor. And second, we are not to be in any doubt about the identity, honour, status and calibre of the one who delivers Israel: Othniel, Israel's war hero (1.11-13) and Yahweh's first judge-deliverer, who is empowered by Yahweh's spirit (3.10) and supported by his new bride (1.13-15).

Ehud vs. King Eglon and a Moabite Coalition (vv. 12-30)

Welcome to an intriguing detective story. The story of a 'perfect murder' is about to unfold as we are presented with the career-best performance of a lone Israelite, who—with one hand behind his back and a little home-made wooden dagger in the other—delivers Israel from another formidable oppressor.

A 'perfect murder' is the taking of a life by an unknown perpetrator when the act of murder is undiscovered and death is thought to be by another cause—in the case of this victim, a natural cause. What an ingenious way to rid the land of a tyrant! Ehud's story is told with relish.

Yahweh disapproves of Israel's behaviour and prepares the next invaders. King Eglon of Moab is mocked with the storyteller's introduction. First, the Moabite king requires the assistance of a coalition army to invade the land. Second, not only does Yahweh strengthen him but he also needs the support of the Ammonites and the Amalekites (an old enemy of Israel, Exod. 17.8-16) in order to take up residence in the city of palms (a popular local name for Jericho). Israelites are pressed into service for eighteen years. Third, invaders are ridiculed further when the King Eglon is described, not only as fat, but *very* fat. The essential description of the king is even more biting. The king's name in Hebrew is the noun for a 'young bull'. Such a description may seem unkind, but would an ancient Israelite storyteller be respectful (or even 'politically correct') about monarchs who invade, oppress and demand tribute? Alternatively, the description 'very fat' may indicate that the king's upholstered constitution is to be understood as robust and healthy, a fine specimen of well-fed manhood. The storyteller also describes the Moabite warriors as corpulent or well-nourished (v. 29). LXX translators thought Eglon to be 'very handsome' and used the same Greek word for the 'pretty' infant Moses (Exod. 2.2) and the 'beautiful' Judith (Jdt. 11.23). 'Fat' in Hebrew also describes the condition of the healthy cows and ears of corn in Pharaoh's dreams (Gen. 41.4, 5) and Solomon's well-fed cattle (1 Kgs 4.23). Moab is also a land in which to 'sojourn' in the time of famine (Ruth 1.1). How are such details to be heard or read? Is the king ridiculed as a royal fatted-calf awaiting sacrificial slaughter or is he a noble healthy specimen who Israelites are wily enough to defeat? Either reading humiliates the invaders and their roly-poly monarch who sits at the top of the Moabite food chain. After eighteen years of serving the Moabites the Israelites remember Yahweh and cry out for help.

Yahweh participates at all levels. Not only does he assist the invader, he also 'raises up' a deliverer who possesses a particular skill suitable to the task ahead. We are not told how Ehud comes to public attention as a tribute bearer because other matters are drawn to our attention.

Ehud is unique. He is a left-handed member of a tribe with a name which means 'son of the right hand'. Ehud is a Benjaminite. He may also be like the 600 Benjaminite warriors who have a particular left-handed skill with a sling (cf. Judg. 20.16) which gives them strategic advantage in combat and is translated by the LXX as 'ambidextrous'. Even though the Benjaminites are unable to expel the inhabitants of Jerusalem (1.21) and settle for co-existence with the Jebusites, the provision of such intriguing details suggests we are on the threshold of an intriguing deliverance story. We are not about to be disappointed.

Ehud makes his own dagger to a precise specification with two edges and a 'gomed' in length (rather than a 'cubit' of English translations; cf. 3.16, NRSV), being the Hebrew measurement from the elbow to the knuckles of his clenched fist. Ehud's dagger is made from hardwood because the forging of a weapon in metal may attract the attention of the invaders. A theme begins to emerge. When Israelites engage in conflict with formidable oppressors, judge-deliverers improvise with makeshift weaponry. Questions arise. What is the purpose of Ehud's dagger which is made to a precise specification? Why is it secreted beneath his clothing and on his right thigh? How will a lone Israelite be able to deliver Israel from a well-fed Moabite army?

The scene is set. Our expectations are raised. Ehud has left-hand expertise; he has made his own blade with two edges and to a precise length. The weapon is concealed about his person. Ehud is Israel's civil servant who personally presents tribute to the exceedingly fat king of Israel's oppressors. To present tribute to occupiers is an acknowledgment that Israel accepts low status and that another king and his god rule the land.

This is a situation which cannot go on. An oppressed Israel awaits deliverance.

The Gilgal stones are passed twice, first from a place of safety into danger, then from danger back to safety. The stones are a reminder to Israelites and to Ehud that the God who helped them to cross the Reed Sea and the Jordan will help him to deliver Israel from the Moabites.

Ehud makes three appearances before Eglon. The first, when accompanied by porters, to present Israel's tribute; the second, on his return, when Ehud reveals that he bears a message, the king calls for silence and his attendants leave; his third audience with Eglon is in a private room in which the king sits alone. Eglon rises, not out of respect for an oracle from the gods, but from shock, that anyone—let alone a tribute-bearing Israelite who has already presented his tribute—should enter his private room.

King and assassin are alone, but there are gaps in the story. We could pry into the text. Is Ehud invited for this third audience? He provides the king with an additional detail about the source of the message perhaps in order to ensure that it receives the full attention of the royal personage when he says, 'I have a message for you *from God*'. The king will hear no such nonsense and rises to evict the intruder. Ehud's opportunity has arrived. He reaches with his left hand to his side for the concealed dagger which he thrusts in an upward movement into the king's stomach—left-handed movements are not expected to signal danger. The dagger's two sides allow it to be smoothly inserted into the king's under-belly and his fat enfolds the dagger and its handle. Ehud withdraws his hand.

Additional gore follows, with the inclusion of sparse but essential details that are significant to the progress of the story and which maximize Moabite humiliation. The king's liquid faeces evacuate his body as he falls to the floor. Before making his escape, Ehud locks himself inside the room with the dead king and makes his unseen escape through a verandah or porch.

We are drawn deeper into the story with the arrival of the king's servants. They wait outside; they continue to wait; they become anxious due to the time their master is taking. Their work is to attend their king, and locked doors prevent them from their duties. Locked doors may not be surprising because the king is in private and thought to be 'covering his feet', a euphemism for using the royal privy.

There is no need for the storyteller to mention the servants or their anxiety, but they are included for the purpose of further mockery: their king is dead, yet his servants think he is relieving himself. Their response borders on slapstick. They are too frightened to open the doors for fear they will interrupt their king doing what their king does in private. Perhaps they also want to relieve themselves! When they can wait no longer, the attendants take a key, open the doors and 'behold', their king lies dead on the floor.

The Moabites dither while Ehud summons Israel's militia. He delivers Israel in two resolute actions which have the same word in Hebrew even though they are very different. Ehud 'thrust' (*tāqa'*) his sword into Eglon; he 'sounded' (*tāqa'*) a trumpet and Israel's militia follow him to the Jordan where the retreating Moabites are slaughtered.

Murder, or Death by Another Cause?

Let's consider the evidence. The king's private room contains the king's massive corpse lying in his own excrement. There is no wound to be seen because, as we have been told, his fat closes over the incision. Moreover, there is no exit wound; no blood; no weapon; no sign of a struggle; no witnesses; no sign of forced entry; no suspect assassin is seen leaving. Furthermore, the doors are locked from the inside; there are no suspects; there is no one to arrest; no one to interview and no one from whom a Moabite investigator may take statements, apart from the king's servants.

So, here is the king's corpse lying in his own excrement which evacuates his body in response to terror and dread at the moment when he realizes that he is dying from the upward internal penetration of an assassin's dagger. Death is instantaneous. We have no details about a further dagger thrust or cut to the throat. Ehud stands before the king; he offers to disclose God's message; he reaches downward to his right side with his left hand to the dagger which he thrusts in an upward movement into the king's abdomen. The dagger is pushed so far internally that it pierces his heart. The king's fat closes over the blade and its hilt as he collapses. Eglon may be dead before he crumples to the floor.

The king's attendants have no reason to suspect foul play. Surely, their roly-poly king has been taken unwell and died. (Modern medical evidence suggests that Eglon could have died from a range of weight-related illnesses such as morbid obesity which is accompanied by serious health effects such as diabetes, hypertension, coronary artery disease and cerebrovascular disease. Moreover, those who are seriously overweight are liable to suffer further from gallstones, osteoarthritis and hiatus hernia.) Poor health may be common among Moabites with deaths at an early age even though the consequences of obesity may have been unknown in the ancient world. Portly King Eglon was a very poorly monarch. Neither wound nor weapon are to be seen. The attendants have no reason to suspect anything other than death from natural causes. Ehud makes his escape having planned and committed a perfect murder!

Thinking about Ehud

What do you think of Israel's second judge-deliverer? Is Ehud deceitful? Sneaky? Cruel? Do you find the story vulgar and repugnant? Or are you impressed by his bravura and admire his tenacity?

We are in the hands of a storyteller who creates his characters and is responsible for their actions as they appear on the page. The story of when 'Ehud met Eglon' is an ethnic joke which is told with a stereotypical cast list: a stupid character who is the foil for a canny hero. The storyteller incites laughter or at least a smile from hearers and readers at Moabite expense. When the story is read aloud—accompanied by the reader's comments and asides in order to mock Israel's enemies—the reading is the cause of laughter and hilarity among listeners. It cannot be denied that Ehud possesses immense inner composure; he is clever, intelligent, shrewd, cool and the possessor of icy nerves. He is courageous and focused when engaged in a conflict that requires not only a dagger concealed about his person, but trickery and deception in order to improve his chances when alone in enemy territory. Ehud is characterized positively as being both courageous and able. To plan an assassination, enter occupied territory alone without back-up and to commit what I read as a 'perfect murder', followed by an exit strategy and then to muster Israel's militia, is a clever act of bravado. When the deed is done, he calls out to Israel's militia, informing them that Yahweh has given their enemies into their hands. If characters are to be judged by how well they bring matters to a conclusion, Ehud triumphs in a climax of energy, flair and panache. After the slaughter of their robust army at the Jordan, the Moabites do not trouble Israel again.

Ehud's story may receive new readings should modern readers be oppressed by oppressors who possess similar dread as these oppressors. Ancient stories are not only evaluated in comfortable homes and libraries situated in peaceful green-field sites; they are also read in countries where readers face the oppressors of the modern world. I suggest, therefore, that the account of Ehud's career-best performance may remain as it is because the storyteller appears to be at ease with his story and his hero. The king's assassination is told with neither regret nor embarrassment, but with relish and delight, suspense and glee. Ehud's violence may be evaluated as legitimate violence when he brings Israel's eighteen years of oppression to an end, after which the land rests for eighty years.

Those who object to Ehud's inclusion in sacred literature would do well to ask what happens in the story as it unfolds and to ask further, who does what to whom and why? I agree that there is something wrong and even immoral in the story. However, it is not the character of Ehud who is immoral. The moral low-ground in the story—as in other Judges stories—is occupied by those who oppress Israel and demand tribute. The storyteller's sympathy is with the powerless who will put up with serving tyrants for only so long.

Israel's invader is mocked in a vulgar tale in which Moabite oppressors are cast as the foils for Israelite humour and scorn. Moabites are a laughable spectacle. Moabites are a pushover. Moabites can be easily defeated by a lone Israelite with one hand behind his back and a little homemade wooden dagger in the other!

Shamgar vs. 600 Philistines (v. 31)

After the heroism of Othniel and the courage of Ehud, a third deliverer is not to be overlooked: Shamgar the son of Anath. The introductory and closing framework formula associated with Othniel and Ehud does not appear and he is not said to be raised up by Yahweh. Shamgar has the introductory phrase which is associated with the consecutive judges (cf. 10.1-5 and 12.7-15), 'after him', which suggests that he chronologically follows what has gone before. The Deborah–Barak–Jael story, which follows, does not mention Shamgar at the beginning but starts with the framework phrase that Israel again did evil after Ehud died.

Israel's oppressors are yet again humiliated when 600 Philistines (a conquest party like the 600 Danites who advance on

Laish, 18.11) are slaughtered—not in honourable combat with suitably armed warriors, but ignobly by a farmer who improvises with an agricultural implement which he uses for prodding oxen on their way as they pull his plough. Shamgar's heroism is so impressive that he is regarded with honour as the son of a deity. Shamgar, whose name may be Canaanite, acquires the matronym: 'son of Anath', the name of the Canaanite goddess of war. Songs are sung about such characters. Shamgar's story fits snugly between Ehud's deliverance and the story about Deborah's team which follows.

Shamgar's improvisation is associated with others who also improvise with weaponry to rid Israel of oppressors. This illustrious hero is mentioned in Deborah's song for 'Victory in Israel Day' (5.6) with Jael who uses a tent peg and hammer. Samson also improvises and humiliates the Philistines with a jaw-bone as his method of slaughter.

The heroic performances of the first three judge-deliverers send a clear warning to those who would invade Israel: you may acquire this people and their land from their God for a few years as a gift or a bargain, but you will be manipulated and used by Yahweh; you will not return home.

The first three chapters demonstrate the storyteller's three purposes: first, exiled Israelite hearers are to be ashamed of themselves and of their past because Israel's exile and expulsion from the land are due to Israel's repeated apostasy. Second, hearers are to be impressed with the calibre and success of the first three judge-deliverers—Othniel, Ehud and Shamgar—who secure the means of Israel's independence in hero stories which form a literature of hope and demonstrate that Yahweh will not give up on Israel but will respond to Israel's cries again and again. And third, exiled Israelites are reminded of their monotheistic religion and are made aware that living peacefully in the land is conditional upon their covenant faithfulness to Yahweh.

In the two chapters that follow, the same story is twice told, as a narrative which is celebrated in song. When Israelites again do evil, the next 'manipulated' oppressor is more formidable than the last and is equipped with 900 iron chariots. However, on this occasion Israel is not delivered by an individual judge-deliver raised up by Yahweh for the purpose, but by a team of three. Once again we are about to be impressed.

Judges 4:
Deborah and Barak and Jael

Again, Yahweh acts like a market trader and offers Israelites for sale when he has good cause to be angry with his people.

We know little about Israel's next oppressor and new 'owner' King Jabin other than that he reigns in Hazor (vv. 2, 17) and is called the 'king of Canaan' (vv. 2, 23, 24 [twice]). We are also introduced to the commander of Jabin's army. Sisera is a dark, bleak, sinister character who oppresses Israel from his lair in the appropriately named 'woodlands of the unbelievers' (*Harosheth-hagoim*, v. 2) with a force of 900 war chariots reinforced with iron fittings. Sisera is equipped with the fearsome weaponry of shock and awe that crushes Israel's life. His chariots are two-wheeled vehicles drawn by one or two horses and driven by skilled elite warriors. King Jabin has somehow acquired sufficient funds to equip and maintain his army of skilful charioteers, horses and chariots with infantry support. Canaanite chariots of iron (*barzel*, cf. 1.19) are the symbols of hostile nastiness that oppress Israelites for twenty years. When, like their ancestors in Egypt, Israelites can stand the intimidation of oppressive taskmasters no longer, they cry to Yahweh. Israel will require a deliverer of exemplary courage to challenge an army of fearsome iron chariots.

Meet Deborah, Israel's judge and prophet. Deborah, whose name means 'bee', resides in the shade of a palm tree in the Ephraimite hills. The tree, with its leaves and shade, is an isolated symbol of life and fertility in an arid landscape. Deborah is Yahweh's representative who is visited by Israelites when they plead for an end to Sisera's prolonged oppression. Deborah's visitors will be advised to take care because she is a fiery character who is more like a wasp than a bee and she does not suffer fools gladly. However, Israel's oppression is about to come to an end; Deborah has a solution. First, she orders Barak—in the name of 'Yahweh the God of Israel'—to muster 10,000 warriors from Israel's militia at Mount Tabor. Second, she will cause Sisera's chariots and infantry to march from their lair to Kishon. Third, the outcome is already decided; the oppressor will be delivered into Barak's hand at the forthcoming Battle of the River Kishon. Israel's oppressors are about to be stung.

A question arises: Barak who? Who is this individual to whom Israel's future is entrusted? Is he a suitable candidate to lead Israel's militia against such a formidable foe? What previous military experience does he have which qualifies him for such a daunting task?

Barak's name means 'lightning' (cf. Exod. 19.16) or a sudden 'flash' of lightning (cf. Ps. 144.6) which is also a metaphor for the flashing or glittering in the sunlight of the cutting edge of Yahweh's sharpened sword of justice (Deut. 32.41; cf. Hab. 3.11). As the 'son of Abinoam'—a quaint family name associated with the characteristics of pleasantness and delight—Barak is known by the colourful name of 'Flash, the son of a delightful father'. However, Barak is not identified as a warrior or a military commander and his combat experience is unknown. Barak's tribe, Naphtali, also lacks a reputation for military success: it is unable to drive out the inhabitants of Beth-shemesh and Beth-anath; it co-exists with the Canaanites and employs them to work in its vineyards (Judg. 1.33). Moreover, Barak himself lacks the reputation of a war hero like Othniel. Barak is called from obscurity and his mettle is untested.

Israel's prospects for military success appear to worsen when Deborah's new general asks her to accompany him to the battle site. When this request is overheard, Israelite warriors may ask among themselves if she has made an error of judgment in her choice of Israel's general. Does his request indicate that he is fainthearted? Is he a wimp? Maybe a coward? Deborah informs Barak that battle honours will not go to him, or to any of his warriors, but to a woman. Does this mean that Deborah will emerge as the battle's heroine? Will she take a sword in hand and lead Israel's militia herself? It does not appear at first that Barak will live up to the dramatic meaning of his name, 'lightning'. Has Israel's judge and prophet made the right appointment? Is Israel about to be defeated? Are Israelites going to be oppressed for another twenty years?

It is not that Barak is fearful about the prospect of war, but he is naturally cautious about engaging 900 enemy iron chariots at the wrong time, which are supported by unknown numbers of infantry. The reason why Barak requests Deborah's company is to appoint her as his army chaplain. As Yahweh's prophet, she knows when the time is right to make an attack. Like anyone facing the prospect of engaging a formidable enemy, Barak is wise to take counsel.

If anyone is wimpish or cowardly in this story, it is Sisera. He has oppressed Israel for twenty years and he is eager to try out his iron chariots and infantry support in the field. His opportunity arrives when he receives intelligence that Israelites—led by a pleasant and delightful general—are mustered at Mount Tabor. Sisera and his army emerge from the woods ready for battle. Barak and his troops will be a pushover!

In the role of Barak's chaplain, Deborah faces Israel's militia. She may be aware of unrest in the ranks. They face a formidable foe and her general lacks experience. Her voice has bite; Sisera's world is about to be rocked; bloodshed and mayhem are demanded. Barak is addressed: 'Arise! Attack! Yahweh has gone ahead of you!'

Without hesitation—with the mindset of a warrior—and in a flash, Barak immediately charges downhill into the enemy as Deborah has ordered. Israel's militia are hostile and dangerous; they follow their general and charge forward into Sisera's chariots and infantry in a frenzy of mutilation and an orgy of hand-to-hand butchery. Swords are stuck into bodies; limbs are severed; lives end. The violence is fast and brutal, chaotic and messy. Within a short time the Kishon flood plain and the road to the 'wood of the unbelievers' is littered with the corpses of Sisera's charioteers, their horses and his infantry. The body count is alarmingly high and there are no survivors. None of Israel's militia are lost. Just one body is missing among the dead. Sisera has abandoned his chariot and run away on foot from the battle site. Barak himself takes up the pursuit.

Sisera—who is dismayed to be suffering defeat—panics and runs in a specific direction for asylum. Heber the Kenite, a metal worker, has set up his business at a well-known oasis landmark called the 'Traveller's Oak' which happens to be near Barak's home in Kedesh. Heber no longer lives among the Kenites who are descendants of Moses but he has made peace with King Jabin who has given him the contract to maintain Sisera's iron chariots. Further repairs are anticipated following the battle. Unfortunately for Sisera, only Mrs Heber is at home.

Jael, whose name means 'mountain goat', observes Sisera's approach. She meets him with a timely offer of sanctuary and safety. He asks for neither but accepts both. Big mistake! Jael is aware of the runner's identity because she has observed him and his charioteers intimidating her Israelite neighbours during their twenty years of oppression. Jael does not address Sisera by name but in his breathless panic he discerns his name in her twice uttered sound-alike invitation, 'turn aside, turn aside', which in Hebrew is like the calling of his name, *sûrāh sûrāh*. Sisera has suffered a military disaster, his chariots are lost, he has run away from the battlefield and, for all he knows, Israelites may be in pursuit. The day is hot and the sides of Jael's tent are tied back revealing an open-plan interior. Jael covers him with a suitable covering which conceals her guest from view. Sisera is on the run and he has arrived at a secure hiding place—or so he thinks.

Sisera's appeal for water, accompanied by the entreaty 'please', may seem a polite request to his host, but it is also pitiful when uttered by a military commander who has oppressed Israel with superior and fearsome weaponry, has run away from the battlefield and is now a fugitive hidden by a woman in a woman's tent. Jael responds to the thirsty escapee with generous hospitality when she opens a fresh skin-container. As Sisera's eyes close from weariness and from the sleepy effect of refreshment, he asks his host to stand at the entrance of her tent and, should she be asked if she has company, not to reveal his presence. Sisera has shelter; he is watched over by an ally; he is safe—or so he thinks.

Jael covers her guest again and as he sleeps she approaches softly (Ruth-like, cf. Ruth 3.7), and with the force of a hammer blow she thrusts (Ehud-like, cf. Judg. 3.21) a tent peg through Sisera's head and into the ground beneath. Tent maintenance is women's work and Jael slaughters her guest with her own domestic implements. The storyteller describes the killing of Sisera in just two verbs: 'she thrust' and that the peg 'descended', in contrast (as we shall see) to the song's staccato of nine different verbs, with repetitions making a total of thirteen action verbs in all. The narrative account is measured and precise: Jael covers her guest, more superior refreshment is offered than requested, milk rather than water. Then she waits until Sisera sleeps before the deed is done with her peg and hammer.

When Barak arrives in pursuit, Jael triumphantly invites him to inspect the lifeless body of Israel's dead oppressor commander secured to the floor of her tent by a peg through his skull. Sisera is going nowhere.

Israel's deliverance is not, on this occasion, due to the individual heroism of a lone judge-deliverer, but is a team effort:

- Deborah is Israel's judge and prophet who calls Barak to be the general of Israel's militia. In the role of Barak's chaplain she informs him when the time is right.
- Barak musters Israel's militia, attacks and slaughters Sisera's army. Barak's courage is outstanding when he charges downhill into iron chariots and infantry with Israel's militia following in pursuit.
- Jael deceives Sisera and slaughters him with a tent peg and hammer as he hides and sleeps in her tent.
- Yahweh 'gives' Sisera's army to Barak and, when acting again like a market trader, 'sells' Sisera to Jael.
- The Canaanite king is humbled and slaughtered by Israel's militia.

Not only is Sisera's army slaughtered in the Battle of the River Kishon, 'King Jabin of Hazor or Canaan' himself is also humbled, trodden underfoot and felled like a tree. *This* 'King Jabin of Hazor' is a different character to the 'King Jabin of Hazor' who assembled a great coalition army against Joshua and Israel at Merom (Josh. 11.1-5). The former King Jabin was a strategic organizer who was respected by other local Canaanite kings and their armies when they responded to his call and joined forces to oppose Israelites as they invaded the land. *That* King Jabin was killed by Joshua in battle (Josh. 11.10). However, *this* King Jabin, who is also styled 'king of Canaan', is mocked for his absence while his army commander is manipulated by Deborah and 'sold' by Yahweh to a woman (Judg. 4.7, 9), and his army is given into Barak's hand (vv. 13, 14). The storyteller wants us to be aware of how soundly the king of Canaan—rather than just the local king of Hazor—is defeated (vv. 23-24). The former King Jabin was a worthy 'hands-on' opponent; *this* King Jabin is mocked as an unworthy 'hands-off' opponent who stays at home while his commander engages in battle.

Israel's oppressors are again regarded with contempt. We are to have no sympathy for commander Sisera who runs from a battlefield defeat into what he assumes to be the safety of an ally's tent where he is killed—not in face-to-face hand-to-hand combat with another warrior, but shamefully killed—by a woman as he hides in a woman's tent. Moreover, Israel has no time for ethical discussions about the niceties of hospitality offered by a woman who kills her guest. An urgent robust engagement with an oppressor is required and in the persons of Deborah and Barak and Jael, Israel is not disappointed. The bee is an inspiration, the 'flash' triumphs gloriously and the honour of taking out the commander of Israel's oppressors goes to a woman with a name like a nanny goat!

We have read a raw story of violence and brutality, gore and woe which tells how Sisera the charioteer commander, who oppresses Israel for twenty years, meets a humiliating end at the hands of a woman. We are to be further impressed when all team members are triumphantly celebrated, as is about to happen in the song that follows.

Judges 5:
Celebrating 'Victory in Israel Day'

This is Deborah's jubilant victory song which she sings as Barak—Israel's heroic general—drags Sisera's lifeless body from Jael's tent, holding the tent peg which is still embedded in the oppressor's skull, to a pyre fuelled with the remains of his chariots. Sisera's corpse is burnt with the amputated limbs and broken bodies of his warriors. The air is filled with the smell of burning meat—the smell of victory—an aroma which soothes Yahweh and his warriors after the butchery of battle. The people of Yahweh dance around the fire and from time to time punctuate the song with exuberant shouts and joyful choruses because their twenty-year oppression is at an end. Oh, the joy of it! Those who are free from Sisera's tyranny have much to sing about.

To celebrate the defeat of an oppressive Canaanite army, combined with the humiliating slaughter of Sisera their commander and the restoration of peace to the land, the storyteller gives way to the voice of a poet or a 'singer of victories'. As the song unfolds, Deborah emerges as a solo 'singer' who elevates herself to the position of team leader and Israel's matriarch. General Barak has a prestigious position of honour as Israel's war hero. Deborah's song is sung in an atmosphere of upbeat euphoria accompanied by abandoned dancing because the intimidation of a foreign oppressor has come to an end: the people of Yahweh have survived and Israel is at long last independent and free, the land rests. A spontaneous celebration bursts out because peaceful independent living can once again resume.

The song is not without its difficulties. Is it acceptable for Deborah to gloat over the humiliating slaughter of Israel's enemies? How are we to account for the differences between the song and the narrative? Responding to such questions will form part of our task. The storyteller as poet treats us like intelligent adults and assumes that we have no sympathy for oppressors or for their women who want to profit from the oppression of others. The song is a celebration of the violent end of Sisera, his charioteers and infantry, which I have already acknowledged, is fast, brutal, chaotic and messy—real violence.

Deborah barely pauses for breath as words tumble over themselves. It may be due to the atmosphere of ecstasy and excited exuberance that the Hebrew text is difficult to follow and translate. Some of the words only appear in the song and are not used elsewhere in the Hebrew Bible; other words have a wide range of meaning.

I offer a reading based upon my own tentative translation (below) in which I step onto thin ice of biblical interpretation by making informed proposals in context, where necessary, which may sometimes agree with English translations and commentators and sometimes differ. I am not too troubled about the finer points of grammar nor the range of possible alternative meanings which are discussed by others. I may just about be able to make out what it is that the storyteller-poet's characters celebrate. When I am uncertain, I will not dither for long like the Reubenites at their campfires (vv. 15b-16); rather I will, like the Naphtalites (v. 18), reveal my colours and enter the fray.

The Song Begins (vv. 2-5)

Israelites were not held back like restrained hair,
they willingly volunteered.
Bless Yahweh!
Listen, you kings;
pay attention, you rulers:
I will sing to Yahweh,
I praise Yahweh the God of Israel:
Yahweh, when you left Seir,
when you marched from the land of Edom
the earth trembled,
the heavens and the clouds poured,
the mountains streamed,
before Yahweh of Sinai,
before Yahweh the God of Israel.

A Time for Heroes and Heroines (vv. 6-12)

In the days of Shamgar son of Anat,
in the days of Jael:
the main roads were closed;
travellers took to winding unfamiliar routes;
village life in Israel stopped,

villages came to a stand-still...
until I arose—Deborah—I arose like a mother in Israel.
When new gods were chosen
the battle came to the gates.
Neither a shield nor spear was to be seen
among 40,000 Israelites!
My heart is with Israel's commanders,
with the people who willingly volunteer.
Bless Yahweh!
Consider this,
you who ride brown donkeys;
you who sit on carpets;
you who walk along the road:
the cry of the water-carriers between the wells
is where the triumphs of Yahweh are celebrated,
the triumphs of Yahweh's villagers in Israel.
Then the people of Yahweh descended to the gates.
Awake! Awake, Deborah!
Awake! Awake!
Sing a song!
Arise, Barak!
Secure your captives,
you son of a delightful father!
The survivors descend against the nobles,
the people of Yahweh
descend against the mighty.

The Mixed Response of Israel's Tribes (vv. 13-23)

Ephraimites were rooted in Amalek.
After you Benjaminites with your people,
commanders from Machir,
marchers from Zebulun with the leader's staff, descended.
Princes of Issachar with Deborah,
Issachar is loyal to Barak:
they followed him where they were sent into the valley!
Reubenite clans were so fainthearted:
why did you dither around camp fires,
listening to the bleating of sheep?
Reubenite clans were so fainthearted.
Gileadites stayed at home across the Jordan.
Danites went fishing!
Asherites went on an outing to the seaside

where they sat on the beach!
Zebulunites were not afraid to risk their lives!
Naphtalites were out in the open!
Kings arrived to fight:
kings of Canaan fought
at Taanach by the waters of Megiddo...
but they were denied spoils of silver!
The stars from their heavenly courses
fought against Sisera.
The Kishon torrent swept them away.
The torrent overthrew them, the Kishon torrent.
My soul trod down the powerful!
The horses' hooves pounded;
the stallions galloped and galloped!
'Curse Meroz!'
says Yahweh's messenger.
'Curse and curse again
all her inhabitants
who failed to turn up
to help Yahweh, to help Yahweh against the mighty.'

Two Domestic Scenes (vv. 24-30)

Blessed among women is Jael
the wife of Heber the Kenite;
blessed among tent-dwelling women!
He asked for water,
she gave milk,
she presented curds in a noble bowl.
She stretched her hand to a tent-peg;
she grasped a hammer with her right hand;
she hammered Sisera;
she annihilated his head;
she crushed him;
she pierced his skull.
He bowed down between her feet;
he fell down;
he lay down between her feet;
he bowed down;
he fell down;
he bowed down;
there he fell.
Dead!

Sisera's mother looked through her window;
she cried out from behind the shutter:
'Why is his chariot so long in coming?
Why can I not hear the sound of his horses?'
Her wise princesses answer...
but she answers:
'Surely, they are finding and dividing the spoils:
a woman or two for each warrior;
dyed cloths of spoil for Sisera,
dyed embroidered cloths spoil,
dyed embroidered cloth spoil around necks.'
May all Yahweh's enemies likewise perish!
May those who love Yahweh shine like the sun!

The Song Begins (vv. 2-5)

Deborah is beside herself with joy due to the enthusiastic turn-out for battle without any reserve or restraint on the part of some (not all) of the people of Yahweh. Hair that hangs loose and is neither tied back nor concealed beneath fashionable head-gear is a metaphor for their free, uninhibited response. Warriors were not pressed but were willing volunteers; there was no holding some Israelites back.

Kings and rulers are to pay attention because Israel has an ally: Yahweh the God of Israel emerged from Seir; the earth trembled as he marched in state from the land of Edom. Yahweh shone upon Israel like the sun as it rises in the east over the mountainous country of Seir (Deut. 33.2). Seir is another name for Edom (Gen. 32.4), indicating that Yahweh also presides over lands which are hostile to Israel (Num. 20.14-21; cf. Judg. 11.17-18). The heavens also participated in the conflict when they produced rainfall which worked to Israel's advantage. Mountain sides streamed with water and produced the Kishon flash-flood and Yahweh battled on Israel's behalf. Israel's enemies were swept away. Yahweh is destructive as well as creative.

A Time for Heroes and Heroines (vv. 6-12)

The phrase 'in the days of' is like the narrative beginning of an epic story (cf. Ruth 1.1) indicating that references are about to be made to known and respected characters: to Shamgar, who acquired the heroic matronym 'son of Anath', a Canaanite

goddess of war (Judg. 3.31), and to Jael, whose initiative is celebrated below. Both are named as the most celebrated characters
of their age.

The times of Shamgar and Jael are recalled as an unstable
era when the economic and social activities of Israel's villages
were restricted and travel from community to community was a
hazardous endeavour. When the main trade routes were occupied by foreign oppressors, trade was disrupted, travellers were
forced to make detours. The lives of peasants who lived in
unwalled villages were impoverished. But that was in the past;
Israel's economic prospects changed when Deborah held office.
She comfortably casts herself (Hebrew: first person singular) in
the role of the nation's matriarch: 'I arose—Deborah—I arose
like a mother in Israel'. Deborah is not raised up by Yahweh like
the judge-deliverers but presides in Israel as judge and prophet.

Deborah's description as 'mother' casts her in a comfortable
image of warmth and well-being. She is the nation's liberator, a
protector who sustains the economic life of her national family.
However, as the lyric hardens, we are made aware that there is
more to this 'mother' than a soft maternal instinct. Deborah
wants her sons to fight. In wartime the fate of women is determined by men. Israel's victory means peace for Israel's women
and a share of the spoils; defeat means despair and the dread of
an approaching victorious foreign male army. When the nation
is threatened, two of Israel's women take initiatives: a mother
coerces her sons to turn-out for battle and a woman who lives in
a tent seizes her opportunity as we are about to be told.

Israelites got themselves into a dire mess: they chose the (new)
resident gods of the land in preference to Yahweh. The invasion
of foreigners entering Israel's 'gates' was understood as Yahweh's
punishment for rejection (Deut. 32.17). Israel's militia was too
poorly equipped to make any kind of defence or attack when
compared with the enemy: Israel's warriors lacked shields and
spears.

As we have discovered, it is a feature of Judges storytelling
that those who oppress Israel are characterized with military
advantage such as the ability to march a long distance from
their homeland (Cushan), the stature of individual troops
(Moabites) and fearsome weaponry (Sisera's 900 iron chariots).
Even though Israel was in crisis and oppressed by 'the mighty',
Deborah neither flinched nor faltered; she had confidence in the

leadership ability of Israel's commanders who lead Israel's willing volunteers for whom she blesses Yahweh and gives heart-felt thanks.

All are made aware of what happened, whether they ride donkeys, sit on carpets, walk from place to place or draw water from wells. Everyone is to make the righteous acts of Yahweh a matter of conversation and joyful celebration. All who ride, sit, walk and draw water are to celebrate what Yahweh has done on their behalf. Cries are heard of others, who may be archers, musicians or singers—what matters is not who they are but what they talk and sing about—as they draw water from wells. Gossip and songs in Israel are about the mighty acts of justice that have taken place: the acts of Yahweh, who powerfully intervenes on Israel's side to restore justice and peace to Israel, supported by those who live in the highland villages who risked their lives by facing a well-equipped army. The people of Yahweh descended from their hill settlements and attacked the very 'gates' of Canaanite cities.

As Sisera's corpse burns on the pyre an exuberant chorus enacts the call to arms because the time for deliverance from years of oppression has arrived. However, it is not implied that Deborah and Barak need to be repeatedly called because they dither or may have over-slept! If Deborah is resting in the shade of her palm tree, this is her urgent call. If Barak, the son of a 'delightfully pleasant father', is also resting this is his call to arms; his moment has arrived to arise and secure his prisoners. However, Deborah needs to be respectfully reminded that Barak does not take prisoners (cf. Judg. 4.16, 23-24). The time to attack the Canaanite oppressor has arrived.

The Mixed Response of Israel's Tribes (vv. 13-23)

The tribes who willingly responded to Deborah's call to engage the enemy are congratulated; those who do not, are reprimanded. The noble people of Yahweh, who heroically survived years of oppression, turned out against the superior force of the oppressor's chariots. There follows a list of Israelite tribes who willingly responded and of others who did not. Judah and Simeon are not mentioned.

The Hebrew phrase about Ephraim is difficult (v. 14). I suggest that the Ephraimites stayed safely at home rooted to the spot in the highlands in Amalekite territory (12.15). Ephraimites are generally reluctant to go to war apart from when they were called to the Jordan crossing by Ehud and allowed none of the Moabite–Ammonite–Amalekite coalition to escape (3.27-29). When they do turn out to join Israel's militia, they arrive late and grumble about missing a share of the spoils (cf. 8.1 and 12.1). However, there is no need to despair because Benjaminites were willing; they followed leaders from Machir (another name for the tribe of Manasseh; Machir was the first son of Manasseh, the predominant clan in the tribe, Josh. 17.1; cf. Gen. 50.23; Num. 26.29). They were accompanied by leaders from Zebulun who possessed authority and carried a staff of office. Leaders from Issachar accompanied Deborah who were also loyal to Barak and did as they were ordered when they followed him and charged downhill into the enemy. Neither were Zebulunites afraid to face the enemy; they were so courageous in the attack that they seemed to have contempt for their own lives even to the point of death. Neither were the Naphtalites (Barak's own tribe) afraid to come face to face with the enemy in open country.

Other tribes were reluctant and stayed at home. The Reubenites were indecisive; they dithered and sat around their campfires listening to the bleating of sheep. The Gileadites stayed out of harm's way at home across the Jordan. The Danites were occupied with boats; it appears they preferred to go fishing rather than help Yahweh. The Danite absence also shows why Samson fights alone (cf. Judg. 14–16). The Asherites were hopeless; they went on an outing to the seaside!

Unnamed Canaanite kings arrived to do battle at Taanach, beside the waters of Megiddo, and failed to win any silver spoil. Israel's tribes had no need to fear; they were not alone because the stars did battle from the heavens on Israel's behalf when they fought against Sisera by swelling the waters of the River Kishon into a sudden raging torrent in which the enemy was swept away. The name of the Kishon is repeated for emphasis and the torrential sweeping action is mentioned three times: this is what happened, this is where it happened and this is to whom it happened.

No wonder Deborah shrieks and jumps for joy when the Hebrew text says literally: 'you will stamp, my soul, mightily'. Even though a variety of amendments for a smoother translation are suggested, I read the text as it is because Deborah has good reason to be delighted: Israel's twenty-year oppression has come to an end. She mimics the hammering of hooves as Sisera's horses attempt to escape the advancing flood waters in frenzied panic. The enemy who arrived with confidence in numbers, drowned in disorder.

Yahweh's messenger makes an appearance and urges celebrants to curse a town and its inhabitants because they failed to 'help' Yahweh. Like the making of a vow, the uttering of a curse is more than mere wishful thinking. No divine or human agent is invoked to *do* anything apart from uttering the curse, but the spoken word possesses a potency to effect results. The curse carries force when it is ordered by Yahweh's messenger and the word 'curse' appears three times in Hebrew, twice in the imperative to express emphasis. We are not told what the Merozites did—or failed to do—to merit such disapproval; we are left to assume that they may have assisted Sisera in his twenty-year oppression of Israel or they may have been passive onlookers as he attempted to escape. It is possible that they behaved as shamefully as the inhabitants of Penuel and Succoth, who deny Gideon support when he requested food while pursuing Israel's enemies fleeing the land (cf. 8.4-9, 13-17). The messenger's curse may have had some effect because the location of Meroz is unknown.

Two Domestic Scenes (vv. 24-30)

An intense curse upon a wayward city and its inhabitants contrasts with a superlative blessing upon an individual female.

Three times Jael is identified simply as 'a woman' in order to shame and humiliate her male guest and victim. Jael is presented with approval as a unique character who is not only blessed but is superlatively blessed. We are about to be told again what she has done to merit such exuberant respect (cf. 4.17-22).

An unidentified male requested water (5.25). Who was this? Might the request have come from Jael's husband? Suspense. Jael generously responded with milk or curds served in a noble bowl which may have been her husband's goblet, a receptacle fit for the man of the tent as well as for noble heroes among the people of Yahweh (cf. v. 13). To whom was Jael so generous? Were Mr and Mrs Heber taking afternoon tea? More suspense. We are not told the man's name or where he has come from. The poetic version of Israel's deliverance contains none of the narrative's background detail. The storyteller-poet is anxious to take us to the mocking detail of a blow-by-blow account of the victim's demise. In the narrative, just two verbs describe the killing (cf. 4.21), but here in the song, a catalogue of thirteen Hebrew verbs describe a frenzy of slaughter activity: five feminine verbs describe what Jael did to her victim, two of which are repeated, followed by eight masculine verbs which describe what her male victim received.

As the man drank, Jael grasped a tent peg in one hand and reached for a hammer with her right hand. Both items were available because they are used for tent maintenance which is the work of nomadic women. The man is identified when he is hit (from behind?) by Jael with the hammer—her victim is not Mr Heber, but none other than Sisera, the one who led Israel's oppression for twenty years! Jael did not hesitate, she struck him on the head, she shattered and split open his skull. Jael destroyed her victim; he sank between her feet, he was prostrate, he fell between her feet; we are told yet again that he sank and yet again that he was prostrate, and to make sure that we have fully understood, we are again informed where he sank, and yet again that he was prostrate. Sisera's knees buckled under Jael's hammer blow and he fell prostrate at her feet. We are to be in no doubt—no doubt at all—Sisera was not only dead, he was decidedly dead! Enemies are swept away in a flood and their lifeless leader crumples at the feet of a woman! Easy!

The peg is only mentioned once and may have split his head apart but we are not told that he is pegged to the floor as in the narrative (4.21). However, each verb describes a subtle violent act followed by a pause for ancient hearers and modern readers to take in what has been done. When we are told in the last line that he was 'dead', we may wonder at the inclusion of such an understatement! However, there he is, there he lies, hammered, broken and destroyed. By its sound, the final Hebrew attack verb (*šādûd*) when uttered aloud has a quieter, more 'measured' sound after Jael's hammering and crushing of her victim's skull. The word begins with the hushed sound of air passing through the teeth and lips which seems to almost whisper in awe: it's done, he's dead, ruined, devastated, undone, annihilated. Look, here he lies, wasted; savour what has taken place, take in what you have heard, be glad at what you see; Israel's oppression is over: *ssssaaadooooood*. Wow!

Jael's encounter with Sisera is sometimes read as a sexual encounter (similar to Judith's preparation to meet Holofernes, cf. Jdt. 10.4), during which he is weakened and after which he sleeps. It is sometimes claimed that Sisera is a sexual opportunist who enters Jael's tent for the purpose of rape. I do not think so! The storyteller-poet's theme is the humiliation of the 'mighty', and the act which Deborah exuberantly celebrates in Jael's tent is neither sex nor a combination of sex and violence, but just brutal violence.

In an abrupt change of scene Deborah humiliates Israel's oppressor further. Sisera's slaughter is followed by a hilarious humiliation of his mother in a second domestic scene at another location. Deborah scorns her female rivals who wait in expectation for the return of their men. It is not her purpose to be subtle.

An imaginative leap is taken as we are brought to Sisera's home where his anxious mother looked from a window; she leant forward anticipating the sound of hoof-beats which announce her boy's approaching chariot and his safe return. Her lad is not expected to be empty handed, but she was worried because he was late. She was unaware that he has already been refreshed, mothered, smothered and dispatched by another woman. She asked aloud if there were reasons for his delay. She was in the company of princesses who are said to be wise (after a fashion) and are ready with answers for the curtain-twitcher's longing. However, before they could respond, she provided her own imaginative reasons for his delay which convinced her of his well-being: he is enjoying his victory; Israelite women and the spoils of battle are being shared among his charioteers. Sisera's mother's anticipation of spoil is bawdy, coarse and contemptuous of Israelite women. She anticipates that her son and his men are delayed because they are ruthlessly enjoying the conquests of women as spoil. Women are not referred to here honourably. Sisera's mother uses the vulgar language of the barrack room when she refers to Israelite women as her son's rape victims. Not only does she imagine the abuse of females by her son and his charioteers, she also anticipates an abundance of Israelite clothing for herself. Neither she nor her female companions consider that being forgotten or disappointed is an option as she leans from her window anxious for the first sound and sighting of her lad. Quality spoils are anticipated: a rape or two for the men and coloured cloth for herself. She longs to see her son's neck adorned with the garments that she will soon be wearing. Deborah gloats with victorious pride that there is neither sight nor sound of the darling boy, only anticipation, silence and longing.

Two Difficulties

Are we meant to approve or disapprove when acts of violence are celebrated? And how are we to understand the differences between the narrative and the celebration in verse?

First, how are we to read this domestic scene of a mother's longing for a son who we know has been hammered and pegged? Clearly this is not a homely tale told to win our sympathy for a mother's anxiety. We may also wonder about Deborah's purpose when gloating with glee over a mother's longing for her son who has already been slaughtered. A prior question may be asked about the purpose of the storyteller-poet for including such a scene.

It is the storyteller-poet who decides what is included and where we are taken. The second domestic scene has the purpose of adding further humiliation to the oppressor's slaughter and of including his mother in the humiliation. Both characters are humiliated in order to shame those who have oppressed Israel and their women who want to profit from that oppression. No sympathy is expressed here for anyone! In both domestic scenes Sisera is twice held in contempt: first, in the shameful manner of his slaughter by a woman in a woman's tent with a woman's domestic implement. Second, as his mother awaits his home-coming with longing, he is further humiliated. Deborah gloats over the imagined coming disappointment of Sisera's women. Not only are kings denied spoil, their women are also empty handed. We too may imagine the action in Jael's tent taking place in slow motion: the camera focuses on the assailant's hands, implements are grasped, music intensifies, the hammer is lifted and descends, the skull is shattered, the victim falls and the camera rests on the body as a mixture of blood and brain fluid slowly oozes from his open skull and stains the tent floor.

Why is the slaughter of Sisera repeated here in an overindulgent catalogue of claret-soaked violence and retold with an accumulation of attack verbs compared to the narrative's brief telling? Casual violence by itself is a stultifying form of behaviour with negative consequences for both perpetrator and victim in which a violent act is met with a violent reaction. However, the storyteller-poet has a specific purpose. This is an account in the form of a ballad about how the one who has led Israel's oppression finally and decisively meets his end. The storyteller is neither a disinterested teller nor an indifferent teller who keeps a safe critical distance aloof from events. The song is included in order to influence us profoundly. We are invited to share the storyteller's point of view that Israel's oppression—which lasts for a deeply unpleasant twenty years—has come to an end and to celebrate with singer(s), chorus and dancers the humiliating demise of the oppressor commander and to mock his soon to be disappointed mother and her companions. Sisera has not died an honourable hero's death in battle following a one-to-one combat; he has been shamefully dispatched by a woman. Sisera has run away from a torrent of bad weather into a torrent of personal trauma. The violence is not casual but purposeful. We are to be in no doubt that Israel's oppression has come to an end.

Some may disapprove when acts of violence without remorse are used to describe the slaughter of enemies and are presented as glorious grown-up fun; however, the storyteller is not so coy and neither is Deborah, the central female character. We cannot dismiss the violence of ch. 5—in which Yahweh is complicit—as the violence of a male image of God which requires the softness of a feminine touch. This is a woman's text in which female characters are in the foreground. The violence of violent people has come to an end and the land is at peace; moreover, the rapes of Israel's women with which a mother anticipates her son is occupied are not committed. I argue, therefore, that violence in ancient biblical storytelling—which some may consider to be morally suspect—is acceptable in two places: first, when Yahweh acts to deliver the oppressed; and second, when the manner of an oppressor's humiliating slaughter is celebrated with approval by the storyteller's 'reliable' characters who possess the status of Israel's judge-prophetess-matriarch and Yahweh's messenger.

There is no discussion in the song about the rights or wrongs of victors gloating over the defeat and slaughter of enemies or whether Jael may have abused ancient hospitality customs or if the slaughter of Sisera may be considered a treacherous act. The storyteller is not embarrassed by what it takes to win Israel's independence. Moreover, a psalmist, who is clearly impressed with Deborah's song, also wants her enemies to be destroyed like Israel's enemies of the past among whom Sisera is listed (Ps. 83.10-11). The battle for independence—by Israel's force of arms and by Yahweh's cosmic and meteorological intervention—is a just war with the aim of removing oppressive invaders and restoring Israel to covenant loyalty. Sisera continued to behave disgracefully when he deserted his command and ran away from the prospect of an honourable last stand. No songs of celebration will be written and sung about the heroism of this cowardly Canaanite charioteer like the exuberant song that here celebrates 'Victory in Israel Day' and records the triumphs of Israel's villagers. We are to be impressed by both narrative and song which tell of a formidable enemy who is successfully defeated by the teamwork of Deborah the judge-prophetess with the collaboration of Barak the courageous general of Israel's willing and noble volunteers and of Jael who seizes the day.

A second difficulty arises when the differences are noted between the narrative and the celebration in verse. In the narrative, Sisera lays down to rest; he is covered, then pegged. In verse, it is while he stands to drink that he is hammered to the floor. The principal difference which I would like to identify between the two accounts is that the battle of the narrative does not appear in verse. In the song, it is Yahweh who marches, the people willingly volunteer, some tribes appear—others make their excuses—but there is no military engagement as in the narrative when the enemy panics under Barak's courageous downhill charge from which Sisera himself runs on foot (Judg. 4.14) and all are slaughtered (v. 16). Other judge-deliverers meet oppressors on the battlefield: Othniel 'went out to battle' (3.10); Ehud, with the Israelites of the hill country, slaughters Moabites (3.28-29); Shamgar slaughters Philistines (3.31). However, in ch. 5 the two armies do not appear to meet face to face. In the song, the 'battle' is won when Sisera's army is routed and swept away by a flash-flood. The explanation for the differences between the narrative and verse is that in the latter the storyteller, with the voice of a poet, is a 'singer of victories' who presents a theological version of Israel's conflict with Sisera's chariots and infantry as an act of 'holy war' which is similar to the 'song of Moses and the Israelites' (cf. Exod. 15). Yahweh's participation is emphasized while Israel's militia does little; when Yahweh is on the march the earth trembles, the mountains stream with rain water and Israel's enemies are swept away.

Deborah's victory song concludes with the chorus's exuberant wish for all Yahweh's enemies to perish and for those who love Yahweh to beam like the rays of the sun. The land rests from conflict for forty years. Deborah's song is a celebration of 'Victory in Israel Day'; Israel's oppression is at an end. May all the world's oppressors likewise perish!

Judges 6:
Gideon: A Commission for a Reluctant Deliverer

We are about to be introduced to a reluctant deliverer who changes overnight from cynic to popular hero. Military leaders who are cool and cautious like Gideon are respected by their followers because they know their lives will not be thrown away on unrealistic combat objectives by an aspiring hero in the reckless pursuit of personal honour.

The stories of Israel's deliverance from formidable oppressors are triumphantly told. We have read the brief story of Israel's war hero who simply 'went out to battle' (3.10) and defeated a world-class oppressor. A 'perfect murder' unfolded as we were presented with the career-best performance of a lone Israelite, who—with one hand behind his back and a little home-made wooden dagger in the other—delivered Israel from a formidable coalition of oppressors (3.7-30). We have not overlooked the one whose heroism was so impressive that he has come to be regarded with honour as the son of a goddess (3.31). We have been invited to sing along with a raucous chorus in celebration of the team effort of the bee, a flash of lightning, and a nanny goat (ch. 5). All risk their lives for the higher purpose of delivering the people of Yahweh from oppressors and we are impressed with their spectacular acts of courage.

We next follow Gideon, the idol destroyer, as he defeats overwhelming numbers of invaders with a few loyal companions by simply standing still and making a lot of noise.

The Characterization of Israel's Next Oppressors (vv. 1-6, 33; 7.1, 12)

When Yahweh decides yet again that the time is right to respond to Israel's apostasy by summoning oppressors, the land is invaded by a nomadic coalition of Midianites, Amalekites (again in a supportive role, cf. 3.13; Exod. 17.8) and hordes of 'Easterners'. Just as Sisera had the military advantage of 'iron' chariots, these invaders have the advantage of overwhelming numbers, their tents are like a plague of migratory locusts, their camp stretches as far south as Gaza and they are accompanied by camels which are too numerous to count. Associated with the Midianites are Ishmaelites who are a camel-breeding tribe of the desert (Judg. 8.24; Gen. 37.28, 36; 39.1). Camels are environmentally adapted to the desert and possess a tolerance for dehydration and drought; they are able to travel without drinking and move at speed over sand on large flat hoof-pads. 'Easterners' is a term applied to the inhabitants of the desert from east of the Jordan. They are also cited for their proverbial wisdom (1 Kgs 4.30 [5.10]) and Job is described as the 'greatest' of all the sons of the east (Job 1.3). However, the invaders do not arrive in the land to impart wisdom but to carry away Israel's harvest secured to the backs of their camels. For seven consecutive years the land is pillaged by desert tribes.

Parallels may be observed between these new nomadic invasions and Yahweh's itemized warnings and curses in Deut. 28 of economic and social hardship which will be brought upon Israelites if they are disloyal to Yahweh. For example, 'you shall build a house but not live in it' (v. 30) may be compared with Israelites who are forced to abandon their homes and hide in caves (cf. Judg. 6.2). 'You shall plant a vineyard but not enjoy its fruit' (v. 30) may be compared with the looting of Israel's produce (cf. Judg. 6.3). 'Your ox shall be butchered before your eyes, but you shall not eat of it; your donkey shall be stolen in front of you and shall not be restored to you; your sheep shall be given to your enemies, without anyone to help you' (v. 31) may be compared with the looting of animal fodder when none of Israel's livestock remains (cf. Judg. 6.4). And, 'a people whom you do not know shall eat up the fruit of your ground and of all your labours, you shall be continually destroyed and crushed' (v. 33) may be compared with Israel's land occupied by strangers who loot its produce (cf. Judg. 6.3).

The results of successive nomadic raids are more than the looting of Israel's annual harvests for their food supply. The nomads are characterized as land-wasters who threaten Israel's very existence through the application of overwhelming force. Israelites hide in inaccessible places in the hills. Israelites have never been so oppressed. Israel requires a deliverer.

Instead of a deliverer—a person of action—Yahweh sends a man of words, an unnamed prophet. Israel appeals for help, but what Israel gets is another reprimand reinforced with abrupt historical reminders of the goodness of Yahweh in the past and Israel's apostasy in the present. Israelites are forcefully reminded of their past and of their obligation not to fear the gods of the Amorites (vv. 7-10; cf. 2.1-5; Exod. 34.11-15; Josh. 24.15).

Gideon and Yahweh's Messenger (vv. 11-24)

In contrast to the terse oracle of an unnamed prophet, the first words of Yahweh's messenger to Gideon are in the form of a courteous and complimentary greeting as he sits in the shade of a tree at Ophrah watching him at work. This tree, like Deborah's palm with its leaves and shade, may be a symbol of life and fertility and the only sign of growth that remains in a landscape picked clean by harvest looters.

Gideon lets the messenger's 'mighty warrior' greeting pass. However, to be told that 'Yahweh is with you' is an absurd proposition which requires comment. Gideon's replies have more than a touch of sarcasm when he protests: if Yahweh were with him and with Israel, he and his people would experience the wonder of rescue from the oppression of looters such as when his ancestors were rescued from Egyptian oppression (cf. Exod. 3.20; 15.11; 34.10). Yahweh's messenger may have spoken to Moses in the past and led Israel through the Reed Sea; however, Gideon protests that neither Yahweh, nor his messengers, have been active recently on Israel's behalf.

Gideon's replies intensify as he moves from sarcasm to cynicism. His 'cynicism' is one of the keys to understanding the storyteller's perspective in the Gideon stories and elsewhere in Judges. A cynic is a passionate person who has been disappointed and does not want to be disappointed again. Gideon's complaint is that Yahweh has abandoned him and his people; their land is now at the mercy of others. He is aware of Yahweh's wonders in the past when Israel was brought up from Egypt, but that was then; where is Yahweh now when Yahweh is needed? Furthermore, Gideon does not want to be a deliverer. Conflict with oppressors is something he is trying to avoid as he prepares wheat in a place associated with grape processing away from the eyes of invaders.

Gideon's response is understandable. He has no evidence that Yahweh is either with him or with Israel. If Yahweh were with him and his people then Israel's land would not be wasted, harvests would be abundant and nomadic looters would have been expelled from the land six harvests ago. Gideon is no one's fool, not even Yahweh's.

Yahweh is not distinguished from his messenger when Gideon is issued with a commission. He is told to deliver Israel because in Yahweh's estimation he is up to the task of delivering his people from the 'grip' of the nomadic coalition. Gideon's scepticism remains even though Yahweh has promised to be with him and that he will be able to smite all the invaders.

Even though this is the first occasion in Judges when Yahweh speaks directly to a potential deliverer, Gideon is either unimpressed with the speaker's confidence in his abilities or he is unaware of the identity of this visitor when he protests that he and his family lack clout. Gideon claims insignificance; he is the youngest son in the smallest family in the tribe of Manasseh. We are given no information about his stature or details of his previous exploits where he may have acquired honour as 'a mighty warrior'. Like Barak at the time of his 'call', Gideon's mettle is untested. When Yahweh wants to get things done, it appears that he calls those who are unwilling and feel their own insignificance: first Moses, then Joshua, now Gideon.

To summarize so far. The task set before Gideon is daunting. Not only does a formidable coalition of nomadic invaders return each harvest for seven successive years, they are numbered like locusts and grains of sand. Israelites are impoverished and hide in the hills while the land is wasted. Gideon knows his place and he tells Yahweh and his messenger that he is not deliverer material. He is unlike former judge-deliverers and their collaborators who take to their tasks without hesitation; he is unlike Othniel, Ehud, Shamgar, Deborah, Barak and Jael. Gideon's response is different; he hesitates, he challenges, he objects. As he says, little people like himself do not become delivers; little people prepare their food in secret away from the eyes of harvest looters.

Could it be that Yahweh is mistaken when attempting to commission a cynic with low morale to deliver his people from the most formidable oppressors so far?

Gideon vs. Baal (vv. 25-32)

Yahweh commands Gideon to demolish the baal altar and cultic pole belonging to his father, Joash the Abiezrite, and to construct a Yahweh-altar upon which he is to sacrifice his father's seven-year-old 'second' bull. How does Yahweh communicate such specific instructions? Has Yahweh's messenger returned or as the communication is made at night, may this be in Gideon's dream? However, it seems to be a series of foolish acts because the bull may be the only live animal that remains in Ophrah. We are aware that Israel is impoverished, that the land is wasted, produce is looted and no livestock remains. Joash's bull may therefore be a rather poor specimen. If the animal is the 'best' bull rather than his father's 'second' bull, it will no doubt be the 'best' that is available while food and fodder are scarce and Israel's food supply is threatened. Gideon does Yahweh's bidding at night with the assistance of ten servants because he is naturally fearful for his own self-preservation and it is no small thing for a son with low self-esteem to destroy what may be the symbols of his father's status.

When the Ophrah early risers discover the deed and who is responsible, they demand of Joash nothing less than the life of his son. Joash chooses to defend Gideon rather than side with the local baal who has done nothing to protect Ophrah's harvest from nomadic looters. We now see that cynicism is a family characteristic and that Joash himself is a satirist when he asks if his neighbours are speaking up for Baal. Joash is not interested in their reply because Baal is capable of making his own self-defence. As he says, 'let him speak up for himself'. Contained in Gideon's newly acquired name—Jerubbaal—is the verb 'contend' with the addition of 'baal' as the subject which identifies him as the person to whom Baal may complain about the vandalism of his cultic furniture if he has a mind: 'let Baal contend with him'.

Gideon obeys Yahweh when he challenges the pagan deity by destroying one altar and building another upon which he sacrifices his father's bull. However, we may wonder if he will be able to smite the nomadic hordes and deliver Israel when he is afraid to act alone in daylight against the cultic possessions of his family and neighbours.

Baal's new opponent is under pressure because the nomadic invaders gather together, cross the Jordan and form their formidable encampment in the Valley of Jezreel.

Gideon's Signs (vv. 36-40)

Gideon has an empowering encounter with the spirit of Yahweh when he is either clothed from the *outside* like a cloak or resided *within* by the spirit when he is worn like an outer garment. The spirit either comes upon Gideon or takes possession of him. The time for Israel's militia to assemble has arrived. Gideon's own Abiezrite clan respond to the call of his ram's horn as does the militia from Asher, Zebulun and Naphtali. However, even though he has an empowering clothing encounter with Yahweh's spirit and is followed by Israel's militia under arms, Gideon still wants further assurances. He asks for signs with a fleece, first wet then dry, as sign-evidence that Yahweh will deliver Israel by his hand as Yahweh has said. Demanding signs from Yahweh with a wool fleece, first one way then another, may not be the language of one who is wearing or being worn by Yahweh's spirit; it is, however, the understandable request of one who is cautious before engaging formidable oppressors.

In summary, Gideon is naturally cool and cautious. He is careful and circumspect about the proposed conflict with nomadic invaders whose numbers are insurmountable. He asks for sign-evidence—first from Yahweh's messenger, then from Yahweh—that he is not called to participate in a fool's errand. In the chapter that follows, the reading demonstrates that Gideon's repeated request for signs do not necessarily reveal timidity and cowardice. They are his means of being reassured—before engaging a formidable foe—that Yahweh will do what Yahweh has promised.

Judges 7:
Gideon and the 300

Even though there is no headcount of Israel's next oppressors, they are threatening and assemble in a vast gathering. Their tents are like a dense swarm of locusts which darkens the land as far as anyone can see even as far south as Gaza (the whole of Canaan, cf. Gen. 10.19). They and their camels are too many to count; they—the Midianites, Amalekites and people from the east—are as uncountable as the sand grains on the beach (Judg. 6.1-6, 33; 7.12). Such is the characterization of the vast numbers who await Israel's next deliverer.

The Reduction of Gideon's Militia
from 32,000 to 300 (vv. 2-8)

Israel's next commissioned deliverer is accompanied by a militia numbering a mere 32,000 who are to engage the locust hoards. Gideon and his army make camp at the Harod water source which is appropriately known locally as the 'Trembling Spring'. The spring's name reflects the militia's state of mind at the prospect of the battle ahead.

Gideon has already received an abundance of reassurances which add up to a substantial list of sign-evidence that he is the one to deliver Israel. Yahweh promises Gideon that he will not be alone, since Yahweh will be with him. He is assured that all the invaders will be struck down. Gideon observes the ascent of fire from the Ophrah rock and the withdrawal of Yahweh's messenger. Moreover, he receives Yahweh's reassurance of peace; he is not to be afraid, he will not die. Gideon's positive response to what he observes and hears at Ophrah shows that he is impressed when he builds an altar which he calls 'Yahweh is peace' and his reassurances continue. Gideon is instructed by Yahweh in a dream to burn the Ophrah Baal furniture and sacrifice his father's bull. He receives support from his father who does not join the townspeople in their outrage against his son.

Baal neither strives nor contends. Gideon is clothed by Yahweh's spirit. When he musters his own clan, the tribes willingly follow. Yahweh obliges with the two fleece signs, first wet, then dry. Gideon is followed to Harod by 32,000 Israelites mustered to engage the nomadic invaders. After encountering Yahweh's spirit, Gideon's repeated requests for signs do not necessarily reveal his fearfulness and timidity or indicate cowardice but are his means of being reassured, before engaging a formidable foe, that Yahweh will do what Yahweh has promised. Israel's next deliverer is almost ready.

However, someone is not satisfied. Gideon has made demands of Yahweh and has no doubt tried his patience. Yahweh also has a trial for Gideon with a time-consuming water test of his own. Gideon is under pressure but Yahweh is in no hurry. Again we wonder how Yahweh 'speaks' to Gideon (vv. 2-8). Gideon has received specific instructions from Yahweh in a dream (6.25) which will occur again (7.9), but how does Yahweh communicate the precise procedure for troop reduction? The storyteller is not troubled by the anomaly of God speaking directly to a mortal without an intermediary such as a priest (1.1), messenger (2.1-4) or prophet (6.7-10); the story of Israel's deliverance is to be told and listeners await the outcome.

Gideon and his militia may tremble at the prospect of engaging an invading army of vastly superior numbers, but Yahweh says that 32,000 Israelites are too numerous to be of any use! If Israel's militia should defeat the nomads, they will forget him and boast about their own achievement. Gideon is, therefore, to send home those who are frightened and who tremble at the prospect of the battle which lies ahead. Two thirds of his militia take the opportunity to escape and 'fly away' to the remote safety of Mount Gilead. Gideon is astonished to be left with a mere 10,000.

However, Yahweh is still not satisfied. What Yahweh requires is a further reduction of the human element. Gideon has tested Yahweh with water tests of sorts; now Yahweh proposes a further test for Gideon also by means of water.

At the edge of the Trembling Spring Gideon is instructed by Yahweh to divide his warriors into two groups. He is to separate those who lap water with their tongues like a dog from those who kneel to drink. Three hundred lap, bringing the water to their mouths as they stand. A bemused Gideon observes the 10,000 as they form a queue to each drink in turn. The drinkers are also bemused as the separation is made. Yahweh whispers in Gideon's ear that those who lap the water while standing are to be put in one group and those who kneel to drink in another.

It is of no concern whether the larger group of 9,700 kneel on one knee or on both knees with their faces to the water. Yahweh's interest is with a few who happen to number 300 and Gideon is to observe whether drinkers stand or kneel to take their refreshment. The drinkers who kneel with their heads dipped to the water or lie flat and drink directly from the water, as is sometimes claimed, do not drink like dogs. Dogs stand when drinking. The numerical refining process separates the few who stand from the many who kneel. Standing is not specified in the text because the posture of a drinking dog is common knowledge. The observation suggests that the 300 stand to drink and bring water to their mouths with their hands like a dog uses its tongue to bring water to its mouth. The test, by water-refinement, is Yahweh's arbitrary means to select a few and eliminate many. A few are required and in Yahweh's battles neither numbers nor skills matter. A minority are required and 300 are selected. Yahweh could make his selection by choosing the minority who wear their hair in a certain style, the minority who wear a type of ear ring, the minority with a particular eye colour or the minority who may guess how many figs are on a particular tree. Refinement by water is Yahweh's natural available means of leisurely making a further reduction.

Yahweh's sense of humour is revealed in the method he uses to prepare Gideon and his men for combat. Gideon is not told to make preparations for battle by giving his men a strict training regime in military techniques or to take them out for desert manoeuvres, but (absurdly) to watch their method of drinking. It is often thought that those who stand to drink are more alert for battle and look around them for the enemy. However, alertness is not required among the members of Gideon's small militia. All that matters is for a small number to be assembled who will follow Yahweh's cautious leader.

Under the circumstances what Yahweh proposes is an absurd waste of time. Let's pry into the text (just a little) and imagine that Gideon observes the drinkers at the rate of, say, two a minute. This means that about 120 drinkers perform before him each hour. Allowing for rest breaks, Gideon will be able to observe about 1,000 drinkers during daylight, which means that the observation of the 10,000 and their separation into two groups takes about ten days. The 22,000 who are too frightened at the prospect of battle may have taken a day or two, to strike camp which means that the total reduction (from 32,000 to 300) may have taken almost two weeks in which time the nomadic hordes could have taken the initiative and either attacked or absconded with Israel's produce. Gideon is dismayed; he shakes his head; he wonders what he has got himself into and how he is going to deliver Israel from hordes of Midianites with just 9,700 warriors! However, Yahweh chuckles to himself as he informs Gideon that it is the larger group of 9,700 who can return to their tents, which they do leaving behind their supplies and ram's horns. Gideon is shocked to discover that he is to lead the remaining 300 in what appears to be a forlorn hope against a formidable enemy.

Gideon's time has come. The nomads are encamped in the valley below and he is to get up and descend to them because Yahweh has given them into his hand. For Gideon to take the initiative and attack such a vast number with a little force of 300 is a terrifying prospect. Yahweh has another sign for Gideon if he is still unsure. If, after receiving all the signs and participating in the tests, he is still fearful of the prospect of battle, Yahweh says that there is still time for him to secretly descend to the nomad's camp and eavesdrop on their conversations. He will be sure to overhear something that will give him confidence. Moreover, he has no need to go alone; he can even take Purah his servant for company.

A Dream and its Interpretation (vv. 9-15)

For the final sign which dispels Gideon's caution, Yahweh invites him to descend to the enemy outposts and listen to a conversation among the Midianites who are discussing a dream and its interpretation. He is accompanied by his servant because no one wants to descend into the valley of death alone, especially if what is discovered is to be disclosed to the 300 on his safe return.

The dream, when it is told and overheard, is surreal and concerns a Midianite calamity; the speaker requests an interpretation: he dreamt of a barley loaf that rolled into camp and flattened a tent. The dreamer does not say if the loaf is big enough to do the flattening or if he is troubled by what is said to occur which does not appear to have been a nightmare, but he is intrigued by such an absurd prospect. The speaker describes a 'symbolic dream' which is generally dreamt by Gentile leaders such as Pharaoh and Nebuchadnezzar. Such dreams—which lack sense or meaning—require interpretations to disclose messages which are ominous and concern future events. It is not certain if his companion is a specialist in dream interpretation to whom the meaning is immediately clear: the 'flattening' is a calamity which the dream interpreter says will be brought upon the Midianites by Gideon.

Even though a certain importance may be attached to dreams and their meanings which are thought to foretell the future and are a way in which the gods communicate to dreamers, *this* particular dream is thought to be of little consequence. It is the dream of 'a man', not the dream of a king which would attract attention. If it had been King Zebah's dream accompanied by King Zalmunna's interpretation (8.5) the Midianites would have struck camp and moved on. They have no cause to be agitated or frightened by the dream or its interpretation; they have security in numbers; Israelites are hiding in caves and the prospect of them being attacked is as absurd as a loaf of barley-bread rolling into their camp and flattening a tent.

However, Gideon takes the dream and its interpretation seriously as a divinely communicated sign which promises him victory. Gideon is so familiar with Yahweh's communications through dreams (7.9; 6.25) that it is natural for him to hold the Midianite's dream in high regard for it to settle the matter of his caution. Midianites dream about their own defeat and about his triumph. Dreaming of defeat and actual defeat are different manifestations of the same idea and the way this dreamer thinks about himself produces a dream and an interpretation which is certain to come to pass. Strong warriors dream of victory; weak warriors dream of defeat. Midianites lack certainty. Dreams and their interpretations create realities. Gideon also overhears his own name and that he is the son of his father. Moreover, he is described as a 'man' of Israel, not a boy or the youngest. Furthermore, he is known among the invaders. Until this disclosure the risk of engagement has been too great; now Gideon's situation is reversed: he knows that the nomads are given into his hands; at last he is reassured of success. Gideon is a changed man.

The dream and its interpretation are the ultimate signs which at last give Gideon the assurance that harvest looters and land-wasters will be defeated. Until now he has been a Yahweh-sceptic, but on his return to the 300, there is urgency in his voice. He informs them that Yahweh has given the nomads into *their* hands—not 'into *my* hands'—and he motivates his little army by sharing with them his newfound certainty.

A Terrifying Midnight Performance of Sound and Light (vv. 16-25)

In order to proceed at night—simultaneously on three sides of the enemy camp in the Valley of Jezreel—Gideon divides the 300 into three groups, which are of equal numbers because he accompanies a group of 100 men.

Gideon issues the 300 with the most inappropriate and absurd equipment for battle: each man is given a ram's horn, an empty earthenware jar and a torch! His instructions to the 300 are precise. They are not to let him out of their sight as they move about the valley; when they are almost on top of the sleeping enemy they are to copy what he does. When Gideon blows his ram's horn the 300 are to blow their ram's horns and shout a battle cry which contains the essential information that the one who has been dreamt about has arrived, his army is rolling into their camp and gathering momentum. The blasts of ram's horns, the shouts and the sudden appearance of 300 lights in the darkness, announce the arrival of Gideon 'the man of Israel' at the head of his army.

The ram's horns are sounded, followed by the 'breaking' of the earthenware jars which reveal the torches as the 300 shout, 'a sword for Yahweh and for Gideon!' The Midianites hear shouts containing a specific detail from the dream of one of their number which adds further authenticity to the atmosphere of fear and dread among the nomads as they awake. The night 'attack' requires careful attention to detail with synchronized timing accompanied by trust and discipline among the 300 and their leader in order to use the darkness and the familiar terrain of the valley to the best advantage. Gideon plans their 'performance' to take place with precision at the beginning of the middle watch at midnight, the most vulnerable time of the Midianite sentry system. A terrifying disturbance is created of shrill noises which echo around the valley: the sounding of 300 ram's horns, the smashing of 300 earthenware jars, the shouting of a war cry announcing the fearful arrival of Gideon and Yahweh combined with the sudden appearance of 300 lights. Items are programmed to follow one another. The simultaneous smashing of jars sounds like thunder. The sudden appearance of 300 lights appears to be of supernatural origin. The torches are rotated, indicating movement and activity. The shout is like a shrill chorus in which each word is clearly enunciated and clearly heard. The ram's horns, which have a flat unmusical sound, are first blown together, followed by further blasts and shouts which are repeated over and over again in a cacophony of sound indicating an advancing army. The results are spectacular. The Midianites wake up in panic. They cry out in alarm. They turn on each other in the darkness and confusion. One night a sentry shares a dream and receives an interpretation about defeat. That same night, or the following night—allowing time for Gideon's preparation—the Midianites attack each other. Survivors flee the land.

Gideon's courage is outstanding. He places himself and the 300 at considerable risk without an exit strategy at the very edge of the enemy's camp which contains overwhelming numbers. The 300 follow a leader who, when he is certain of success, makes a specific decision to confront hordes of harvest looters—not after consultation about strategy with commanders pouring over military charts—but after he overhears, of all things, the telling of a dream by one of the enemy and the interpretation of the dream by another. Such a plan, founded upon a suspect source of intelligence, seems foolhardy. Moreover, the 300 are to engage the locust hordes equipped, not with the latest weaponry, but with domestic implements! Furthermore, the instructions that the 300 are to obey reveal their position at the very edge of the enemy camp at night with lights and noise and shouts. When Israel's militia is recalled, a specific call is made to the Ephraimites to take the strategic Jordan crossing where two nomad leaders are captured and executed. Their heads are presented to Israel's triumphant deliverer.

In summary, Gideon's leadership and the performance of the 300 is impressive, but victory honours belong to Yahweh who in the confusion of the enemy camp sets every man against the other. Gideon's 'sword' is acknowledged but is unused. Neither he nor the 300 shed enemy blood in a deliverance in which Yahweh fights for Israel and Israelites simply stand and watch. Gideon and the 300 create a terrifying midnight disturbance of sound and light, then do no more than stand still and listen to the panic in the darkness.

One of the difficulties with making a positive reading of Gideon is to account for what is often referred to as the violent act of a sadist when it is claimed that he treats the Israelite inhabitants of Succoth and Penuel like his enemies. May Gideon's vengeance upon two wayward Israelite cities mean that a positive reading of his character cannot be made?

Judges 8:
Gideon's Defence of the Pastures of God

The Gideon story, which unfolds with humour and absurdity, now becomes dark and bleak. Enemy kings are executed and Gideon responds in kind to taunts from Israelites. He treats the inhabitants of Succoth and Penuel like his enemies because they behave like his enemies.

Succoth and Penuel (vv. 1-17)

When the Ephraimites present Gideon with the severed heads of two nomad leaders, Oreb and Zeeb ('the raven' and 'the wolf'), they complain that they were not included in an invitation to engage the Midianite hordes. The Ephraimites whinge because they have been denied spoil. Apparently they did not hear or they chose to ignore Gideon's call to join his militia. Gideon's response is non-confrontational and diplomatic. He compliments them on the capture and execution of the nomad leaders which he says is more impressive than his own endeavours. So far Gideon has not killed anyone. Furthermore, he reminds the Ephraimites that the success of their military endeavours is not in their hands, but it is Yahweh who has enabled them to capture enemy leaders.

When Gideon and the 300 cross the Jordan valley in pursuit of fleeing nomadic survivors and their kings, they face dire conditions. They are thirsty, hungry and exhausted, which explains his request to the local inhabitants for food, first from Succoth—a city associated with Jacob (Gen. 33.17)—and from Penuel, a city also associated with Jacob's travels where he encounters 'the face of God' (Gen. 32.30). The enemy kings whom Gideon pursues possess names that suggest they are formidable opponents even though they flee the land. Zebah means 'sacrifice' and Zalmunna has a hostile name associated with the refusal of hospitality in the shade. Citizens of both cities are unimpressed. Their refusals to give support are accompanied by personal taunts. A taunt is fighting talk, a ritualistic challenge which is not to be ignored unless the person on the receiving end backs down.

Even though Gideon makes a reasonable request for provisions, his appeal is understood by the inhabitants of both Succoth and Penuel as a boast that his quarries are already in his possession. His request is refused. Big mistake! However, honour is at stake. Gideon and his weary army leave Succoth and Penuel empty handed uttering threats of reprisals on their return once their mission is complete. The elders of Succoth will be taught the lesson of loyalty; they will be thrown into thorns and trampled and Penuel's tower will be pulled down because both Israelite communities fail to provide food for a militia who are at war on behalf of Israel and are far from home. Moreover, they fail to fulfil the obligation and expectation of hospitality with the provision of refreshment for warriors in a harsh environment. They will be humiliated and treated with contempt by Gideon on his return.

Meanwhile, the Midianite body-count is alarmingly high. An invading force of 135,000 armed nomads has been reduced by 120,000 to a terrified fleeing remnant of 15,000, a loss of about 90 per cent in Gideon's midnight performance of sound and light in the valley of Jezreel combined with the attack by Naphtali, Asher and Manasseh and Ephraim at the Jordan. The nomadic survivors are pursued along the familiar 'tent-dwellers' road' where they consider themselves to be safely out of Gideon's reach and in home territory. However, when they are attacked, the dispirited nomads are too terrified to mount a defence; they panic and run because they are terrified by the mere threat of Gideon's approach. The two nomadic kings, Zebah and Zalmunna, are captured; survivors flee. It is of course in Gideon's interests that a few terrified empty-handed nomads survive to tell other nomads on their return home how they have been expelled from the land by 'Gideon, a man of Israel' so that they will be too frightened to invade and loot the land at Israel's next harvest. Israel's looters are soundly defeated.

Before leaving the Jordan, Gideon has unfinished business with the inhabitants of two wayward Israelite cities. Penuel is passed by in order to deal first with Succoth. A Succoth youth is interrogated who supplies a list of their leaders and elders amounting to seventy-seven men. The young man has sympathy with Gideon who now possesses a precise register of Succoth rulers and elders in order to bring them to account.

Gideon displays the two captured enemy kings to the 'men of Succoth', to the ones who said they were not obliged to provision an empty-handed leader of exhausted men. They are called to account because of their public taunts and insults as is the practice of warriors in pre-combat stories (cf. 1 Sam. 17.8-10, 43-47; 2 Sam. 21.21). As promised in the earlier taunting exchange, they are thrashed by Gideon with thorns and briers. What is evident from Gideon's threat and the threat being carried out is that he gives the elders of Succoth a humiliating and public punishment—a beating with thorn branches from the desert flora.

Gideon returns to Penuel and again he does as he promised and pulls down their tower. He has not threatened to kill the inhabitants. He threatens only their tower's demolition in reprisal for their mockery and refusal to provide support. Evidently the men of the city attempt to defend their property and suffer the consequences.

The Execution of Two Enemy Kings (vv. 18-21)

Gideon also has unfinished family business with the captured kings, Zebah 'the sacrifice' and Zalmunna 'the inhospitable', whose lives he would have spared had they not been responsible for the murder of his brothers. Although the Tabor killings refer to an incident unrecorded by the storyteller, the kings are well aware of those to whom Gideon refers. They answer diplomatically that their victims had the appearance of princes, like Gideon himself. When Gideon says they were his kin the kings realize their time is limited. He unwisely uses the family vendetta to initiate Jether, his eldest son, in the harsh realities of conflict resolution when he proposes a dishonourable and humiliating death for the two kings at the hands of the boy. Even though it is an honour for his son to kill kings who have led the nomadic invasions of the land and murdered his uncles, Gideon's firstborn lets his father down badly. Jether has no heart for execution. Their final words are a taunt to the lad and to his father because slaying noble nomadic kings such as themselves is a man's task. Gideon executes them himself and takes their camel's decorations as spoil. The name of both kings is reflected in their fate. Zebah is slaughtered like a sacrificial victim. Zalmunna, who has denied shade to others, is denied his life.

To summarize so far: even though Yahweh delivers Israel, it is Gideon himself, accompanied by a reduced force of a mere 300, who faces the hordes of nomads in the valley of Jezreel equipped with domestic implements. Succoth and Penuel are not attacked without cause. Gideon serves Yahweh's purpose in the interests of Israel's welfare when he becomes the cause of the slaughter of foreign oppressors and expels survivors from the land. Israelites can now descend from their caves and hiding places and Gideon himself can thresh his wheat where it should be threshed and clean his wine press in preparation for the next grape harvest. He refuses the offer to be Israel's dynastic king and reminds the 'men of Israel' that they live in a theocracy, Yahweh rules over them and they are to remain in covenant loyalty. He simply asks for his share of the gold rings taken from the Ishmaelites and their camels (Judg. 8.24).

Further questions are raised by the closing episodes which could indicate that a positive evaluation of Gideon's character, the focus of the reading, is not possible. For example, why does he make an ephod? How does the ephod become a cause of Israel's unfaithfulness and a 'snare' to Gideon himself and to his family?

Why does Gideon Make his Own Ephod? (vv. 22-28)

An ephod is a high priest's vest or tunic around which other garments are fitted when serving Yahweh in the Tabernacle (Exod. 28, 35, 39; Lev. 8). It is a revered item of beauty made with care and skill from fine materials. An ephod can also be made of fine linen such as that worn by the boy Samuel (1 Sam. 2.18) and by David as he dances (2 Sam. 6.14; 1 Chron. 15.27). It appears to be worn by a priest when making a specific request to Yahweh and when a decisive answer is required. An ephod may be worn to insure that a specific answer will be forthcoming. For example, David requests Abiather the priest that he bring the ephod which he carries and he asks Yahweh about the pursuit of the Philistines and on another occasion about the pursuit of the Amalkites (1 Sam. 23.6, 9-12; 30.1-8); on both occasions Yahweh gives specific answers. Phinehas the priest also carries an ephod (1 Sam. 14.3).

Two characters in Judges make their own ephod, Gideon and Micah (chs. 17 and 18). Micah is sponsored in business by his crafty mother as a religious entrepreneur who fills a gap in the market with a means of assisting Israelites to consult an ephod and idols about matters of concern, no doubt for a fee. Even though an ephod appears to be a visible garment, it is uncertain what Gideon's ephod looks like which he makes from his share of the Midianite spoils. The storyteller does not say that he builds a shrine at Ophrah; however, his ephod does appear to have an oracle-function like Micah's but with a difference: Micah is a businessman; Gideon's ephod is made for a more noble purpose.

Gideon makes his own ephod as his means of direct access to Yahweh in the hope that he will receive specific replies when required. His commission was to a daunting task. He has survived a prolonged engagement with a terrifying and formidable invading foe. He has faced insurmountable problems. He has made decisions while in action and remained calm in a crisis. He has received no training nor engaged in any planning exercises. Now with the land at peace and the provision of his own personal ephod—which he may consult should the need of Yahweh's counsel arise—Gideon has no need for further visits from Yahweh's messenger with absurd proposals. He has no need to rely upon foolish and humiliating water tests with a fleece. He has no need to participate in ridiculous time-consuming drinking experiments with 22,000 participants or to rely on overhearing the dreams and interpretations of enemies. Gideon makes his own direct and secure means of access to Yahweh.

However, Gideon's retirement with his personal ephod—if retirement it is—is not without its problems. The ephod, which is not made with devious intent, attracts similar misplaced veneration and devotion that the Israelites gave to the golden calf at Sinai (Exod. 32.4). The charge of 'fornicating'—which is one of the storyteller's unequivocally strong verbs of disapproval of Israel's conduct (Judg. 8.27, 33; cf. 2.17)—is applied again to Israel because of Israel's attraction to the ephod. Gideon's ephod is also the cause of further trouble when it becomes a 'snare' not only to Israelites but also to him and his family. We need to note that this is what the ephod *becomes*, it is not that Gideon makes or uses it with the intention to entrap anyone or to draw Israelites into apostasy. We are not told specifically how the ephod becomes a snare, but it may fail to provide the clear communication from Yahweh which is anticipated and it may be used by apostate Israelites in an attempt to access the reinstated Ophrah Baal. As in the theological perspective (ch. 2) Israelites are held accountable for their own apostasy.

Thinking about Gideon

Unlike Yahweh's previous judge-deliverers—Othniel and Ehud—Gideon is reluctant to be 'raised up', but evidently Yahweh knows

his man and persists with his commission when providing him
with signs and reassurances on request. Gideon progresses in his
response to Yahweh from being at first bemused, then cynical.
Cynicism gives way to caution and caution allows him, in his
own time, not only to destroy the altar of the local Ophrah baal,
of which his father is custodian, but to act decisively against the
nomadic invaders when he accepts Yahweh's commission.
Requests for reassurance after the spirit's clothing are understood by some readers and hearers to be indications of weakness,
revealing that he is cowardly and hesitant. But Gideon asks for
signs because of his natural caution for self-preservation; moreover, he is wise to avoid confrontation with an enemy until he is
certain of victory. Yahweh's purpose is to prevent Israelites from
claiming they have won their deliverance by their own hand;
therefore, a deliverer is selected who naturally feels his own
inferiority when compared with the hordes of harvest looters
whose fearsome presence we are reminded of (6.33; 7.1, 12).
Gideon's requests for signs, which are all granted, are themselves signs of divine favour (cf. 6.17) and signal the storyteller's
approval. He is the only deliverer to receive Yahweh's direct
commission and to be 'clothed' by Yahweh's spirit.

Gideon is neither a coward nor a bully; he is, rather, a successful
warrior who achieves goals. The 300 follow a leader who, when
he is certain, is able to think quickly under pressure, not after
consultation about strategy with commanders pouring over military maps, but after he overhears (of all things) the telling of a
dream by one of the enemy and the interpretation of the dream
by another. Moreover, the 300 are led into battle armed, not with
the latest weaponry, but (absurdly) with domestic implements!
Furthermore, the instructions that the 300 are to obey reveals
their positions to the enemy. After Jezreel, Gideon's exhausted
little army cross the Jordan and capture two nomad kings, survivors flee in terror, two wayward Israelite cities are reprimanded
and Gideon's men return victorious to Ophrah with spoil aplenty
to share with their leader. Gideon and the 300 achieve almost
impossible military objectives. Neither injury nor fatality is
reported among their company. Gideon's leadership is so esteemed
that he is invited by the 'men of Israel' to be their hereditary
ruler. Yahweh may win Israel's battles but it is Gideon himself
and his companions—possessing neither military qualifications
nor abilities other than standing like dogs when they drink—who
together face overwhelming numbers and, with the participation
of Yahweh, succeed against the odds. He is respected by Israel's

tribal militia who trust him, follow him and obey him. Gideon is a military strategist. His diplomacy with the Ephraimites avoids civil war. He acknowledges Yahweh's participation when Yahweh does what Yahweh has promised and the enemy is given into his hands. He chases invaders from the land into their own territory from which they do not return. He captures their kings who are executed for war crimes. Gideon is presented as a character with honour and status, a war hero whose hand is used by Yahweh to successfully expel a horde of invaders and bring peace to the land.

The inhabitants of Succoth and Penuel are not punished without cause. They have taunted Gideon and to issue taunts is to declare the recipient an enemy. He is more lenient with Succoth and Penuel than Joshua is with Canaanite cities. Seventy-seven town elders receive a beating and a tower is demolished just as Gideon threatened would happen. Had he dealt with these cities in the way that Israel is said to have dealt with the Canaanites in the conquest narratives, both settlements would have been raised to the ground, all adults would have been killed and young women and spoils taken. He deals with Succoth and Penuel with the restraint of a noble and just visiting magistrate who responds to taunts, challenges and insults and acts with the nobility and presence of the mighty warrior he has become. He preserves his status and honour and punishes those who deserve punishment. The humiliating thrashing of seventy-seven rulers and elders who are precisely listed, the demolition of Penuel's tower and the killing of their men serve as vivid reminders in biblical storytelling: those who act with Yahweh's commission, who are empowered with the clothing of his spirit, who deliver Israel from formidable oppressors and bring peace to the land, are to be obeyed, honoured and provisioned.

Gideon is not to know that his ephod will become an object of religious attraction or be the cause of Israel's unfaithfulness to Yahweh or that it will be a snare to himself and his family. Moreover, it is not his purpose to lead Israel back into apostasy. Israelites themselves are consistently held accountable for their own behaviour. Israelites are wilful; they have the ability to turn from Yahweh to serve the local baals without any leadership. Gideon makes and places his own ephod at Ophrah in order to secure the means of obtaining direct instructions from Yahweh about how to respond in a future crisis without relying on others. However, it appears that the ephod does not work for him or for his family who experience internal rivalry and tragedy when, in the chapter that follows, Gideon's son Abimelech is held account-able for his own crime of infanticide (9.24, 56). Gideon's 'many wives' do not turn his heart away from Yahweh as anticipated in the deuteronomic cautions (Deut. 17.17) and as with Solomon (cf. 1 Kgs 11.3-6).

The Gideon story concludes with three unequivocal state-ments of character approval. First, the land rests for forty years during his lifetime. Second, he dies 'in a good old age', which is a sign of Yahweh's blessing and is also an achievement for one whose life is characterized by conflict. And third, Gideon did 'good' to Israel.

Sadly, Gideon is forgotten and no lasting loyalty or kindness is shown to him or his family. However, the victory on the 'day of Midian'—against a formidable coalition of nomadic Midianites, Amalekites and Easterners—is recalled with approval at a later date when Israel is threatened and others attempt to take posses-sion of the 'pastures of God' (Ps. 83.9-12; Isa. 9.4; 10.26).

As well as having a large family of 'many wives' and seventy sons, Gideon also has a concubine in Shechem by whom he has a son. Abimelech has nothing in his favour that commends him to others apart from being the son of Israel's war hero which he is about to exploit in a ruthless bid for self-advancement.

Judges 9:
Abimelech

The theme of the Abimelech story is disclosed when Gideon's youngest son, the traumatized lone survivor of an act of fratricide, appeals for retribution upon the murderers of his brothers. He demands that the memory of his father, Israel's deliverer and war hero, be honoured. In a long and complicated story a noble character (Zebul) carries the theme forward towards a satisfying conclusion when an unnamed woman, armed with her domestic upper millstone, inflicts the final act of retribution. Emotions run high; we will be horrified at Abimelech's slaughter of his rival half-brothers but we are invited to beam with delight as the wheel of retribution crushes him with its brutal bruising edge.

The Characterization of Abimelech (vv. 1-5)

Abimelech, who is Gideon-Jerubbaal's son by his Shechemite concubine, is not a judge-deliverer but a ruthless opportunist who makes his poisonous contribution to the sum total of human misery when he acts like a tyrant and seizes an opportunity to be the ruler of Shechem. He asks his uncles from his mother's Shechemite family to present a proposition on his behalf to the city's leaders, that one ruler (himself) is better than seventy rulers (his half-brothers). Abimelech reinforces his proposal by reminding the Shechemites that he expects his proposition to succeed with their support and sponsorship because he and they are family.

Abimelech's status is marginal. In Gideon-Jerubbaal's posterity, there are seventy sons, and Abimelech, as half-brother, whose mother is described as Gideon's Shechemite 'concubine' (8.31), appears to be the seventy-first. Abimelech has not done anything that would suggest his suitability as a regal candidate; he is not identified as a mighty warrior like his father; he is not characterized as an imposing Saul-like figure (cf. 1 Sam. 10.24); he has no honour or prestige; he is not called judge or deliverer; he is not 'raised up' by Yahweh or by anyone else. Abimelech is not identified as anyone's choice for anything. The opportunist possesses no qualities in his favour. What Abimelech does have is a Shechemite family connection which he exploits with his name that means 'my father is king', characterizing him as a prince, an impatient king, in waiting.

The citizens of Shechem accept Abimelech's proposal and he is sponsored with the sum of seventy pieces of silver from the Baal-berith temple treasury which he uses to hire men who are described as empty and reckless. Abimelech's hirelings are not to be thought of in the same way as Jephthah's rootless associates (Judg. 11.3) to whom we will be shortly introduced. They are merciless unprincipled characters who are available to anyone to do anything for a price. The slaughter of his half-brothers lacks any finesse. At Ophrah each brother is brought in turn to a stone which is stained with the blood of the previous victim. How will such a gruesome slaughter be avenged?

One of the brothers, who hid or was hidden by someone, survives. Jotham is ready to cite a familiar local tree-fable to which he adds his own personal retribution application when he demands justice for himself, for his brothers, their wives and mothers and for the memory of Israel's war hero, his father Gideon-Jerubbaal. Our storyteller brings us, with Jotham the survivor, to an uncomfortable place of rage.

Jotham's Fable (vv. 6-21)

Abimelech is not anointed or kissed as in the manner of Samuel's king-making (1 Sam. 10.1), or anointed and accompanied by the 'rush' of the spirit (1 Sam. 16.13), and he is called neither 'king of Shechem' nor 'king of Israel'. His 'coronation' takes place at Mount Gerizim where Jotham, the lone survivor of the Ophrah stone fratricide, intends to be heard. The Shechemites are addressed and God (*ĕlōhîm* in Hebrew but I suggest Yahweh is here intended) is to take notice. The place that was designated by Moses as a place of blessing (Deut. 27.12) now becomes a place of rage where the process of retribution is initiated.

Jotham tells a fable about the olive, fig and vine trees, which, with their fruits, are among the 'seven staples' of the land (Deut. 8.7-9). The trees are invited in turn by an assembly of trees to rule over them. However, they already have their own prestigious and useful functions which they will not abandon in order to merely wave their branches in gestures of nodding regal acknowledgment over other trees. Only the bramble is available, to whom the invitation to rule is at last made. However, the trees are to be cautious. The bramble warns the tree assembly that if they are not sincere in their invitation, they are to beware because the bramble can produce fire enough to devour even the cedars of Lebanon. What may the fable mean in such a context?

The principal points of reference are the bramble's (Abimelech's) unsuitability to be king and the Shechemites (the tree assembly) who have not acted in 'good faith' with Gideon-Jerubbaal's family when they appointed Abimelech king. The emphasis shifts between the inadequacy of Abimelech to the question of Shechemite sincerity. The fable is used as a sharp criticism of those who are foolish enough to anoint a worthless individual as their king, and used against the worthless king himself. The additions of 'cedars' and 'fire' warn the Shechemites of inevitable ruin.

One intended victim, Jotham, has escaped the slaughter of his family and he dramatically reveals his identity when he calls Jerubbaal 'my father'. He uses the fable to attack Abimelech and the Shechemites for abusing the honour of a deliverer who did good to Israel when he risked his life for the community and brought peace to the land. His father is a war hero who fought with disregard for his own personal safety. The memory of those whom Yahweh commissions is not to be so dishonoured. Jotham rages as he accuses the Shechemites of acting treacherously against his father by cooperating in the killing of his sons— Jotham's brothers—and making a ruthless tyrant their king. Jotham is dismayed; he has only contempt for Abimelech, whom he calls the son of Jerubbaal's slave. He protests that if this is acting 'in faithfulness and in honour', then Abimelech and the Shechemites deserve each other. Neither faithfulness nor honour are present in their king-making; may king and citizens produce a fire to devour them all.

Jotham's emotions have been assaulted, his brothers have been murdered and there has been no time to say goodbye. He rages and protests. He is bereaved and vulnerable, his world has become a dark place and his fable unfolds in surges of grief. He is a shocked and traumatized survivor of terror. He cries out as the spokesman for the surviving members of his traumatized extended family. What Gideon-Jerubbaal's youngest son demands is justice and retribution for himself, for his family and for his father. Moreover, Abimelech the mass-murderer and the Shechemites

are all complicit in the slaughter and they will burn. Once Jotham
has stated his case, he flees beyond Abimelech's reach.

In summary, Jotham uses the fable as a tragic account of
injustice, about the restoration of the good name and honour of
one who has delivered Israel from oppressors. Those who misuse
the memory of Israel's heroes and slaughter their families will
not get far; treachery is combustible. Other fables are also effec-
tively used by storytellers in which they allow story characters
within stories to carry their interests: Nathan to David (2 Sam.
12.1-4) and Jehoash to Amaziah (2 Kgs 14.9-10).

The wheels of retribution begin to turn with the introduction
of other characters. Yahweh sends a 'troublesome' or 'hostile'
spirit—perhaps the translation 'evil' in Judg. 9.23 is too strong—
between characters. The storyteller also introduces a 'noble'
character and an unpleasant individual.

How Retribution Becomes the Theme
of the Abimelech Story (vv. 22-57)

Abimelech rules for three years and Yahweh manipulates characters towards retribution in order that the blood of Jerubbaal's
seventy sons might be 'put' where we know it belongs: upon
Abimelech and his sponsors. Yahweh sends his 'troublesome'
spirit between Abimelech and the Shechemites who betray him
when Yahweh participates in Israel's life on Israel's behalf.
Acts of injustice are not neglected. The 'troublesome spirit' cultivates hostility and suspicion between Abimelech and the
Shechemites.

Abimelech is challenged when the Shechemites make plots
and act treacherously by sponsoring look-outs who lie in wait for
passing caravans to be robbed of their produce. They have sponsored murder in order to establish Abimelech; now they betray
him by sponsoring robbery. The function of Yahweh's 'troublesome spirit' is to plant the seedlings of retribution. Abimelech is
informed about the robberies and the informant is revealed as
Zebul, who is later disparagingly referred to as his city
governor.

We may wonder about Zebul's function and status. Abimelech
is called 'a ruler' and Zebul is also 'a ruler'. Zebul sends messengers to Abimelech warning that Gaal (who is about to be introduced), accompanied by his brothers or kinsmen, is making
trouble for him. He forcefully informs Abimelech how he may
win the day. Zebul's role is often understated when it is said that

he sends messengers to Abimelech to give his advice and that
Abimelech acts on his advice. However, Zebul gives more than
mere 'advice'; he is forceful and his instructions are reinforced
with commands such as when he orders others to 'arise' and to
'lie in wait'. The detail for Abimelech's attack is presented in the
form of Zebul's precise military instructions which are to be
carried out at dawn. Abimelech is also 'informed' when the
Shechemites are working in the filds and he is informed again
when the Shechemites retreat into their tower, which are further
examples of Zebul's informing work. Zebul is present at the city
gate when he mocks and taunts Gaal, Abimelech's rival, and
Zebul himself is also able to expel Gaal's accomplices after their
cowardly leader absconds. Who is Zebul and what is his function
in the story? He is not identified like other characters by
patronym, nor is the name of his tribe disclosed. He appears to
be Abimelech's man in Shechem who possesses a 'noble' name.
Zebul's name in Hebrew as a verb means 'to honour'; as a noun
his name suggests a large elevated place which draws the eyes
upwards, such as the Jerusalem temple where heaven and earth
meet (1 Kgs 8.13; cf. 2 Chron. 6.2) and to Yahweh's heavenly
throne (Isa. 63.15).

Zebul functions as the 'troublesome spirit' sent by Yahweh
who, as a human character, moves among the various parties in
order to bring characters into conflict with one another leading
them towards the retribution conclusion. Bringing characters
into conflict appears to be Zebul's function each time he appears
in the story. Zebul is placed between Abimelech and the
Shechemites in order to pass on information that will lead to the
destruction of first one party, then another. Zebul is not actually
described as a spirit; however, his character gives the story
momentum and carries the plot forward. Zebul does nothing
himself which can be described as evil and he does not slaughter
the innocent as does Abimelech. He does, however, pass on information and give precise instructions which are instantly obeyed,
both by Abimelech and Gaal. Zebul, the nobleman, is in a
commanding position and is always in the right place at the right
time. It appears that Zebul is none other than Yahweh's agent,
the 'troublesome' or 'hostile' spirit in the story.

The mood of the story darkens further when Gaal arrives in
Shechem accompanied by his brothers or kinsmen. Gaal is
carefully characterized as another nasty piece of work who—with
his 'gang'—is just the sort of base character that the Shechemites

will enlist for their treacherous purposes. Gaal's name means 'to loathe, to feel disgust, to be unpleasant', a name that may also be related to the Arabic *ju'al*, 'dung beetle'. Gaal is further identified by the patronym 'son of Ebed', the 'son of a slave', which always accompanies his name in the story (Judg. 9.26, 28, 30, 31, 35). Gaal's characterization suggests nothing that is positive or likable. It may be the storyteller's way to identify contemptuous characters as the sons of slaves, first Abimelech, now Gaal. It is not Gaal's fault that his father or mother or both are slaves but readers expect bad things of one whose name is associated with a dung beetle.

The loathsome son of a slave arrives with his 'gang' and, in a drunken state, begins to curse Shechem's new king. Grapes have been gathered and trod, wine is available and Gaal and his men drink, eat and make merry in the house of their god. However, they are not participating in a religious festival. Gaal and his companions enjoy an exuberant drunken binge during which he publicly mocks the city's absentee ruler. He boasts that the Shechemites will find in him a more suitable leader; the Shechemites have more nobility than to serve a son of Jerubbaal. Gaal incites trouble and unrest in a bid to replace Abimelech as Shechem's king. Moreover, he issues a challenge: who is this Abimelech that he should be served? Gaal asks why he and the Shechemites are to be subject to the likes of Abimelech. He evidently considers himself a Shechemite and incites an insurrection against a mere half-Israelite when he asks why they should serve the usurper. Zebul sends messengers to inform Abimelech that Gaal is turning the city against him.

Zebul is also on hand to present Abimelech with a solution to Gaal's threat and to propose an ambush opportunity: he is to draw near to the city at night, lie in wait in a field and at sunrise make a dawn attack. Zebul assures Abimelech that he will gain an easy victory. Abimelech does exactly as Zebul says; he waits in the field until dawn until the 'hung-over' Gaal stands at the gate of the city. Gaal is inspecting the place he will occupy among the city leaders when he replaces Abimelech. But there is a disturbance. Gaal is unsure what he sees through the morning desert haze. He notifies Zebul that people are descending upon him from the mountains. Zebul takes advantage of Gaal's fragile condition and suggests that he is seeing shadows; surely he imagines people where there are none. Gaal protests; he rubs his eyes; he looks again; he is sure visitors are approaching. He points in the direction of Mount Gerizim 'the centre of the land' or perhaps he points in the general direction of Jerusalem (v. 37; cf. Ezek. 5.5; 38.12). He panics when he perceives he is ill-prepared and under attack. No doubt his men also suffer the effects of the previous night's festivities. Zebul issues a choice reply for our delight which may be paraphrased as follows:

> *Where is your big mouth now?*
> *You wanted to know, "Who is Abimelech that we should serve him?"*
> *Well, there he is, the very one you despised!*
> *Out you go!*
> *Go on, have a go if you think you are hard enough!*

Zebul's taunt is cutting. We could pry (just a little) into the text and picture him prodding the 'dung beetle' in the ribs as he challenges him to carry out his boast of the previous night. The Shechemites still have confidence in Gaal when they follow him out of the city to confront Abimelech. Gaal cannot openly face the one he has challenged; he runs away and does not appear again in the story. Abimelech evidently knows where he is not wanted; he takes the battle no further than the city gate and returns to Arumah. Zebul mops up and expels the dung beetle's gang from the city.

The story continues to advance towards its retribution conclusion. The next day Abimelech is informed (Judg. 9.42) that the men of Shechem have resumed their normal agricultural duties in the fields. Evidently Zebul is the source of further information. Like his father at Jezreel, Abimelech divides his men into three groups and lies in wait. When the Shechemites emerge from the city, equipped to work in the fields rather than armed to defend themselves against an attack, Abimelech blockades the city gate while his other two companies attack the unarmed field workers. This is the second occasion Abimelech slaughters those who are in his way. He destroys the city and sows the site with salt. It is a ruthless tyrant who makes Shechem a desolate and uninhabitable place (cf. Deut. 29.23; Ps. 107.34; Jer. 17.6).

When Shechem's leaders within the city are told about the destruction, they hide in a stronghold in the 'house' of the god El-berit, and Abimelech is informed (Judg. 9.47) about their hiding place. Zebul evidently carries the story still further by informing and sending messages. Abimelech and his men take their axes and cut branches from trees which are piled in bundles against the Shechemite's refuge and set on fire. A thousand men and women die from the combined effects of fire and smoke. Retribution comes to the Shechemites when flames of ruin and destruction come out from Abimelech and devour them just as Jotham in his rage-fable anticipated. Furthermore, the violence and the blood of Jerubbaal's sons is 'put' where it belongs, upon the city leaders. Characters become the ruin of each other, first Gaal, then the Shechemites. Zebul the informer has done his work; he is not heard of again.

However, the process of retribution, which has a little further to travel, gathers momentum. Abimelech moves on and, for reasons which are not disclosed, he captures the city of Thebez where the inhabitants shut themselves inside a well-fortified tower and climb onto the roof. At Thebez Abimelech attempts a similar strategy as at Shechem: to burn the tower and those who seek sanctuary within.

Retribution finally comes upon Abimelech when an unnamed woman throws an upper millstone from the tower which crushes his skull. We may ask why a woman takes an upper millstone with her to the top of the tower? Do all the women of Thebez carry their millstones? The place for a domestic millstone is in the home at ground level. A millstone is rectangular in shape and is worked back and forth, by a kneeling miller with both hands, forwards and backwards, across a larger stone upon which grain is placed. This woman has taken her stone to the tower so that it is not mislaid in the confusion of an attack because it the means by which she provides food for her family. To lose her stone or to have it taken threatens the provision of food for her family (Deut. 24.6). There is, however, one occasion when a woman may consider actually throwing away her upper millstone and that occasion has arrived. It is to rid her community of a threatening tyrant, to save her own life, to save the lives of her family and to save the lives of her neighbours. Her arms have acquired strength from daily hand-milling and she is well able to throw her stone which hits Abimelech on the head. However, the drama of trauma and retribution is not yet over. Abimelech is still alive and even though his skull is crushed, he calls for his young armour bearer to draw his sword and finish him off. Abimelech does not want to be remembered in Israel's posterity as the warrior who was shame-fully killed by a woman wielding an item of kitchen equipment!

We may be amused to know that the story of the ignominious death of Abimelech at the hands of a woman is used by another biblical storyteller which shows that the mode of his death is preserved as a proverbial warning among Israel's warriors. On the occasion that the Israelites besiege the Ammonites at Rabbah (2 Sam. 11.18-22) some of King David's valiant men are killed and among them Uriah the Hittite is also slain as the king himself has ruthlessly planned. Joab, the king's field commander, instructs a messenger to inform the king about the loss of his men. Joab warns the messenger that should the king be angry with his report and demand to know why provision was not made by his warriors to avoid a hazard of siege-warfare—missiles thrown from the wall and thus evading the same fate as Abimelech—the messenger is to calm the king by informing him that Uriah has also died in the siege as planned. The story of Abimelech, whose skull is crushed by an upper-millstone thrower, is preserved as an example among military instructions for ancient siege warfare as one of the hazards besiegers are warned to avoid when attacking city walls: they are to take care when fighting close to the wall or they may be struck by an item of kitchen equipment and a death-by-upper-millstone could befall them also!

When Judge-Deliverers and their Families are Dishonoured

The story of Abimelech and the Shechemites takes place in a hard-hat area. Despite the inclusion of gruesome murders, the abuse of Yahweh's war hero and characters who act with insincerity, the reading demonstrates the story's impeccable moral credentials. We are informed how Yahweh operates in good faith: neither a mass-murderer nor his sponsors are permitted to get away with their crimes. Moreover, Zebul, who may be understood as Yahweh's noble agent and 'troublesome spirit', carries the plot forward by strategically manipulating characters into position in order to bring about events which lead to the final act of retribution. The evil that Abimelech does to the family of a judge-deliverer and Israel's war hero returns to him and the evil of the Shechemites returns upon them, literally upon all their heads and the fire of Jotham's fable devours all.

The Abimelech story demonstrates what happens when Yahweh's deliverers and their families are dishonoured and that evil-doers will suffer much the same volume of evil that they inflict upon others, suggesting a correspondence of the initial act with the just consequences that follow. Earlier we saw that a similar fate befell Adoni-bezek who, unlike Abimelech, submitted to what he accepted as a just retribution (cf. Judg. 1.5-7). The storyteller meticulously structures and arranges episodes in sequence in order to show that the shape of their deeds returns to Abimelech and the Shechemites: Gaal's conspiracy with the Shechemites against Abimelech is similar to Abimelech's earlier conspiracy with the Shechemites against his brothers. Gaal's character serves the retribution theme. Abimelech uses his close ties with Shechem against his brothers to achieve his own ambitions; Gaal uses his ties with the Shechemites against Abimelech. Shechem's leaders turn against Jerubbaal in favour of Abimelech; the Shechemites turn against Abimelech in favour of Gaal. The skull-smashing-by-upper-millstone episode shows that retribution appropriately returns: the Ophrah massacre of Jerubbaal's sons takes place upon one stone; Abimelech's skull is crushed by a woman thrower of one stone at Thebez. Even though the Hebrew words for 'stone' differ, both are stones.

To conclude, the reading has argued for retribution as the theological theme of the Abimelech story and that the memories of those whom Yahweh commissions to deliver Israel from oppressors and their families are not to be abused, but honoured. Even though there is a delay when Abimelech rules for three years and it appears that Yahweh does nothing, Yahweh still participates in Israel's life when neither the abuse of Gideon-Jerubbaal's name nor the evil of Abimelech and the Shechemites are forgotten. In storytelling, no one has to wait until the afterlife for justice. Exilic listeners are to note that Yahweh remembers acts of injustice and will respond with retribution in his own time. Israel has, therefore, a secure future in the land: pretenders who run amok (Abimelech), scheming city leaders (Shechemites) and opportunists who are characterized as loathsome 'dung beetles' and the sons of slaves (Gaal) will be the ruin of each other.

Judges 9, however, is an account of ancient story-world justice. We may wish that the modern world worked this way. It is to be acknowledged that fair-play and satisfying endings that exist in distant story-worlds are elusive in our own.

Judges 10:
The First Part of a 'Consecutive Judges' List and Yahweh's Rejection of Israel

Some of the stories of judge-deliverers are told, others are not. The stories of some characters are too pedestrian to be expanded by the storyteller when compared with the ingenuity of judge-deliverers whose stories are accompanied by framework introductory phrases. Dramatic stories of deliverance make good storytelling; family details about marriages, administration and donkeys do not.

'Consecutive Judges' (vv. 1-6)

There are two categories of leaders in the book of Judges. First, the warriors who are raised up by Yahweh and empowered to deliver Israel, and second, those whom I call 'consecutive judges' (sometimes referred to as 'minor' judges) who are briefly listed one after another in two lists and each linked in a chronological scheme with the phrase 'after him'. The consecutive judges are Israel's officials whose duty is to decide disputes between individual Israelites (cf. Exod. 18.13-26) and to preside over the peace and stability of the land. Jephthah appears in both lists when he features in his own story (Judg. 10.6–12.6) and in a brief listing, 'Jephthah judged Israel for six years, then Jephthah the Gileadite died and was buried in the town(s) of Gilead' (12.7). Jephthah's longer story begins with the familiar framework of other judge-deliverer stories and the words, 'Israel again did what was evil' (10.6) and concludes with a short entry containing the brief information that he judged Israel for six years, an entry which is as brief as that of other consecutive judges.

Characters in the short listings possess a prestigious role in Israel's life. Their brief entries are set in a distinct abbreviated framework, which, as well as a chronological connection, gives the number of their judging years, some family details, that they died and their place of burial. It might be assumed that their brief listings are their death notices. We are not told that Israel does evil or that Yahweh has cause to be angry. They are not raised up, they are not commissioned, there are no oppressors and no stories of deliverance unfold. Shamgar may be considered among the consecutive judges even though in our final form of the text he is placed after Ehud and before the teamwork of Deborah and Barak and Jael in which he is also mentioned (5.6).

Like previous judge-deliverers, we are informed that Tola arose to deliver Israel, but we are not told who he delivered Israel from. His 'biography' is a brief pedestrian listing, not an intriguing deliverance story. He is given a patronym which includes the name of his tribe, his place of residence, the number of years that he judged Israel, that he died and his place of burial. Yahweh does not 'sell' or 'give' Israel to others from whom they cry out for deliverance and from whom they are delivered. A clue to the nature of Tola's deliverance is that he arose 'after Abimelech' (10.1). He therefore delivered Israel by maintaining peace and stability in the land for twenty-three years after the 'men of Israel' returned home (9.55) following Abimelech's demise.

Tola is followed by Jair the Gileadite who judged Israel for twenty-two years during which the 'men of Israel' continue to live in peace and stability. Jair is not called a deliverer but his progeny of thirty sons who ride their own donkeys characterize him as the head of a family who possess wealth and status with the ability to maintain the stability of the land. Heads turn when the nobility ride by on their donkeys; they possess a status which is like the modern equivalent of each riding a prestigious Harley Davidson motorcycle. Jair's sons are mayors of towns or villages which are called 'Jairstown' (10.4) after their father. Israelites live in peace and stability for a total of forty-five years during the judgeship of Tola and Jair; however, when Israel again does evil and is 'sold' to the Ammonites for eighteen years, the sons of Jair the Gileadite lack the courage to expel their new 'owners' (v. 8).

Yahweh Rejects Israel (vv. 5-18)

The familiar pattern of apostasy resumes. Even after Yahweh has delivered Israel from Cushan, from the Moabites, from Sisera and his 900 iron chariots and from hordes of nomadic tribesmen, Israelites continue to be disloyal to Yahweh. Curiously, Israelites not only return to the Canaanite Baals and Astartes, but also to the gods of the nations from which they have been delivered: the gods of Aram and Moab as well as the gods of Sidon. Israelites also serve the gods of the Ammonites and the Philistines to whom they are next 'sold' by Yahweh and by whom they are beaten into subjection and oppressed (v. 8). After eighteen years, Israel's cry to Yahweh is accompanied by a unique admission of guilt when for the first time the storyteller says that Israel admits to abandoning Yahweh in favour of the Baals.

However, it is too late. Yahweh has done enough for his wayward people and repeats the same reminders, reprimands and accusations made by his messenger at Bochim (2.1-5) and by his prophet (6.8-10). How does Yahweh 'speak' to Israel? Again the storyteller appears to be untroubled by the anomaly of God speaking directly without an intermediary (cf. 7.2-11); no priest, messenger or prophet appears, yet Yahweh speaks directly with devastating finality. Israel is formally rejected and dismissed and the covenant is concluded. Yahweh is unequivocal: 'I will no longer deliver you' (10.13). Moreover, Israel is brushed aside and told to petition the gods to whom they show preference for assistance, 'let them deliver you!' In the past the Israelites had good intentions when they arrived in the land and were focused on conquest. After a promising beginning, Israel lapsed into apostasy and showed no commitment to Yahweh who chose them, delivered them and gave them land as he promised their ancestors. Israel has consistently shown disloyalty and ingratitude to Yahweh. Yahweh is now finished with his people.

Israel's reply to Yahweh's rejection is urgent and intense. The Israelites admit their guilt; they agree they have sinned, Yahweh can do whatever he likes (Yahweh can even give them up) but before he does, he must do something. Rescue us today! The favoured gods are discarded and Israelites make a big show of returning to Yahweh. However, Yahweh will have none of it. He is weary and exasperated by Israel's repetitive behaviour and from constantly contending with their apostasy. Yahweh will not tolerate Israel any longer (v. 16; cf. 16.16).

Matters for Israel go from bad to worse. An Ammonite army crosses the Jordan with intentions of engaging Judah, Benjamin and Ephraim. Israelites and oppressors face each other: Ammonites equipped for battle in residence in Gilead, Israelites at Mizpah (10.9, 17). Israel is under pressure and is lost without sponsorship by Yahweh who could raise up a deliverer as he did many times in the past. The Gileadites themselves have got to *do* something; their future is threatened and their commanders ask if anyone from among their own number will lead their militia against the oppressors. A substantial reward is offered: the one who leads an attack will be appointed their tribal leader. Neither judge Jair nor any of his thirty sons show any interest (vv. 3-5).

Has Yahweh given up on Israel? Can this really mean the close of the covenant? Will Yahweh never again raise up an Othniel, an Ehud, a Barak or a Gideon and empower them with his spirit to deliver his people? May Yahweh's dismissal be his last word?

The future looks bleak. Israelites are 'owned' by two new oppressors, the Ammonites and the Philistines. Israelites are abandoned to their fate.

Judges 11: Jephthah

Can anything positive be said about Jephthah the Gileadite? No one has a good word to say for a character who is said to be terrifying and is generally evaluated to be anything from stupid and self-centred to something more serious such as child abuser and murderer. Jephthah also fails, or so it is said, to act with the assurance of one who is empowered by the spirit when he attempts to manipulate Yahweh, who he does not trust, with a vow. Moreover, it is also claimed that he reaches the depths when he makes an unnecessary vow, particularly when the victim turns out to be his innocent daughter—his only beloved child who emerges from the house to welcome her victorious father home from war—and he carries out his vow and sacrifices her even though he has other options. After sacrificing his daughter he ruthlessly slaughters Israelites. A nasty man, a very nasty man, or so it is said.

The focus of my reading of Judges is to attempt positive evaluations of judge-deliverers as each character is considered in turn. May the proposition fail with Jephthah? It is my purpose to argue that Jephthah is portrayed as a cautious character. His story needs to be carefully read again with our prejudices and assumptions put to one side. We are not going to shy away from what we read nor are we going to make the story acceptable for sensitive readers. Let's read what the storyteller presents.

Jephthah's Characterization (vv. 1-3)

When he is first introduced, Jephthah is sympathetically characterized. The storyteller's approval of Jephthah is revealed in narrative signals with information that he is a victim who becomes a worthy character and then becomes a victim again.

Unlike previous judge-deliverers, Jephthah is socially disadvantaged. As well as having Gilead as his father, his mother is a prostitute and it is for this reason that his half-brothers expel him from the family home and deny him an inheritance. The son of another woman is unwanted. Jephthah flees into exile to live in a land called Good (*Tob*) or the 'Goodlands' (rather than the mythical 'Badlands') where he associates with others who are also outcasts and 'empty' like himself which need not imply that they are like the 'empty and reckless men' (cf. 9.4) whom Abimelech hires as assassins. Jephthah's associates are displaced persons who have 'withdrawn' out of necessity or, like himself, have been expelled from society. They are not necessarily outlaws, robbers or brigands as is often claimed, but they lack the qualities which command success in leading a regular life in their story-world; they lack inheritance and material goods such as property and tribal status. The storyteller simply says that Jephthah and those with whom he associates 'go out together' (Hebrew *yāsā*, v. 3) which is a common word that simply means 'to go out' and could refer to going out to do battle, like Israel (cf. 2.15; 20.28), Othniel (cf. 3.10) and Yahweh (cf. 4.14; 5.4). The Goodlands invokes a fortuitous backdrop where alienated men who are out of favour in their own land discover a home. In exile Jephthah acquires an honourable status while living in a land which is evidently 'good' for him and for others. Jephthah is a noble character, like Boaz, Kish and Jeroboam (cf. Ruth 2.1; 1 Sam. 9.1; 1 Kgs 11.28), to whom is given the impressive epithet 'mighty warrior', which means he possesses wealth, honour and status and suggests he is their leader.

The storyteller's brief introductory biographical disclosures about Jephthah (Judg. 11.1-3) have narrative purpose. Betrayal by his half-brothers makes it difficult for him to trust others in the future. What is described in just a few words of background detail, about expulsion from the family home, is more than a storyteller's interesting aside; it is the description of a traumatic early life. Jephthah makes good, but he has a problem: he is called upon to take enormous risks with his life when he has an inability to trust anyone.

Jephthah's Reinstatement (vv. 4-11)

When Israelites at Mizpah are threatened by the Ammonites, no one in the Gileadite army is willing to take defensive action until the elders discover that the exiled Jephthah has the required qualifications of leadership. He is head-hunted with the proposition that he accept the appointment of commander of their army.

The Gileadite elders are desperate for his expertise even though—as it turns out—they are his half-brothers, the very ones who hated him and expelled him from the family home! Jephthah enjoys their predicament. However, can he believe their offer to be genuine? Can they be trusted? They have betrayed him in the past; will they betray him again? Jephthah regards their offer with some suspicion. He requests a clarification and he is right to do so because they have already made a more substantial offer that if anyone from among their own company comes forward to lead an attack on the Ammonites, that person will be made their tribal chief (10.18). Jephthah is not going to settle for being a mere army commander and he uses their appeal for help as a legitimate opportunity for his personal reinstatement and as a means of acquiring further honour. In desperation the elders return to their original offer of tribal chief of all Gilead. There is still, however, the matter of trust and Jephthah requests further assurances from the elders who bring Yahweh into their negotiation as a guarantee that they will keep their word. Jephthah's appointment as army commander and tribal chief is confirmed before Yahweh at Mizpah.

Jephthah's Negotiations for Peace (vv. 12-28)

As the newly appointed tribal chief and army commander, the reinstated Jephthah makes two attempts at negotiating for peace with the Ammonite invaders. He first sends messengers to ask their unnamed king the obvious question, 'why have you invaded my land?' His question is short and terse in order to put the invader on the defensive. The Ammonite king answers that he wants the territory—which the Israelites took on their arrival from Egypt—returned. He is specific about the geographical boundaries of the land in question which is the area north of the River Arnon, south of the River Jabbok and east of the River Jordan which Sihon had taken from the Moabites. The king makes what seems to be a reasonable claim in order to restore peace. Negotiations are made on geographical rather than ideological grounds when both refer to the area in question as 'my land' (vv. 12 and 13). Even though armies face each other and are ready to do battle, the correspondence is at first diplomatic rather than warlike. Peace is a likely prospect.

According to Jephthah, the Ammonites have no just claim to the land and his second message contains a history lesson for their king (vv. 15-27) which may be paraphrased as follows:

Thus says Jephthah, chief of all Gilead and army commander, to the king of the Ammonites:

You must be aware that when we arrived from Egypt—through the Sea of Reeds and the wilderness to Kadesh—we did not take anything from Moab or Ammon. We respected their land rights. We even asked permission to pass through their territory and through Edom. When they refused, we made a wide detour around their lands at great inconvenience to ourselves. We also asked permission from Sihon, king of the Amorites, to pass through his land, but he did not trust us. We were attacked at Jahaz and Yahweh gave us victory. We were therefore able to take possession of Amorite land by right of conquest which covered the area you are now claiming: the territory from the River Arnon in the south to the River Jabbok in the north with the wilderness to the east and the River Jordan to the west. You need to be aware that we also respected the well-protected Ammonite border which we did not cross.

Let me ask you a question. Are you taking Moab's side and intending to recover their land which was taken from them by the Amorites? This would not be a good move. Look, we are both reasonable men. Let's be content with what our gods have given us. Chemosh will be good to you. Yahweh has been good to us.

On second thoughts, I hope you are not going to be so arrogant as to carry through your claim by actually attacking us. Such a course of action would be an error of judgment on your part. For example, you must have heard about Balak the king of Moab who was too frightened to attack us and backed down when he could not get support.

Come to think of it, you Ammonites have had lots of time to press your claim, why now? Look, we are already established in Heshbon, Aroer and along the River Arnon. Surely, your claim is 300 years too late!

Let's bring this matter to a conclusion. I have not wronged you but you have initiated hostilities by attacking me. This is what we will do: Yahweh the judge will decide the matter between us.

Even though his message is intimidating, Jephthah is to be commended as the only judge-deliverer in Judges who attempts to avoid the slaughter of open battle by negotiating with invaders. He reminds the Ammonite king that Israelites courteously asked permission to pass through foreign territory on their way from the desert onto the land. When permission was not forthcoming, Israel made a wide detour. If permission had been forthcoming the Israelites would have respected property and territory and would not even have touched their fields and vineyards or drawn water from their wells; they would have kept strictly to the 'King's Road' (Num. 21.22). Moreover, the Ammonite king is presumptuous to think that he can defeat Israel in open battle when others in the past were frightened by the prospect (Num. 22–24). Also, Jephthah implies that the Ammonites have invaded Gilead—rather than at any time in the past 300 years of Israel's ownership—when they were leaderless and their elders lacked fighting spirit (Judg. 10.18). Jephthah's reference to the Moabite god Chemosh as the god of the Ammonite king (11.24) need not trouble us as an error. Chemosh may not have been an exclusively Moabite god as is supposed, but worshipped by others. What Jephthah does is to entice the invader to recover land which once belonged to Moab and thereby to be enriched by Chemosh, the land's prior patron deity.

Sadly, Jephthah's negotiations for peace with the Ammonite king are less successful than his negotiations with the Gileadites about leadership and their king is not intimidated by the reference to a rival deity. When Jephthah's messengers return empty handed, war is inevitable. Yahweh will decide.

As with Othniel, Yahweh's empowering spirit comes upon Jephthah and he marches through Gilead and Manasseh and musters the army at Mizpah where he faces the Ammonites. Jephthah makes a vow of victory to Yahweh; he offers a sacrifice of whatever/whoever comes out from the doors of his house to meet him when he returns home in peace. Why does he find it necessary to vow a make when everything seems to be in place for his victory over the Ammonites and for his spectacular restoration as the Gileadite's chief of men?

Jephthah's Vow (vv. 30-31)
Does Jephthah vow an animal or a human as a sacrifice for victory over the Ammonites? The wording of the vow in the Hebrew text can be translated either as '*whatever* comes out of the door of my house' or '*whoever* comes out of the door of my house'. However, I have yet to be convinced that Jephthah offers Yahweh a human sacrifice.

The words of Jephthah's vow indicate that he lives in a house with doors or gates to which he anticipates he will safely return following his victory over the Ammonites. His dwelling may be an Israelite stone and cedar pillared house (as indicated by archaeological discoveries) in which livestock are stabled on the ground floor and he and his family live in rooms above. Tribal chiefs possess the prestige to live in stone and wooden houses which require a substantial investment in materials and manpower to construct. Does Jephthah further anticipate that an animal will be the first to emerge on his return?

The identity of the sacrifice is indicated when Jephthah uses the Hebrew cultic words specifically associated with animals. He says he will offer an ascending sacrifice, an *'ōlâ* which refers to the burning or holocaust of an animal, such as a whole ram on an altar, and the ascension of the flames, smoke and aroma to Yahweh (cf. Exod. 29.18; Lev. 1). There is no uncertainty about the fate of Jephthah's vow-victim should Yahweh oblige by giving him victory: an animal sacrifice will ascend to an altar and ascend in fire and smoke to Yahweh. He does not vow a human sacrifice which is condemned as an abomination (Deut. 12.31; 18.9-10). The Hebrew word *'ōlâ* is not used in the prohibitions of human sacrifice; rather the prohibition is that Israel may not 'give' (*nātan,* Lev. 18.21; 20.2-5) children to a heathen god. Other prohibitions of human sacrifice do not use the specific animal sacrificing word *'ōlâ* apart from Jer. 19.5 which is associated with fire and Baal. Jephthah's vow is word-specific when he uses the language of animal sacrifice. His vow, therefore, concerns an unspecified animal, not a human sacrifice; *'ōlâ* is the legitimate Levitical offering associated with animals (Lev. 1).

The sacrifice of an animal has not been made in Israel since Joshua's victory at Ai when he built an altar at Mount Ebal accompanied by burnt offerings and peace offerings (Josh. 8.31). It is to be remembered that Gideon's burnt offering is an individual matter made at night (Judg. 6.27). What Jephthah proposes is not a forbidden pagan human sacrifice, but an appropriate acknowledgment of Yahweh who gives (or will give) victory against the Ammonites. The purpose of *'ōlâ* sacrifices are to activate the covenant and to restore the relationship between Yahweh and his people. Jephthah proposes nothing less than Israel's return to Yahweh and covenant loyalty accompanied by an appropriate animal sacrifice.

Yahweh gives Jephthah a very great victory over the Ammonites who are forced to submit to Israel (11.33). On his return home, it is not an appropriate animal which appears, but his only daughter who comes out of his house alone to meet him dancing with timbrels, to present herself as the vow victim. Jephthah has no large progeny like the consecutive judges, no sons, just one daughter and here she is (v. 34). As an only child she is special, too special for sacrifice. When Jephthah sees his daughter, he is beside himself with grief and he informs her that he has opened his mouth to Yahweh and he cannot take back what he has opened his mouth about. Jephthah's daughter informs her father that he must 'do to me' what he has said because Yahweh has given him victory against his enemies. She says further that he is to 'let this thing be done to me' and she requests a delay of two months in order to grieve in the company of her companions. When she returns to her father, he sacrifices her according to his vow. We are spared the details but are informed that she is remembered every year by the women of Israel.

Why Jephthah Makes a Vow

Once Yahweh's spirit comes upon Jephthah, we anticipate Israel's deliverance will follow because the storyteller has brought us here before with Othniel (3.10) and Gideon (6.34). However, is it really necessary for Gilead's newly appointed tribal chief and commander, who possesses the spirit, to make a vow?

A vow may be defined as a plea for divine assistance motivated by special need with a promise of payment or deed. Vows to the gods were serious matters in ancient cultures and were not regarded as the mere wishful thoughts of supplicants. Vows were to be verbalized, articulated and distinctly pronounced, not merely conceived in the mind (Deut. 23.24). The fulfilment of a vow was also a public matter and meeting the terms of the vow was essential with a sacred obligation to be fulfilled. Vows were binding and irrevocable (Num. 30.2). Fulfilment was not to be delayed (Deut. 23.22; cf. Eccl. 5.3-4) because the one who vows is in debt to Yahweh when the request is granted and Yahweh is a creditor who requires settlement.

Jephthah makes his vow for three reasons: first, because he is unable to trust anyone, including Yahweh who has said he will no longer deliver Israel (Judg. 10.13), and has not yet said that he will change his mind or make an exception by delivering the Ammonites into Jephthah's hand. He therefore makes his vow to secure Yahweh's support. Second, he makes a vow because his future is at stake and he is under intense pressure to secure victory. And third, the *'ōlâ* will be a legitimate cultic ceremony to mark Israel's return to Yahweh and to covenant loyalty following deliverance from the Ammonites. Jephthah's vow also follows a precedent. Yahweh granted victory to Israel in response to Israel's vow when faced with resistance from the Canaanite king of Arad (Num. 21), an episode which occurs just before the events recalled in Jephthah's second message to the Ammonite king.

Jephthah vows an animal, not a person. Jephthah's vow is neither rash nor unnecessary. He is a skilled negotiator who is able to argue Israel's case and he is well aware of the power of words. Jephthah makes a vow with the purpose of securing his own personal reassurance of victory against Israel's formidable oppressor who claims to have right on his side and makes no reply to Jephthah's second attempt at peaceful negotiation.

The account of initial trauma of family betrayal, which introduces his story, does not make Jephthah a bad man. However, he now faces the formidable task of combat with an uncertain outcome. The Ammonite army is not characterized as a formidable force like previous oppressors but Israel is dominated for eighteen years and no Gileadite is courageous enough to initiate an attack. Jephthah makes his vow *in extremis* in order to secure personal survival and victory. His life is at risk. Will he be defeated? Will he be betrayed again by his own people? Jephthah is vulnerable and in a dangerous place. He entrusts the outcome of the battle to Yahweh with no safety net or 'plan B'. He is characterized as one who has learnt about human nature and the rawness of life through living with the consequences of family betrayal. As a result he does not trust anyone, including Yahweh, unless he has guarantees and assurances that what he undertakes will succeed.

Jephthah's vow is no doubt posted and publicized and becomes a matter of public discussion at the gate and at village wells throughout Gilead and beyond. The vow may be announced before the Israelite army at Mizpah in order to give his warriors fighting spirit. When Yahweh gives the Ammonites into Jephthah's hands, the Gileadites are aware that he has a debt of divine assistance to publicly acknowledge.

A Daughter's Act of Self-Sacrifice (vv. 34-40)

Something is wrong with the appearance of Jephthah's daughter. Why is she alone and unaccompanied by Gileadite women? There are no dancers with tambourines such as those who accompany

Miriam on the bank of the Reed Sea (cf. Exod. 15.20) and those who welcome Saul and David home with joyful singing and dancing from their victories over the Philistines (cf. 1 Sam. 18.6-7). Is she innocently welcoming her victorious father back from war or may she be doing something else in her own interests?

It is clear that she already knows and understands that a public Yahweh-vow concerning a sacrifice has been made by her father for victory over the Ammonites. When she emerges from the family home I propose that she willingly offers herself as her father's vow-victim. Furthermore, she specifically requests her fate and returns for the same purpose. Why does she present herself twice for sacrifice? What explanation may be given for a daughter's joyful acceptance of a father's vow and the presentation of herself as vow-victim? Is she idealistic, fanatical, depressed, confused? Does she have romantic ideas about the after-life? Might she be an adolescent with raging hormones? The suggestion of her dutiful submission to the will of her father will not do. This girl is not so timid; she dances joyfully towards her father at the prospect of her own sacrifice. She is more than submissive to her father; she is submissive to the idea of sacrifice. Jephthah's dilemma is not, therefore, about breaking or keeping his vow. He faces a situation of a more delicate nature: is he to obey his daughter?

When she emerges to meet her father, it is a natural reaction for him to protest that her appearance causes him to double over with grief; no wonder Jephthah says she is one of his 'troublers'. She is unexpected. He is grief-stricken. The girl is now the story-teller's prime-mover; she is in control. All Jephthah says to his daughter is that her appearance has cast him down, because:

'I have opened my mouth to Yahweh and I am not able to return' (Judg. 11.35b, my translation).

The word 'vow' (*neder*) does not appear in the Hebrew text or in the two Greek translations (LXX A & B) of Jephthah's statement of regret when he first meets his daughter, as suggested by some English translations:

'For I have opened my mouth to the LORD, and I cannot take back my vow' (v. 35b, NRSV).

However, she is well aware what he has 'opened his mouth to Yahweh' about when she says:

'Do to me what came out from your mouth now that Yahweh has wrought vengeance for you upon your enemies the Ammonites' (v. 36b, my translation).

Jephthah's phrase 'opened my mouth' does not appear to be an ancient metaphor for making a vow that informs her that a vow has been vowed, but the words of a distraught father admitting that he has said something he cannot withdraw. She is aware of the vow and deliberately exits the family home in order to present herself for sacrifice for her own reasons about which we can only speculate. She makes a final request when she asks to be allowed to spend two months walking in the hills in order to feel sorry for herself with her friends because she is to die young, unmarried and childless. Jephthah's life is composed of episodes of harsh conflict: with his brothers, with the Gilead elders, with the Ammonites, now with his daughter. It's all too much and he tells her to 'go!'

The storyteller drives the daughter's character forward and informs us that she positively and pro-actively accepts her fate, not in an act of submission to her father, but as her own independent act of will. She willingly returns to her father after being left alone for two months, even though her return is unmarked by either timbrels or dancing. We imagine a distraught father dreading a daughter's return.

When it comes to making the sacrifice, Jephthah does not use an alternative form of 'offering' such as consigning his daughter to a solitary life in a sanctuary where she is denied the prospect of marriage or children. He does not use the get-out-of-a-vow-for-a-fee option (Lev. 27.1-8). He does not refuse to fulfil his vow which may save his daughter but bring retribution upon himself. His refusal to carry out the vow may also have wider implications and bring calamity upon his fellow Israelites. For example, at Sinai when Yahweh complains that his people are corrupt and have quickly turned away from him in preference for a golden calf and are out of control, Moses orders the Levites to carry out random executions (Exod. 32.1-8, 25-29). Yahweh also says that no record will be kept of those who sin against him (Judg. 11.33). On other occasions the earth swallows up Korah and his family for his rebellion against Yahweh (Num. 16), and Israelites are defeated in battle when Achan takes Yahweh's produce (Josh. 7). Jephthah has no wish to offend the God of Israel who will surely deal with him, his family and with the Gileadites if he does not keep his vow. Had a 'clean' animal made an appearance—rather than his daughter—on his return home, Jephthah's reinstatement to a position of honour and status would have been an outstanding personal accomplishment. His plans are cautiously made. He would have moved from exile in the company of fellow outcasts to be the commander of Israel's militia, the chief of the Gileadites, a war hero who defeated the Ammonites and the one who led Israel back to Yahweh and to covenant faithfulness marked with a suitable cultic sacrifice. But on his return home, his daughter appears. Readers may protest at the outrageous proposition of a daughter presenting herself to her father as a human sacrifice, but such I argue is the storyteller's story. Women's self-sacrifice for a cause, which has become a feature of the modern world, may not have been unknown in the ancient world. Jephthah's daughter is manipulative and intent on her own self-sacrifice for reasons which are not disclosed. The imperatives in her speech are the demands of one who is independent and unconcerned about her own survival. She knows what she wants when she demands: 'do to me' (Judg. 11.36), 'let this thing be done for me' (v. 37), and 'leave me alone for two months' (v. 37). That Jephthah intends no harm to her, or to anyone (apart from the Ammonites), when he makes his vow is clear from his grief-stricken response at her appearance. Her mother does not make an appearance armed with her upper millstone (9.53) to protect her only daughter or to reprimand her husband for opening his mouth. The girl does not run away and she does not object or refuse her father. When she goes to the hills for two months, she does not use the opportunity to escape to a 'good' land of exile of her own. Moreover, Jephthah does not have to go in search of her and bring her home by force and in shame to her fate. She is not taken to a place of safety by her companions. Her response is more than mere passive acceptance of her fate as a submissive, dutiful daughter; Hebrew women in Judges are not such obliging pawns in patriarchal hands.

What do Israel's women think of the daughter of Jephthah the Gileadite? Is her sacrifice lamented or celebrated; is she thought of positively or negatively in the customs of women? For her to be lamented for four days every year suggests she is remembered with sorrow and mourned as an unnamed victim. However, to be annually celebrated (*tānâ*, 11.40; cf. 5.11) suggests that she is highly esteemed and that her sacrifice is remembered with approval. Either way, she is not forgotten.

Two matters are particularly alarming in the text. First, the storyteller does not say that Yahweh finds the prospect of child sacrifice unacceptable. It is outrageous for ritual sacrifice—the slaughter of an animal and the whole totally consumed by fire

(Lev. 1)—to be applied to a human. The sacrifice of Jephthah's daughter recalls God's instructions to Abraham to offer his son as a burnt offering followed by Yahweh's messenger telling him—just in time—to desist with the provision of a ram (Gen. 22.1-13). However, Jephthah hears no voice from heaven and no substitute animal appears. Yahweh is silent. The second shocking matter in the story is that the storyteller's attitude, stance or point of view is not disclosed. We have to repeatedly comb the text in a bid to uncover implied negative criticism of Jephthah (which may not be present) and impose our own morality and ethics upon the text in support of our own disapproving evaluation of his character. We are right to protest that the very idea of child sacrifice is horrific and abhorrent; however, the storyteller moves on to the next episode without making an editorial comment, apparently unmoved. Even though Jephthah is not condemned in subsequent biblical tradition (1 Sam. 12.11; cf. Heb. 11.32), it is the Judges storyteller who emerges as a terrifying character.

Meanwhile, Jephthah's problems continue. Like Gideon, he is about to be challenged by the Ephraimites (cf. Judg. 8.1) who fail to support him against the Ammonites. They complain merely because they are denied the opportunity of spoil. How will Jephthah respond to their challenge? Will he be diplomatic like Gideon? Will he attempt a peaceful solution as he does on two occasions with the Ammonite king? Will he—with his full authority as judge-deliverer, army commander, chief of Gilead and Israel's war hero—make a just response? Jephthah's life is punctuated by triumph and tragedy: Yahweh gives a great victory against the Ammonites and Jephthah survives, but he is denied the honour of leading Israel's return to Yahweh accompanied by appropriate sacrifices, and his personal reinstatement among the Gileadites is marred by the loss of a daughter. Jephthah inherits a new life of guilt and remorse from which he may not recover. He is a damaged and isolated individual who is in no mood to trifle with Ephraimite whingers.

Judges 12:
Jephthah and the Ephraimites with the Remainder of a 'Consecutive Judges' List

The exiled Jephthah almost succeeds when he grasps the opportunity of full reinstatement among the Gileadites to a position of honour as their tribal chief who restores Israel's covenant with Yahweh accompanied by appropriate sacrifices.

Jephthah has been expelled from the family home by his half-brothers because he is the son of another mother, a prostitute. He achieves honour as a warrior in the 'Goodlands' in exile with others who are also rootless and who live on the margins. His opportunity arrives when the land is invaded by the Ammonites and he is head-hunted by the Gileadite elders who happen to be the half-brothers who expelled him from the family home. Not only does he accept the post of commander of their army but he also becomes their tribal chief. He makes a vow to secure Yahweh's support and he will mark the return of Israelites to Yahweh and covenant loyalty with a burnt offering if he is able to defeat the Ammonite invaders. However, on his victorious return, his daughter has other ideas. For her own reasons, she joyfully presents herself as a sacrifice victim.

Jephthah's problems continue when he is challenged by the Ephraimites. An earlier challenge to Gideon (8.1) characterizes them as arrogant latecomers who are not only slow to respond to a call to arms but lack the urgency of those who are required to respond to the call for Israel's deliverance. There has been plenty of time for them to consider their loyalties and to muster a militia while Jephthah is cautious and does not rush into battle but negotiates for a peaceful withdrawal of the Ammonite invaders and awaits their replies.

Four reasons account for Jephthah's robust response. First, the Ephraimites are armed and show no respect when they issue a high-handed challenge directly to Jephthah who is the newly appointed tribal chief of Gilead and their army commander with the prestige of defeating the Ammonite invaders and winning a great victory. Second, when he called to them out of desperation for help they failed to assist him; he was an isolated man of conflict (v. 2; cf. Jer. 15.10) who risked his life for Israel. Third, threatening to burn his house with him inside is an inappropriate way to address Israel's deliverer and war hero. And fourth, when Jephthah and the Gileadites are taunted as 'Ephraimite fugitives', it appears that there are old scores to settle.

Jephthah is in no mood to trifle with whingers; as he says, he risked his life to rid the land of the Ammonite invaders while the Ephraimites stayed out of harm's way (cf. Judg. 5.14; 8.1). The matter is decided in the battle which follows in which the Ephraimites are defeated. When they attempt to flee the land of Gilead, Jephthah makes a strategic military manoeuvre by cutting off their retreat and at the Jordan crossing they are identified when battle survivors fail a word pronunciation test. Each person at the crossing is asked in turn to articulate the word 'shibboleth' which Ephraimites pronounce as 'sibboleth'. It appears that their dialect phonetically pronounces the Hebrew consonant *šîn* as *sāmek*. The meaning of the test-word—whether 'flowing stream' or 'ear of corn'—does not matter; any word with the same initial letter is enough to catch out the visitors.

The Ephraimite episode in which a total of 42,000 are slaughtered is told as a harsh satire that ridicules an arrogant tribe. A force of more than 42,000 armed men are unable to burn Jephthah's house. They are unable to pronounce a simple test-word—they are not subtle enough to modify their pronunciation in order to survive. The Ephraimite-Gilead episode makes a similar point to the stories of Gideon and the inhabitants of Succoth and Penuel and the abuse of Gideon's memory in the Abimelech story, which is this: those who deliver Israel from invaders and oppressors are to be provisioned, supported and honoured, not abandoned, abused and threatened.

It is to be noted that the storyteller does not conclude the Jephthah story with any negative evaluations of his character. None of the unequivocal verbs of disapproval that are applied to Israel are applied when he makes a vow, sacrifices his daughter and makes a robust response to the Ephraimites.

'Consecutive Judges' (vv. 7-15)

Jephthah's story concludes with his short listing among the 'consecutive judges', which is attached like an appendix with the brief information that he judged Israel for six years and that he was buried in the towns (plural) of Gilead (12.7). It is rumoured that in later life his limbs fell from his body and they were buried where they dropped as he travelled around his land, but I could not possibly comment.

The three other consecutive judges who appear in the second list are, like Tola and Jair (10.1-5), distinguished by their wealth and status. After Jephthah, Ibzan judges Israel for seven years and is able to maintain peace and stability in the land by making marriage arrangements for his sixty children. He arranges for thirty brides to marry his thirty sons and plans similar arrangements for his thirty daughters. Matrimonial arrangements are made outside his own tribe but we are not told if they are within Israel or with Canaanite families as is said earlier of Israelite families (3.6). When Ibzan dies, he is buried in Bethlehem.

No information is provided about the nature of the participation in the life of Israel of Elon of Zebulun who follows Ibzan, apart from his being a judge for ten years and that he is buried in Aijalon in his home territory. Abdon, who judges Israel for eight years, has forty sons and thirty grandsons; they ride a total of seventy donkeys which indicates that they are, like the members of Jair's family, men of wealth and status who turn heads.

The odd details of the consecutive judges, which describe donkey husbandry and marriage arrangements, are too pedestrian to be expanded by the storyteller when compared with the daring ingenuity of Ehud, the exuberant celebration of Deborah's song, the ingenious defeat of the Midianite coalition and the submission of the Ammonites by the reinstated chief of Gilead. Dramatic stories of deliverance make good storytelling; family details about marriage, donkey riding, wealth and administration, do not.

Israelites still have a problem. The land is not said to rest at the conclusion of Jephthah's story or within his brief consecutive listing because it is still occupied by the Philistines. Israelites are again beaten into subjection and this time they are oppressed for forty years (10.7-8; cf. 13.1). They cry out in desperation to Yahweh for help (10.10, 15) and Jephthah is awarded a great victory over the Ammonite oppressors. Will a deliverer arise to free Israel from the Philistines?

Judges 13:
Mr Wonderful's Visit

Manoah was not best pleased. In fact he was very annoyed and for good reason.

He did not like the idea of strangers walking into his field, especially an unannounced visitor who proceeded to give his wife daft ideas of a personal nature about getting pregnant, having a holy son and then making rules about what she can and cannot eat and drink. She had said he was a man of God who looked like a messenger from God which was another daft notion because there had not been anyone of that description around for a very long time. The man was obviously an impostor. Or was he?

Manoah decided that caution was his best option. So, when he had a quiet moment, he asked Yahweh to send the visitor back in order to say his piece face to face and clarify if they were to do anything special when (if) the lad was born. If this so-called 'man of God' dared to show up, Manoah would sort him out, man to man. He would listen to what he had to say, then he would kick his backside and send him on his way!

He yawned and put his feet up. He was too tired to deal with these matters now and it was hot outside, too hot to work. It was time for his afternoon nap and a rest in the shade. She could dig up the vegetables from the field and pick some fruit for the evening meal. He yawned and closed his eyes. Soon he slept and his wife heard his snores as she sat on a stool in the field and cleaned the root vegetables she had pulled from the ground.

Manoah was woken by his wife's shouts as she ran back into the house saying that the visitor was back. He got up from his armchair, rolled up his sleeves and followed her out of the house into their field grumbling about being woken up. He would tell this individual to clear off and leave his wife alone.

They came face to face in the field in the heat of the day. Standing before Manoah was a smartly dressed man about his own height wearing a long white robe with his hair covered by a silk cloth in the desert style. He smiled as Manoah approached.

"'Ere, I want a word with you. Are you the man who has been filling my wife up with daft ideas about getting pregnant?' Manoah's angry words were sharp and were uttered with the intention of intimidating the visitor. Manoah wanted him to feel embarrassed and awkward.

The visitor stood his ground, continued to smile and offered a hand which Manoah regarded with disdain. Manoah's abruptness appeared to have no effect.

'Yes, I am,' the stranger said and quickly added, 'how do you do?'

Such an outright admission was unexpected. His wife had thought the visitor frightening but Manoah was not going to be taken in by a smug smile and slippery words.

He would play for time. He scratched his beard. He took a sharp intake of breath through his teeth. He stood his ground, held himself to his full height and slowly looked the stranger up and down with narrowed eyes. Manoah grew in confidence. He felt himself to be a strong intimidating presence standing on his own land.

'All right', he said at last, 'you obviously don't know that my wife can't have children—not that it's any business of yours!' The visitor's chest was prodded several times by a pointed finger. 'But if, and I only say if, what you say happens, what are we to do with the lad? What is to become of him when he grows up?'

The visitor's eyes also narrowed. The smile changed to a frown. His face became grey and threatening. His hand, extended in greeting, became an extended finger which was prodded into Manoah's chest.

Manoah's eyes widened. He took a step back, then another. The visitor stepped forward. The finger was poked again. Their noses almost touched. The stranger continued to advance and Manoah was forced to take another backward step. He swallowed. His mouth was dry. His bowels felt fragile. He felt small and intimidated as his wife looked on.

'Now hear this', announced the visitor. 'Your wife is not going to drink any vine products. That means no wine and no strong drink. Understand? She is not going to eat any unclean foods. If you do not know what unclean foods are, any priest will give you a list. She is to do exactly what I have told her! Got it?'

Each word was uttered with authority in a firm clipped tone which informed Manoah that the speaker expected not only to be listened to, but obeyed. He and his wife were to do as they were told.

The visitor repeated: 'Make sure your wife does everything I say!'

Manoah felt a finger drill into his chest as each word was uttered. All he could do was to listen and nod in wide-eyed agreement.

The visitor's eyes were narrow and full of menacing intent. Manoah did not know where to look, first down at his feet and then into the visitor's face. This was his field but the stranger's words and his presence made him feel small and disorientated. He had followed his wife out of the house with every intention of briskly sending the visitor on his way. He still had a mind to do something. All he could think of was to continue playing for time.

When at last he spoke, all he could say was, 'Perhaps we should talk about this sensibly over some refreshment. You must be thirsty? Hungry, even?'

The visitor was impatient and gave the rudest of replies: 'You can entertain me if that's what you want to do. But I will not eat your food.'

Who did this bad-mannered individual think he was speaking to? This was his field and his wife!

Then the visitor added, almost as an afterthought: 'I'll tell you what you can do. Prepare a burnt offering and offer it to Yahweh, just here on top of your stone wall.'

Manoah had heard enough of this individual's personal demands and disrespect. He wanted answers.

'Tell me something. What's your name? How can we let you know when the lad is born?'

'Why do you want to know my name? If I told you, you wouldn't understand it you wouldn't belive me.'

Manoah was gazed upon by the furrowed brow and pursed-lip expression of a teacher who was impatient with a naughty boy. Clearly the visitor did not suffer fools gladly.

'I'll tell you what you can call me', he said at last with a smile and a raised finger, 'call me Mr Wonderful.'

Well, that was it. Manoah had heard enough. This Mr Wonderful had it coming. He clenched his fists and gritted his teeth. His wife could see his anger rising and as his face began to redden she thought he might make himself unwell. It was now up to her to do something. She firmly took his arm and steered him into their kitchen leaving the visitor alone in the field.

Poor Manoah; he was expected to make an offering to mark what he considered to be a daft conversation with an ignorant individual with a limp-wristed name.

As the couple prepared a kid as a food offering, Manoah was full of questions. He could understand about the drinking and eating prohibitions and about a lad being dedicated to Yahweh. But why? What for? There must be more to this. So she told him that the boy would be dedicated to the specific task of attacking the Philistines.

Manoah was dismayed. His jaw dropped. He wanted a son and he did not mind any son of his having long hair and being holy, but picking a fight with the Philistines was another matter altogether.

He considered the Philistines to be 'uncircumcised' louts but they were not a pushover. They were armed, armoured and moody. What would a son of his be able to do on his own against so many? Everyone accepted the Philistines as their rulers. The Israelites had at last settled down. The land was at peace and there was no further necessity for war.

Most of Manoah's tribe, the Danites, had gone north and others were at last enjoying some peace in the lowlands. The Israelites were farming and planting their land with vines and olives. Harvests were good. Neither the Philistines nor the Canaanites were as bad as they were led to believe. They all got on reasonably well together. Times were good and getting better. The future was co-existence. But here was this smug stranger talking about a son of theirs becoming a troublemaker! He shook his head. He was not sure about it, not sure at all. Manoah the Danite was discombobulated.

The couple emerged from their kitchen with embarrassed smiles each carrying a tray to face the waiting visitor. They laid their offering on top of the stone wall and stood back.

Then it happened.

Crackling flames and smoke suddenly ascended from the food. The visitor said nothing, not even 'thank you' or 'goodbye'. He just leaped onto the wall, dived up into the flames and smoke and disappeared.

Manoah stood and looked, his mouth wide. Husband and wife were shocked. They looked at each other, then they fell to the ground in fright and dismay covering their heads with their hands.

Suddenly, in the silence, the shekel dropped. Manoah understood the identity of their visitor. Mr Wonderful was none other than a messenger from Yahweh and messengers were to be treated with honour as though they were the very people who had sent them. He began to panic; he was in big trouble. No one insulted Yahweh—the God of Israel—and survived!

'What are we going to do!' he cried into the ground. 'I've seen Yahweh! What have I done? What have I said? To think that I was going to kick his backside! Help! We are going to die!'

For a moment both were silent and still.

'Don't be daft', his wife said at last as she stood to her feet brushing the dust from her clothes. 'If Yahweh was going to kill us he would not have told us about our little boy and he wouldn't have fired our offering.'

When at last Manoah allowed himself to be pulled to his feet he saw that all that remained of their visitor and food offering was a mass of charred smoking debris on the wall. They were neither harmed nor scorched. Manoah's face was white; he felt unwell, embarrassed and disorientated. He had no idea what to think about what he had heard and seen. He felt like protesting to someone, but there was no one, they were alone. This sort of thing did not happen to people like them. Yahweh had no business interrupting their lives like this. They were little people, hard-working honest folk. They were not priests or prophets. However, Manoah's wife understood only too well. She drew close and squeezed her husband's hand.

'Did you hear that, dear? We are going to have a little boy.'

She smiled sweetly, gave a knowing nod and said, 'We must have an early night.'

In time Manoah and his wife have a son just as Yahweh's messenger said they would. His mother called him 'Samson' which some claim to be associated with the sun and a local cult of the sun. While it is correct that Samson's name can mean 'sun', the storyteller does not associate him with either the sun or with sun worship; there is no mention of a sun-cult, sun-goddess or Beth-shemesh, 'the house of the sun' (Judg. 1.33; cf. Josh. 19.41) which is said to be located near the family home in Zorah. There is no reference to the sun in connection with nazirite provisions or with Samson's deliverance task. His name is less mythical and has a more positive characterization than a solar hero or a sun worshipper. Samson's name is from ancient words which mean 'strong', 'fat' and 'to serve' because that is just what he becomes: Yahweh's strong servant, who shines with strength like the rays of the sun, a noble, powerful and distinguished hero. Manoah's wife named her child in anticipation of the fulfilment of what has been disclosed by Yahweh's messenger about his character, his strength and his designated task. The *on* ending of his name is an ancient affectionate form meaning 'little' (like 'Gide*on*', Judg. 6.11), and for this couple—who at one time lived with the ancient stigma of being childless—the gift of a little boy, even a strange little boy with an isolated hazardous destiny, may have been thought of in the family home as their 'little ray of sunshine'. But here any association with the sun ends.

Samson and his family live in a Danite camp situated between Zorah and Eshtaol, where he is not only blessed by Yahweh but he is encountered by Yahweh's spirit. Both are signs of divine approval. The Hebrew verb *pā'am*—which is translated 'to stir him' (v. 25, NRSV) and describes Yahweh's work with Samson—is used by other storytellers to describe the responses of those who are troubled in their dreams, such as Pharaoh (Gen. 41.8), Nebuchadnezzar (Dan. 2.1, 3) and a psalmist (Ps. 77.5). Is Samson also 'troubled' by Yahweh's spirit in his formative years? If he is troubled, what form may the spirit's troubling take and for what reason?

Samson is nurtured by a mother who, during her pregnancy, does not drink wine and is careful not to eat 'unclean' foods while neighbouring families in Dan and beyond no doubt eat and drink whatever they choose and live how they like. Moreover, Samson himself does not cut his hair which becomes a sign that he is a 'nazirite', meaning he is dedicated to Yahweh for life to fulfil a specific assignment. The 'stirring' of the spirit is Yahweh's unique reminder that he has a future deliverance task of conflict with Israel's Philistine overlords. The spirit's encounter is for the young Samson a unique disturbance and discipline in order to keep a growing lad loyal to his unique designated future in an age when adult members of Israel's tribes give poor examples to their children by doing evil 'in the eyes of Yahweh', forgetting the God of their ancestors and serving the gods of the local Philistine counterculture (Judg. 10.6).Yahweh is not content for Israel to be dominated by others or for Israelites to serve their gods even though he has 'sold' them into the hands of the Philistines (10.7). Yahweh's judge-deliverer in waiting is uniquely prepared by Yahweh's spirit for the formidable one-man task that awaits.

What Sort of Nazirite is Samson?

Does Samson break his nazirite vow when he comes into contact with the dead, when he kills the young lion, when he returns to inspect the lion's carcass and extracts honey and when he kills the thirty men of Ashkelon and strips the dead of their clothing as is generally assumed? Does he break the vow of a nazirite when he arranges a drinking feast for his Philistine guests? Moreover, does Samson violate deuteronomic marriage prohibitions when marrying a Philistine?

The word 'nazirite' (*nāzîr*) means 'devotee'. Samson is generally thought to be devoted to Yahweh in the sense of Num. 6 which describes the self-imposed disciplines of a **temporary** nature. There are, however, differences between the vow-making temporary devotee of Num. 6 and Samson's mother and her son.

According to the provisions of Num. 6.1-21 men and women make precise vows to Yahweh to live under certain strict limitations for a limited period. During the duration of their vow they are called nazirites. They are not to consume produce of the vine including wine and intoxicating by-products such as sour wine and juice. They may not eat fresh or dried grapes and they are not to eat the seeds or skins of grapes. Nazirites are not to cut or trim their hair which is to be left growing and uncut like unpruned vines (cf. Lev. 25.5, 11; Judg. 5.2). Uncut hair is the distinctive visible sign of one who has made a vow and is dedicated to Yahweh. Furthermore, a nazirite must not come into the vicinity of a corpse. Even if a close family member—father, mother, brother or sister—dies during the duration of their vow, those who are dedicated to Yahweh must not become unclean as they are holy and possess a sign (uncut hair) of their dedication. They are holy for the duration of their vow because they agree to the limitations for themselves. If a devotee inadvertently comes into contact with a corpse due to someone's sudden death, they are to submit to an elaborate form of purification and are to offer sacrificial gifts to a priest. The vow is concluded with rites and offerings when the devotee is 'brought' to the sanctuary (Num. 6.13), presumably by witnesses who are able to attest that all the provisions of the vow have been kept during its duration.

The requirements asked of Samson's mother during her pregnancy differ from the provisions of Num. 6. Yahweh's messenger says she is to abstain from wine and vine and grape by-products. However, her first difference is an addition: she is to abstain from eating unclean foods in general, not just vines and grapes.

She is not instructed to have no contact with the dead nor to leave her hair uncut. She is not called a nazirite. The specification for Samson's mother suggests that her son is to be protected in the womb; however, this does not necessarily imply that during his lifetime he remains under the same obligations that are imposed upon his mother during her pregnancy. Samson's limitations, such as they are, are specific to him and to his task.

The only limitation specified by Yahweh's messenger for Samson himself is that his hair is not to be cut. Samson's nazirite designation is not temporary but life-long for the purpose of a specific, unique and specialist task. His uncut hair is associated with a deliverance assignment against the Philistines. Samson, the unique life-long nazirite, and the temporary nazirite of Numbers 6, share just two similarities. First, both are referred to by the noun 'nazirite' which is the word for one who is devoted to Yahweh. And second, Samson's hair is to be uncut which is a nazirite's outward designation. Samson shares no other similarity with the nazirite of Num. 6. Yahweh's messenger gives neither Manoah nor his wife any instructions about their son's future food and drink; however, when Manoah requests clarification about caring for his unique son as an infant, no additional prohibitions are made. Manoah only receives a repetition of his wife's pregnancy restrictions which are extended to include vine by-products. Neither his mother nor Samson himself make vows. Samson's characterization is one of a temporary holy devotee and he is unlike religious nazirites elsewhere associated with prophets (Amos 2.11-12) and priests (1 Macc. 4.9). It is of necessity that Samson comes into contact with the dead and participates in his wedding drinking feast in Timnah because both form part of his assignment to 'begin' Israel's deliverance. Samson is therefore loyal to his specific designated nazirite task.

Samson does not violate deuteronomic marriage prohibitions when he marries a woman from Timnah because Philistines are not listed among the 'stronger and more numerous nations' with whom marriage is forbidden (Deut. 7.1). Moreover, marriage is permitted to 'beautiful' foreign women who are taken captive in war (Deut. 21.10-14) and Samson is at war with Israel's 'uncircumcised' overlords. Despite a marriage of sorts to a Philistine woman which may be unconsummated, Samson remains faithful to Yahweh. He is not drawn to Dagon or to Canaanite baals as are Israelites (cf. Judg. 3.5-6). Samson's own prayers and laments are addressed to Yahweh the God of Israel and to none other.

The Philistines are the descendants of the Caphtorim (Gen. 10.14) from Caphtor—which is also understood to be the island of Crete (Deut. 2.23; Jer. 47.4; Amos 9.7)—who were among the 'Sea Peoples' who attempted to invade Egypt in the twelfth and thirteenth centuries BCE. They were defeated at sea and on land by Pharaoh Ramesses III and settled in a confederation of five city-states: Gaza, Ashkelon, Ashdod, Gath and Ekron (Josh. 13.2-3). Even though they are a formidable militaristic force that may already possess the monopoly of metal working (1 Sam. 13.19-22), the Philistines have good reason to be cautious of lone Israelites who appear at first to be unarmed but are able to improvise with their weaponry (Judg. 3.31).

When he 'descends' to the Philistines to look for an opportunity to begin Israel's deliverance—and when he descends deeper into their territory to Ashkelon and Gaza—Samson follows his own specialized, unique nazirite destiny by accepting the commission from Yahweh's messenger. Samson is a warrior, a terminator who participates in raw, physical acts of violence against those whom the Israelites should regard as enemies. Even though deliverance from the Philistines is Yahweh's agenda, the Israelites are no longer interested.

Judges 14:
Samson 'the Outsider'

How are we to think of Samson? Is he different from other judges or does he have a similar deliverance task? Is he the mythological character of folklore like Hercules the Greek strong-man and Enkidu the Babylonian wild-man of *The Gilgamesh Epic*? Are we to understand him as a lone super-hero who inhabits a popular adventure story? May he be thought of as a mythological sun-hero whose story is adapted by the storyteller for religious purposes? Are we to think of him negatively as an over-sexed womanizer who is enslaved by physical passion? Is he to be dismissed as a violent brute with a spiteful nature? Is he an uncontrollable juvenile delinquent who throws away his life?

A negative evaluation of Samson seems to be the prevailing view among readers: negative evaluations are heaped upon his character, as high as the Philistine dead are heaped at Lehi (15.14-17). However, I wonder, is he misunderstood? Is it possible for credible evaluations of a more generous nature to emerge from a further consideration of his story? The focus of the reading is to attempt positive evaluations of judge-deliverers and their collaborators. It is, therefore, my purpose to read the Samson story—not as an intrusion into the book's structure, but—as part of the Judges narrative in which it is set because he is Israel's next judge and deliverer. I also understand him as an 'outsider', because even though Israel has cried out to Yahweh for rescue from Philistine oppression (10.7-10), Israel no longer wants to be delivered. As we are about to discover, Samson is unable to lead an army like Othniel, Barak, Gideon and Jephthah; he acts alone for reasons that the storyteller is about to reveal. Let's read the story of Samson 'the outsider'.

Samson's Strategy against the Philistines (vv. 1-4)
A birth announcement by Yahweh's messenger—made to a woman who is unable to have children—raises our expectations that an outstanding character is about to be introduced.

Samson's mother does as she is told and adheres to specific nazirite-like prohibitions during her pregnancy that are specified by Yahweh's messenger. The specification to leave her son's hair uncut is reinforced in Samson's formative years by his encounters with Yahweh's spirit. However, as Samson gets older he faces a formidable task.

Even though the Israelites have initially cried out to Yahweh for deliverance from the Philistines, their appeal is not repeated as the change of ownership extends to forty years (13.1). The Judahites are content to submit to Philistine rule and the Philistines become their new 'owners' (10.7) and rulers (15.11). The Danites, Samson's own tribe who are reprimanded by Deborah— as she celebrates Israel's victory—for their lack of fighting spirit (5.17) unless they face an easy target (18.10), may have already migrated north. The Israelites accept Yahweh's rejection and settle for co-existence under the rule of others and by implication under the Philistine patron deity: Dagon rules the land.

How can Samson 'begin' (13.5) to deliver the Israelites—who no longer want to be delivered—from oppressors who have the power to crush and beat them down? Such a task for a lone judge-deliverer, albeit one empowered by Yahweh's spirit, would seem to lack viability, unless he is able to devise his own unique methods of conflict.

When Samson first descends into Philistine territory, it is for reasons other than mere infatuation with foreign women. He has the cool effrontery to create a conflict opportunity by infiltrating the Timnah community and joining a Philistine family by marriage. He selects a girl. He tells his parents that she is suitable for his purpose and, according to custom, he asks them to make arrangements. He does not simply 'take her' or 'go in to her'. We are not told if the girl is attractive, only that she is a suitable candidate for Yahweh's and Samson's purpose. The storyteller is unconcerned that Samson's courtship deceives a girl who no doubt has expectations of matrimony, nor is there any respect for the Philistine residents of Timnah who are crudely characterized as 'uncircumcised' (14.3; 15.18). Samson's parents, however, object to his choice of marriage partner; they evidently want their son to settle down with a nice girl from among their own. They are unaware that Yahweh and Samson have begun to work together and that marriage is an opportunity to provoke the Philistines and to do them harm.

Samson's First Kill (vv. 5-11)

While walking through a local Timnah vineyard Samson has an empowering encounter with Yahweh's spirit which for him is both affirming and enabling. When he is confronted by a young roaring lion he does not run away or climb a tree to safety. He stands his ground, he meets the attack and when empowered by the spirit who rushes to his assistance, he is able to courageously defend himself.

The killing of a young lion with his bare hands is a metaphor for the formidable task against the Philistines that lies ahead. His ability to kill the creature and to pull it apart with his bare hands is Yahweh's sign to a young Danite judge-deliverer-in-waiting that he is capable of taking on the Philistines single-handedly. The arrival of Yahweh's spirit at the right time when he faces a threat is also for his own personal encouragement. If he can kill an attacking lion, he can kill Philistines. Samson may lack Israelite support, but he is not alone. He returns on a later occasion to inspect the lion's carcass, and his discovery of a sweet delicacy reminds him of what he is able to accomplish with Yahweh's assistance against overwhelming odds. He makes his way home basking in his achievement and enjoying the refreshing honey. Sharing his find with his parents is a good omen for the future but he does not inform them about the lion's attack which may be interpreted by them as a bad omen.

Samson returns to Timnah for his marriage and—as is the custom—he arranges a seven-day drinking feast for young Philistines who are friends of his new family and may be among his future relations by marriage. Thirty so-called Philistine 'friends' are appointed as security guards or minders to keep him under observation. Long-haired Israelites pose a possible threat even though Samson's hair is tidily styled in seven plaited braids (16.19).

Samson's Riddles (vv. 12-20)

An opportunity presents itself for Samson to needle and humiliate the Philistines and to provoke his guests into conflict. He opens the feast with the proposition of a riddle and challenges them to provide the explanation. To make the riddle more interesting he includes a wager with desirable terms. He will give each of his thirty guests a complete change of clothes—including underwear and top clothes, an outfit for each of his minders—if they are able to explain his riddle. If they cannot provide an answer by the end of the feast, they must each give him a complete outfit. Much is at stake and neither can afford to lose face. Both parties are intent on humiliating the other. Samson announces his riddle:

> From out of the eater came something to eat;
> And from out of the strong came sweet.

His Philistine minders are unevenly matched against a sharp Israelite wordsmith. They have seven days; but they are crass. They take the bait and accept the groom's wager to attempt to explain an unanswerable conundrum. Samson even tips the size of his wager in *their* favour in order to provoke their interest, but the riddle itself is weighed in *his* favour because they are unaware of the background details. They were not in the vineyard when he had the good fortune to make the discovery of honey in the lion's carcass.

The Philistines are stuck. For the first three days of the feast they are unable to explain the riddle. They are so desperate to avoid humiliation that they threaten Samson's wife: they will burn her and her father in their house if she does not manipulate the answer to the riddle from her husband. The Philistines have no intention of suffering a humiliation at the hands of an Israelite who needs a haircut.

Samson's wife cries and nags her husband for the entire seven days of the feast for the riddle's answer. She cries during the first three days in order to satisfy her *own* curiosity and nags him for the remaining four days because of the Philistine's threat. Will Yahweh's strong judge-deliverer—who is able to kill a lion and humiliate his Philistine guests with an unanswerable riddle—be able to resist his tearful nagging wife? Of course he gives in to her, the poor man is unable to do otherwise. On the last day of the feast he tells her the answer even though he has not disclosed it to anyone else including his parents.

Interest in the wager becomes intense. Perhaps we can imagine a crowd gathering to hear the riddle's explanation by Samson's triumphant minders just before the wager closes at dusk on the last day:

> What is sweeter than honey,
> and what is stronger than a lion?

If the answer is the same as Samson has disclosed to his wife, it does not appear to be an answer to his riddle, but another riddle. He accepts the answer and admits defeat. However, Samson has the final word when he responds with a further poetic riddle which is a contemptuous dismissal of his guests and of his wife:

> If you had not plowed with my heifer
> you would have not found out my riddle.

Samson does not impoverish himself by paying the debt from his own wardrobe or by financing a public and humiliating shopping trip with his triumphant Philistine minders to the local Timnah bazaar. As in the Timnah vineyard, when he was threatened by the young lion, he is empowered by the spirit of Yahweh who hastens to his aid. Samson descends deeper into Philistine territory and in Ashkelon he kills thirty of their number, strips the dead of their outer garments, and returns to Timnah. He gives the clothes to the guests who explained his riddle. Samson omits the under garments from the riddle payment and his Philistine minders do not care to press the riddle's full penalty. They are content to have humiliated a hairy Israelite.

Let's summarize. It is with great self-confidence that Samson mocks his Philistine wedding guests in Timnah when he proposes the fool's errand of an unanswerable riddle. They rise to the challenge when they spend three days trying to solve the riddle even though they lack the essential information—revealed to us—which links honey with a lion's carcass. Samson contrives first to humiliate the Philistines—who attempt to answer his unanswerable riddle—and consequently to provoke conflict. The Ashkelon slaughter follows. Samson attacks Philistines, takes their clothing as spoil and pays his wager debt with Philistine property. He does not rob the thirty Ashkelonites because what he takes from them is spoil. Samson is not a thief. Yahweh's judge-deliverer is at war and the victor takes the spoils. Samson has been humiliated in his marriage feast among Yahweh's enemies; his only consolation is that he has provoked a confrontation and drawn first blood. He is angered by the limitations of being a lone deliverer and he returns alone to his father's house. As a final insult Samson's wife is given to one of his Philistine minders. We may imagine Manoah greeting his son on his return home with the words:

'Son, you have learnt a lesson. Be warned. Philistines don't play by the rules.'

However, Samson is not alone. The availability of Yahweh's spirit when engaging a lion and the thirty Ashlelonites is confirmation for a lone Israelite 'outsider' that he is employing proper methods to make his beginning against the Philistines.

Judges 15:
Samson vs. the Philistines

Samson is dedicated to Yahweh for the specific task of beginning Israel's deliverance from their new 'owners', the Philistines (13.5; cf. 10.7). However, the Israelites are no longer interested in being delivered and settle for peaceful co-existence. Philistines rule. Samson is alone but for the empowering of Yahweh's spirit. He therefore chooses his own deliverance methods when he has the cool effrontery to create conflict opportunities by infiltrating the Timnah community and joining a Philistine family by marriage. His Philistines guests deceive him when they obtain the answer to his riddle by threatening his new bride. The only satisfaction for Samson is that he is able to kill thirty Ashkelonites and take their clothing as spoil to pay his wager. Samson returns home in a rage. But he will be back.

A Second Visit to Timnah (vv. 1-8)
The wheat harvest seems as good an occasion as any for the charismatic charmer to make a return visit to stir up a further opportunity for conflict with the Philistines. There also is the matter of his wife. So, with a kid under his arm (rather like a select bunch of flowers) as a gesture of reconciliation, Samson presents himself in Timnah on the doorstep of the family home:

'I'm going to our bedroom.'
'Oh no you're not', said the girl's father standing in the doorway as he folded his arms. 'It was obvious to all of us that you hated her. You abandoned her, so I gave her to one of the guests at the wedding feast and a very happy couple they are too. Leave them alone.'
'You did what?'
Samson's face reddened. The man of the house had to think quickly. Clearly his now ex-son-in-law was not best pleased. Israelites are unpredictable especially this one who needs to tidy up his hair.

'I tell you what I'll do', said his father-in-law. 'You can have her younger sister. Look, isn't she gorgeous? Me and her mother consider her to be the better of the two.'

This is not what Samson wanted to hear. He took hold of the man, grabbed a handful of clothing, lifted him off his feet and his head hit the door lintel. Samson looked the man in the eye and said to him, and to his younger daughter who cowered behind him, 'The next time I attack Philistines, no one will be able to lay any charges against me.'

Samson let go of his father-in-law who fell in a heap on the doorstep.

The kid, which Samson carried under his arm as a gift for his wife, bleated with alarm, wriggled free and ran away.

Samson obviously takes what his Philistine ex-father-in-law does with his wife as a personal insult which is useful for his long-term purposes. He provokes another argument which presents the justification for further conflict.

Samson may not be able to lead Israel's militia into battle but he does enlist an army of sorts when he catches 300 foxes (or perhaps jackals) who are scavenging for harvest leftovers in the Philistine wheat fields. Some may think of Samson's response as an impulsive act of revenge. However, the burning of enemy produce is the smart military tactic of a guerrilla fighter and a threatening act of intimidation which requires strategic planning and considerable preparation for its several stages: catching 300 wild foxes, moving them to the required sites, tying the tails, fixing a torch in each tie, firing the torches and letting the incendiaries loose to burn harvest produce. We are not informed how Samson catches and releases 150 incendiary pairs into the Philistine fields to burn their ripe standing corn, their harvested sheaves and all their vineyards and olives. When secured in pairs with a firebrand the foxes scream repeatedly in terror and run around in circles. Not only does Samson inflict an economic disaster upon the Philistine food supply but the burning represents an intimidating and fearful destruction when he destroys their agricultural symbol of eternal rest. Harvested sheaves are compared to a man's full life at the time of his death (cf. Job 5.26).

A terrifying act of vengeance follows. The Philistines respond by burning to death Samson's ex-wife and her father whom they consider to be the cause of their harvest disaster. We may wonder about the fate of the attractive younger sister but we are not informed. The Philistines find soft targets to blame for their loss of produce.

Samson is outraged at the burning and acts like a just judge on behalf of his innocent ex-wife and her father. The Philistines burn their own people in an act which Samson himself finds repellent and offensive to his own sense of justice. He may have been betrayed by his wife (who discloses his riddle) and insulted by his now ex-father-in-law (who gives her to another), but neither deserve such a horrific fate. Samson says to those who did the burning, 'I will only stop when I have taken my vengeance on you.' In other words he says, 'if you are capable of doing such a dreadful act upon the innocent, then I too will punish you and I will not be held to account'. Samson makes an exact judgment or retribution in a measured act of justice that is not designed to spill over into an uncontrolled blood-fest. The method of Yahweh's judge-deliverer—when unarmed, alone and outnumbered in enemy territory—is raw and harsh. The so-called civilized conventions of combat are cast aside as he humiliates the Philistines who are responsible for burning his family by kicking them to death.

To summarize so far. Samson is now a combat survivor who has experienced total isolation as he fights alone against the odds when engaging with an uncivilized enemy. He witnesses their so-called acts of justice when Philistines burn innocent parties. His solo attack is grim and deeply traumatic for both parties. He has become aware of the fragility of human life in the face of extreme danger, which has come upon him as a consequence of accepting Yahweh's commission to begin to deliver unwilling Israelites.

Samson acts alone and chooses his own methods. He attempts to marry into a Philistine family. He comes close to humiliating them in a public riddle contest. He slaughters thirty of their neighbours from Ashkelon and takes their garments. He does not pay the full wager when he leaves their underclothes. He abandons his Timnite wife. He burns the Philistine harvest and kicks to death those of their number who are responsible for burning the innocent. Samson becomes Israel's outsider who retreats and lives in solitude in a cave as a desert recluse where he bides his time to await a further conflict opportunity. This is an Israelite renegade who must be brought to justice, to Philistine justice. The Philistines themselves take the initiative.

Slaughter at 'Jaw-Bone Hill' (vv. 9-20)

When a Philistine army enters Judah and surrounds Lehi the inhabitants are dismayed and ask what they have done to deserve such intimidation. The Philistines say that they have come for Samson and to do to him what he has done to them. The Juda- hites do not protest further nor do anything to defend themselves nor do they make excuses for Samson. Three thousand of their men promptly go to the Etam cave to demand an explanation and Samson is forcefully reprimanded and reminded by the Judahites that Israel is now subject to Philistine rule. The Juda- hites are content to serve others and no longer want to do battle for the land. The Judahites have settled for peaceful co-exist- ence. Moreover, they are equipped with new ropes to betray rather than with weapons to fight. When they demand an expla- nation, Samson replies that he has done no more than repay them in kind with acts of justice.

The Judahites display a lack of patriotic valour when they disclose that their purpose is to tie him up and give him to the Philistines. Judahites no longer act like the foremost Israelite tribe who are designated to take their inheritance from the Canaanites (Judg. 1.2). They act like Philistine security guards when they arrest and betray Yahweh's judge-deliverer to the uncircumcised. Samson does not resist or attack them in self- defence. He merely requests their word on oath that they will not deceive him or harm him if he allows himself to be bound with their two new ropes. The ropes are described as 'new' because they are freshly made from natural fibres, which are still moist and will tighten as they dry and are therefore stronger than dried ropes. Samson gives way and places himself in their hands rather than slay his own people.

When the Philistines see the Israelite procession approach they leave the safety of their camp with shouts of triumph at the spectacle of a tied-up violent Israelite renegade made powerless and betrayed by his own people. Samson is surrounded by his enemies and by Yahweh's enemies, but he is not alone. As in the Timnah vineyards and at Ashkelon, the spirit of Yahweh is avail- able for him at just the right moment. As he moves, both ropes dissolve as though they are no more than threads of linen touched by the heat of a flame. He shakes himself free. Samson simply stands before the Philistines ready for combat with the ropes in pieces at his feet. How does a 'fresh' donkey's jaw-bone just happen to be at hand? Is there a carcass, like that of the lion,

lying on the ground conveniently with reach from which he takes
the jaw-bone? Or does he first kill a donkey in order to extract a
suitable weapon which is not only 'fresh' but warm? It is with the
donkey's jaw-bone that Samson kills a thousand 'men' whom we
assume are Philistines rather than his Judahite betrayers.

Like others who participate in Israel's deliverance, Samson
improvises when meeting challenges. Ehud makes his own small
wooden dagger. Shamgar uses an agricultural tool for prodding
oxen. Jael uses a hammer and tent peg. Gideon uses trumpets,
jars and torches. Samson uses his bare hands to kill a lion and the
thirty Philistines of Ashkelon. He kicks the Philistine incendiaries
to death. He has improvised with fire and foxes tied in pairs. At
Lehi, he improvises again and the Philistines suffer a third humiliating slaughter by a lone Danite armed with only a dog's dinner,
a jaw-bone extracted from a freshly slaughtered donkey!

Surrounded by his dead enemies and sprayed with their blood,
as his feet slip and slide in the gore and swill of spilled human
entrails, I imagine that Samson dances as he sings for joy that
he has survived betrayal by his own people and that he has begun
to deliver Israel single-handed. He is fulfilling the commission
of Yahweh's messenger. Samson's victory rhyme, with which he
celebrates the humiliating slaughter, is a play on four words
which are all similar in Hebrew: donkey (the jaw-bone), red
(blood-stained bodies), heap (piles of corpses), and flay (torn
flesh). He sings:

> 'With the jawbone of a *donkey, heaps* upon *heaps,* with
> the jawbone of a *donkey* I have slain a thousand men'
> (v. 16, NRSV);

or perhaps,

> 'with the jaw-bone of a *donkey*, I *flayed* them in a *heap*,
> they are *reddened* with a *blooded* jaw-bone, I have slaugh-
> tered a thousand men';

or even,

> 'with a *red* one's jaw-bone, *heaps* of *blooded* corpses, I
> *donkeyed* them with a jawbone, I have slaughtered a
> thousand men'.

The rhyme could refer to the wounds inflicted upon his victims
who are a *heap* of bodies (or broken bodies collapsed in *heaps*)

which are covered in *blood* because they are scythed or *flayed* by Samson's swings of the *donkey's* jaw-bone. When the jaw-bone was a lower incisor and a functional part of a living donkey's head, it tore plant food from the ground and crushed corn. Now in Samson's hand and used as a weapon it cuts into flesh as the Philistines are slaughtered in swathes of bloody violence. Samson reddens or stains them with their own blood which sprays from their open wounds. Samson enjoys the puns of his rhyme which combines the delight of combat success with his thankfulness for deliverance and the ridicule of his defeated foe. He positively relishes his victory, celebrateing survival after taking on overwhelming odds. He and Yahweh are a team. He dances for joy as he recites his victory rhyme again and again over the dead in order to humiliate survivors (if there are any) and to ridicule the cowardly Judahites who not only betray him but simply stand by and watch from a safe distance. Under Samson's leadership, the 3,000 could have attacked the Philistines at Lehi and pushed the 'sea people' back into the sea in a triumphant war of independence. Lehi makes the tribe of Judah look bad.

Samson has no interest in the jaw-bone as a combat souvenir which he throws away because it is soiled with the blood of the uncircumcised. Locals give the site a suitable name, 'Jaw-bone Hill', a place where a terrifying slaughter with a high body-count took place. It is clear that judge-deliverers do not participate in the wars of gentlemen: Jephthah inflicts a 'great slaughter' on the Ammonites, as does Samson upon the Philistines when he says that Yahweh has given him 'a great deliverance', a phrase that is used elsewhere by storytellers to describe other heroic victories against the Philistines such as David's defeat of Goliath (1 Sam. 19.5), Eleazar's victory at Pas Dammim (2 Sam. 23.10) and Shammah's victory 'in a field full of lentils' (2 Sam. 23.12).

Samson is covered in sweat and Philistine blood; he is exhausted, dehydrated and thirsty and may be in further danger from the uncircumcised. Yahweh's servant needs refreshment and in response to his appeals for water Yahweh splits open a rock from which water flows, where Samson drinks and revives. The new desert water source is still known locally as the 'Caller's Spring'.

This chapter of the Samson story closes with an indication that the storyteller approves of his character and of the foregoing events when we are told that he judged Israel for the twenty years during which the Philistines occupied the land.

Samson acts alone out of necessity. He engages in a conflict that Judah does not own even though Israelites cried to Yahweh for a deliverance (Judg. 10.10). Yahweh's answer is provided in the person of Samson. Judah is content to be ruled by others, to act in collaboration with their foreign overlords and to stand by like frightened spectators while Yahweh's judge-deliverer fights alone for his life. Samson has little chance of doing any more than make a *beginning* of delivering Israel without tribal support. However, he has begun (13.5) and there is more slaughter yet to come.

Judges 16:
Samson in Gaza

Samson and Yahweh function as a team. When he 'descends' to the uncircumcised, to the Philistines who are Israel's latest 'owners' and oppressors (cf. 10.8), he follows his own specialized unique lone nazirite destiny to begin Israel's deliverance. Samson is a warrior, a terminator who participates in raw, physical violence against those whom Israelites should regard as their enemies. Even though he lacks the support of Israel's tribes, who are no longer interested in the exclusive possession of their land inheritance, and is an outsider, he is not alone. He is prepared by Yahweh's spirit as a young man at home in a Danite camp and is empowered on three conflict occasions. He acknowledges that Yahweh has given him a great deliverance when he is pitched against overwhelming Philistine numbers. After combat he is refreshed by Yahweh with a unique provision of water.

When Samson provokes the Philistines, their body-count is alarmingly high and the conflicts are not without personal cost to himself:

- He is humiliated among his Philistine wedding guests when the explanation of his riddle is disclosed.
- He kills thirty Ashkelonites.
- His wife is given to another.
- He destroys the Philistine harvest with wildlife incendiaries.
- His ex-wife and her father are burnt to death.
- He attacks the Philistines who are responsible for the burning by kicking them to death.
- He becomes Israel's outsider who retreats to live in solitude in a desert cave without the supportive human systems of tribe and family, care and protection which can sustain his life.
- He is betrayed by his own people when he is reprimanded, bound and handed over to the Philistines by the Judahites.

- He improvises when using the jaw-bone of a donkey as a weapon with which he kills a thousand Philistines. He flays their flesh, breaks their bones and hears their screams as they die.
- After the slaughter at Lehi we may imagine him to be covered in sweat and Philistine blood; he is exhausted, dehydrated and thirsty and may be in further danger.
- Even though Samson celebrates his survival in song and dance, he may be aware that final victory and peace in the land are impossible objectives.

As the curtain rises on the final act of the Samson story we need to read carefully or we may lose sympathy with Yahweh's judge-deliverer when he is next alone among the Philistines looking for further conflict opportunities.

Bed and Breakfast (vv. 1-3)

How are we to evaluate the information that Samson visits a prostitute and that 'he went into her', a phrase which storytellers generally use to indicate sexual intercourse? The storyteller is not troubled as the encounter is disclosed in three brisk verses.

Samson is again among the Philistines and this time he visits Gaza for the same reason as he visits Timnah, to create a conflict opportunity. He goes to a prostitute, that is, to her house, a safe-house in a Philistine city. If he had visited an Israelite prostitute we may think that this isolated war-weary deliverer was only interested in sexual gratification. However, the woman he 'goes into' is a Philistine with the same occupation as Rahab who also receives Hebrew male visitors (cf. Josh. 2.1). Samson not only sees a woman but he also sees the possibility of biding his time secretly among the Philistines.

The phrase, 'and he went into her' implies that Samson has sex with the prostitute and may indicate that we are to think less of him. However, the phrase could be read as Samson entering her house and not as a phrase of a more crude nature. For example, the storyteller also says that Barak 'went into her' when he enters Jael's tent (the Hebrew text of Judg. 4.22) where a sexual encounter between the two is not generally assumed. The NRSV translators add the words 'her tent' in v. 22 in order to indicate what it is that Barak enters, a detail which does not appear in the Hebrew or Greek texts. However, English translators do not add the words 'her house' (or 'her tent') for Samson's 'entry' in Gaza. It appears that the NRSV translators offer an innocent translation for the meeting of Barak and Jael with the addition of 'her tent', but allow a disapproving translation for the meeting of Samson and the Gaza prostitute by not adding her residence which implies that his concern is with the woman and her occupation.

Is sex the reason for Samson's visit to an enemy city as is often assumed or may Samson visit Gaza for the same reason that he visits Timnah? When he sees the prostitute he also sees a further strategic guerrilla opportunity, the use of a safe house in enemy territory. Furthermore, may the woman also be an innkeeper-prostitute who combines the two occupations of a hostelry with other services in one establishment as is sometimes proposed? What the storyteller says is that Samson settles for spending part of the night in a Gaza hostelry followed by his vandalism of the city gates. On this occasion he settles for humiliating his enemies rather than creating another slaughter episode. The repetition of 'the night' occurs four times in the brief Gaza story. Samson sleeps for half the night, until mid*night* and at mid*night* he is on the move with the city gates on his shoulders while the Philistines continue to wait all *night* in silence all *night* (as they intend) until the morning.

Look how stupid the Philistines are. Not only do they attempt to answer an unanswerable riddle, they keep a silent nocturnal vigil in Gaza to entrap an absentee Israelite! Samson also takes the opportunity to humiliate the Judahites when he places the gates of a city located in their inheritance area of land (1.18)— which is now occupied by others—on a hill facing Hebron in Judah's territory for all to see.

In Gaza, Samson settles for a part-night bed-and-breakfast in a hostelry followed by his midnight vandalism of the city gates, and on this occasion he humiliates—rather than slaughters—the Philistines. He decides not to return for his breakfast.

The Lehi slaughter makes the Judahites look bad and the vandalism of the Gaza gates makes Samson look good.

Samson and Delilah (vv. 4-22)

If Delilah's name is Hebrew and if she is an Israelite, her act of betrayal fits well with the Judahites who also pacify their rulers by betraying their judge-deliverer. Alternatively, Delilah may be a Philistine because until now Samson has associated with their women and she is on good terms with the five lords of the Philistine cities (Gaza, Ashkelon, Ashdod, Gath and Ekron) who present her with a substantial financial offer.

Delilah is the only woman in the Samson story who is named and she is characterized as independent and possessing a house with rooms. This is a savvy lady who is able to look after herself, an opportunist who takes initiatives. Delilah has no male attachment, no father, no husband, no family, no patronym. However, like other female characters—Deborah, Jael and Jephthah's daughter—she is given the focus of the story as she drives the plot forward. We are not told if she is another prostitute as assumed by some, but Delilah is portrayed as a temptress who uses her feminine allure as power when she betrays Samson for a price as she whines and pesters the poor man for answers.

Samson in Delilah's company is a combat survivor who has happened upon a safe refuge. He is at ease in a comfortable place (or so he thinks) where his fatigue and his wounds (if he has any) can be healed. He is simply resting in a homely alternative to the isolation of his Etam cave. The Philistine lords each present his hostess with a substantial financial proposition of 1,100 pieces of silver if she will entice Samson to reveal what makes him so strong and by what means he can be overpowered so that he can be tied up and humiliated. Samson has been in this position with a woman before. His Philistine wife was also told to coax information from him but was not offered money; she was threatened with burning if she did not discover the explanation to his riddle.

Delilah is not subtle. When alone with Samson she begins her task with a gentle probing question:

'Darling.'
'Emmm.'
'What makes you so strong and what can I tie you up with so that I've got you in my power?'

Delilah's questions and his replies are at first like a relaxed private conversation of lovers who engage in a teasing game. The world-weary Samson humours her by pretending to disclose what she can do to make him as weak as other men. Three times she produces the specified items. Three times she is frustrated and annoyed. Delilah becomes more persuasive and demanding as the story proceeds.

When, in his first answer, Samson says 'if *they* bind me', he discloses that he is aware of her accomplices. First, he says that if he is bound with seven cords made from fresh *yitran* fibres, a plant used for making ropes, he will be as weak as other men. Tying with *yitran*, particularly when fresh or moist—dry stock items from the Philistine stores will not do—is a plausible method of making him secure because the cord will tighten as it dries and he will be unable to break free. To gather the quantities of fresh fibres from plants and weave them into seven cords is a labour-intensive task; the work takes considerable time, perhaps days and may be observed by others. Interest is aroused among the people of Gaza and I imagine that a crowd watches for the outcome, from a safe distance, of course. When the seven cords are delivered to Delilah, Samson allows himself to be bound. The Philistine lords eagerly await the outcome in her private room (cf. 3.24). When she warns Samson that the Philistines are about to pounce, he snaps the bindings like a thread which dissolves when it is held close to the heat of a flame. Even after all the work of gathering and weaving, the reason for his strength is still unknown. Delilah is publicly humiliated. She protests that Samson has told her lies. She does not give up but persists. She wants to know what will hold him.

Samson again refers to accomplices when he says, 'if *they* bind me', this time with new ropes. The number of ropes are not specified but they are to be used exactly like the two ropes with which the Judahites bound him at Etam (cf. 15.11-14). When bound, Samson says he will be as weak as other men. We are not told if the Philistine lords supply the ropes, but they await the outcome as before in Delilah's inner room. Philistines are about to be humiliated yet again. Samson has already been tied with new ropes which had no more strength than threads of dissolving linen when held close to heat, but they wait expecting him to be weakened! Delilah binds him and announces again that the Philistines are about to pounce. Onlookers watch in anticipation. When Samson pulls the ropes from his arms like pieces of thread, Delilah complains that yet again she has been deceived. She persists and asks again how can be restrained.

This time Samson says that if Delilah weaves the seven locks of his head into a web as it is worked on a loom and if his hair is secured with a peg he will be as weak as any other man.

Delilah leads the smiling Danite to the location of a suitable loom. Onlookers follow. They arrive at a weaving shed where she tells him to lay down next to a loom. His hair is secured as he takes a nap. When she calls to him, he wakes from his sleep and simply pulls out the pin; spectators applaud as he demolishes the loom and frees his hair. Delilah protests. She cries with frustration. How can he say that he loves her when he is so heartless; three times he has told her lies and she still does not know what makes him strong or how he can be restrained.

Delilah nags him day after day until he is exhausted with her demands and his lack of sleep. The game has ceased to be amusing and Delilah has become a pest. Samson contends with women; Yahweh contends with Israel (cf. 10.16). He is now tired and weary of her whining so he gives in and tells her:

'a razor has`never come upon my head because I am God's nazirite from birth. If I am shaved my strength will go and I will become as weak as other men' (16.17, my translation).

When Samson includes God (Yahweh) in his explanation together with precise details about himself, Delilah at last realizes that she has achieved her objective and has coaxed out of him how he can become as weak as others, which is not by being tied up with anything, but by having his hair cut. The Philistine lords, who have become bored and no longer wait in her private room, are sent for and informed. All five appear and carefully count out their agreed sums.

Delilah simply stops her nagging so that Samson can rest in peace. As he gently sleeps with his head in her lap she shouts and tries to wake him. When she is sure he is sleeping soundly, she shaves him herself. First she cut his seven locks, then shaves his head and beard and he weakens. When Samson awakes he is disorientated. At first he thinks he is tied as on previous occasions with cords, ropes or a loom and can shake himself free. He is confused and in disarray. He is not aware that he is untied. He does not know that Yahweh has left him. He is unaware that anything has happened to his hair while he slept.

It is to be acknowledged that a positive evaluation of Samson—which is the focus of the reading—now becomes problematic. We could think that he gives up on his task which has become impossible for him to achieve alone and the disclosure of the information—that he did not know if he was tied or untied or that Yahweh had left him—is the storyteller's negative evaluation. However, I suggest that these details are the storyteller's way of informing us that as he awakes from sleep, which is so deep that he is able not only to have his hair cut but to be shaved, Samson is unaware of what is happening to him. It is not that he discloses a secret about himself that he is not to reveal. He does inform Delilah about the significance of his uncut hair and he does not disclose the nature of the task to which he is specifically dedicated. The Philistine lords may have killed him there and then—rather than disable and humiliate him with blinding and binding—if he had disclosed that killing them was his specific unique Yahweh-sponsored life-long nazirite task.

The Philistine lords, who have paid for the information and awaited the outcome of Delilah's shaving, appear and restrain him. Samson is knocked to the ground where he is sat upon as his head is held still and his eye sockets are gouged clean. Even though he is their enemy, onlookers recoil in horror at the disabling assault. Delilah pays no attention to his screams as she carefully counts her 5,500 pieces of silver. The Philistines do not take another chance with cords or ropes, but bind him with metal chains and put him to work on his knees grinding with a hand-millstone in the Gaza prison. However, the Philistines are subtly mocked by the storyteller for their methods because the only way they are able to overpower Samson is by paying a woman of unknown origin—who lacks honour—to betray him into their hands.

Samson shows little discernment in his choice of women who all prove to be disloyal. He is betrayed by all three. His wife nags him for seven days in order to satisfy her own curiosity about his riddle and when her nagging becomes more intense, he tells her. It is possible that the prostitute reported Samson's presence to the Gazaites. Delilah becomes more insistent with her nagging and drains the life from a man who loves her in order to discover what makes him strong. Of course he gives in; he is unable to do otherwise. He is worn out with Delilah's importunity.

However, Samson and Yahweh are not parted for long because we are informed that in time his hair begins to grow.

Dancing for Dagon (vv. 23-31)

'Samson! Samson! Samson! Samson!'

He could hear the chanting of his name accompanied by the stamping of feet and the clapping of hands by the crowd over and over again as he was pulled up from the prison floor where he had been grinding corn, forwards and backwards, on his knees doing the domestic work of women and slaves all day, every day.

'You're wanted', a rough voice abruptly announced from the darkness. 'You are very popular. Lots of people want to see you. They want to look at the one who has single-handedly wasted our harvest and killed our young men. We're having a party and you are invited. You are going to dance for Dagon. You are a star. First you are going to entertain us, then you will have the honour of being sacrificed to our god.'

Once Samson was steady on his feet the lad who threw the corn onto the lower millstone for him to grind led him by the hand from the prison and he stumbled across the Gaza street.

As he staggered into Dagon's house the chant from the Philistine assembly became a deafening roar. Shouts and screams were followed by the shrill mocking laughter of women and children.

The Philistines were enjoying a family day out. He saw nothing but heard everything. He heard his name and other shouts that he could not quite make out followed by more laughter and jeering. There seemed to be music and singing but it was all a loud cacophony of ugliness which made his head throb with pain. His eye sockets throbbed and he felt a liquid mixture of blood and sweat and tears descend down his cheeks and nose where it congealed in his beard. He was exhausted from working in the darkness of his own personal world of terror. His back ached from pushing and pulling the hand-millstone over the wheat that the boy cast on the lower stone. It was the humiliating work of women and he hated it.

Something sharp was prodded into his back. He staggered forward. He felt the sharp point again as he was ordered to dance. He tried. He hopped from one foot to another. Each time he lowered a foot to the ground pain vibrated within the blackened spaces which once held his eyes. He lifted his arms from his sides. He danced around in circles. As he fell with a cry of pain to his knees, the crowd roared with delight.

He was breathless. He asked the wheat-lad to take his hand, 'Let me rest against one of the pillars which support the roof so that I can feel the coolness of the stone.'

Sitting and leaning with his back to the pillar with the jeering of the Philistines in his ears, he whispered words which were barely audible. His mouth was dry, his lips were cracked.

'Yahweh, are you listening?' His lips barely moved. 'Do you remember me? Do you know who I am? Listen. Please help me just once more. Allow me an act of vengeance against the Philistines for the loss of my eyes.'

As he slowly stood to his feet and supported himself against the pillar, there was an expectation of impending violence. He stretched out his arms and felt the pillar on either side. In desperation he took a sharp intake of breath through his gritted teeth and screamed his final words, 'Let me die with the Philistines!' His cry echoed around the building as the crowd fell silent. All eyes were fixed on him.

As he pushed against the pillars with his outstretched arms, they moved...

The Philistine lords organize a great sacrifice to acknowledge Dagon their god who has enabled them to overpower and humiliate Samson the renegade Israelite. All agree that their god has given their enemy—the waster of their land and the one who has killed many of their warriors—into their hands. We imagine a large arena with an open roof supported by pillars which covers the encircled seating. Every seat is taken and even the roof is occupied by as many as 3,000 men and women. This is not a solemn festival but a party into which Samson is dragged to be offered by the Philistines as a sacrifice to their god.

Before 'Samson the sacrifice' the programme features 'Samson in cabaret'. He has options. He could lay down and wait for the inevitable. He could simply give up and acknowledge Dagon. Samson goes out in his own way; he gives up his life—a life which is now lived in isolation and uncertainty at the edge of a dark painful abyss—in a powerful final act of human will and defiance. It is the final deliberate action of a man who is worn out. Samson looks for retribution and achieves it in a doomed blaze of glory. When he pushes on the pillars with all his returning strength, the debris of Dagon's house falls upon Dagon's devotees and upon the Philistine lords who have laughed at his pain and his misery; all die in a mass of screaming pandemonium. In this one all or nothing moment, Samson is able to kill more Philistines in his death than during his life.

Thinking about Samson

Samson 'the outsider' completes the commission of Yahweh's messenger when he slaughters unknown numbers of Philistines.

He successfully 'begins' (13.5) the combat task of freeing unwilling Israelites from the rule of the Philistines—a task that will be completed by others—however, it is at the high cost of his own life.

Samson is not quite the over-sexed womanizer who is enslaved by physical passion as thought by some readers. I argue that he seeks the company of Philistine women in order to enter their society in order to create conflict opportunities. He is more reserved in his encounters with females than is often assumed. For example, he does not crudely 'go into' the women he sees in Timnah. His marriage is arranged by his parents at his request and he submits to matrimonial customs. He does not 'go into' his wife's sister but ignores her father's crude offer. His association with the Gaza prostitute is for the part of one night only and it is plausible—as I have suggested—that he uses her residence as a safe house within a Philistine city as he looks for further conflict opportunities. When he is in the company of Delilah, the woman he loves, he is at ease in a comfortable and safe alternative to the harshness of the Etam cave, or so he is led to believe.

Engaging in episodes of violence and brutality are part of his task as Israel's judge-deliverer who fights alone and unarmed against formidable odds. When he 'descends' alone to the Philistines, Samson follows his own specialized unique nazirite destiny to which he is commissioned by Yahweh's messenger. Samson is a warrior, a terminator, who participates in raw, physical violence against those whom Israel should regard as enemies.

Samson is worthy of a positive reading when he demonstrates fortitude by fighting alone without the stimulus of comradeship. In Dagon's house Samson is in a raw and uncomfortable place where there are no judges, priests or elders sitting in the gate to consider his case and decide in his favour. He is humiliated, abused and in pain; beyond his darkness he hears only the jeering contempt of his enemies. Dagon's house is a pit of misery where he is surrounded by those who enjoy his discomfort and humiliation. He is disorientated, traumatized and alone. He petitions Yahweh to level the scales of justice against the Philistines for the extraction of his eyes and his loss of sight. He requests a judgment for a dreadful disabling assault. Like Abraham's appeal to Yahweh's sense of justice for an innocent minority in Sodom (cf. Gen. 18.25-26), Samson's appeal to Yahweh for his eyes in Dagon's house also contains a motive clause appealing to the God who rights wrongs, to the God of vengeance to give him an act of revenge. Samson requests divine retribution; his cry is more than a brutal demand for a personal vendetta. All his words and actions are directed towards the forlorn hope of beginning to deliver Israelites who no longer want to be delivered. Even when blinded and ridiculed in Dagon's house, he is still focused on Yahweh's higher purpose when in his death he takes Philistines with him. As he leans upon a stone pillar, Samson requests empowerment; he wants justice from Yahweh the judge for what the Philistines have done to him. Samson's appeal presupposes that Yahweh is personally touched by the injustice of his situation and has not finally abandoned him but will act to restore justice. When Samson prays, it is to Yahweh and to no other. Had he petitioned Dagon, a positive evaluation for his character could not be made. However, in Dagon's house, where he is disabled, ridiculed and alone, he is still focused on his task.

The storyteller draws the Samson story to a close with a positive theological conclusion: Yahweh and his judge-deliverer expose the non-existence of one of the gods to whom Israel gives preference (Judg. 10.6). If the blinded Samson does not act, the Philistines— and we—will have evidence not only of Dagon's existence but also of Dagon's lordship over Yahweh, over Israel and over the land. The Philistines foolishly boast that he has been given to them by their fish and grain fertility god (16.24). We know better. There is no contest. Not only does Baal fail to show up in Ophrah (6.31), Dagon does not make an appearance in Gaza; he does not exist to act or to defend himself. Yahweh exists. Yahweh acts. Yahweh strengthens his judge-deliverer to deal with Dagon and to deal with Dagon's devotees in Dagon's house at Dagon's festival. We have been here before: Gideon destroys Baal's altar (6.25-27) and Dagon's house is pulled down by just one bound, blind and disabled Israelite.

Not only is Samson esteemed for the number of Philistines he kills during his life and at his death, the storyteller also records Samson's honourable family burial in the family tomb. His body is not left to be shamefully buried with the uncircumcised, nor is he denied burial with his father like Jeroboam, king of Israel (1 Kgs 13.22), and Jehoiakim, king of Judah (Jer. 22.19; 36.30). Samson judged Israel for twenty years.

It is to Israel's shame that the Israelites fail to support a judge-deliverer who is equipped with almost everything necessary to deliver Israel. Samson possesses the status that accompanies a birth announcement by Yahweh's messenger. The spirit of Yahweh monitors him from birth and equips him when required. He possesses the will to go alone among the Philistines in order to create conflict opportunities. He possesses the wit to humiliate them and the ability to slaughter them in great numbers. He is able (even without Yahweh's spirit) to carry away the Gaza gates which leaves the city open and defenceless. When bound, unarmed and disabled he inflicts significant casualties. Samson successfully 'begins' Israel's deliverance when he surrenders his life without hope of recognition. What Samson lacks is the support of Israel's tribes. The Danites have other interests; the Judahites settle for co-existence with their Philistine overlords and are content to live under their rule. Samson is the isolated judge-deliverer who lacks support and is betrayed by his own people—an outsider.

The storyteller's positive conclusion of the Samson story also concludes the cyclical stories of judge-deliverers in the central narratives. The chapters that follow contain two stories told in different styles. There are no heroes or heroines, no messengers or prophets, just Israelites who, strangely, are not negatively evaluated by the storyteller as they have been so far in Judges. Yahweh no longer acts as Israel's proactive disapproving God. Yahweh does not get angry even though a lot happens for a God to be angry about.

Judges 17:
'Micah & Sons'

'Micah & Sons' is the story of a crafty mother who sponsors her son in business as a shrine proprietor, providing the background for the tribe of Dan to acquire a new home.

Our reading of Judges began with the storyteller's account of Israel's conquest success when some of the Canaanite inhabitants of the land are slaughtered. Israel's initial success is short-lived and is followed by failure when other tribes are unable to exclusively occupy their inheritance and settle for co-existence among the Canaanites. The storyteller's bleak side emerges in theological statements where the Israelites are described as 'evil' because they forget Yahweh and fail to keep their oaths of loyalty to his covenant. Intermarriage with the inhabitants follows. When Israelites 'serve' the local Canaanite gods in preference to Yahweh, the storyteller points the reader's sympathy—not to the threatened or displaced inhabitants, but to Israel's abandoned deity. Yahweh responds by 'selling' and 'giving' his people to successive oppressive invaders in a series of bids to win them back by means of intimidation and violence. When oppressed Israelites cry out for help, Yahweh responds by sending deliverers. We are given good reasons to be impressed with the performances of the deliverers in the central narratives: Othniel is Israel's war hero; Ehud plans a perfect murder; Shamgar's heroism is not to be overlooked; Deborah and Barak and Jael are exuberantly celebrated on 'Victory in Israel Day'; Gideon and the 300 expel hordes of nomadic harvest looters; Jephthah's attempts to negotiate for peace may fail but he wins a great victory; Samson fights alone out of necessity. We have noticed that the storyteller is unequivocally critical of the Israelites for their apostasy and wants us to share his opinion. We have also noticed that none of the negative terms or phrases that are applied to Israelites are applied to those who fight for Israel's deliverance from oppressors.

There are no hissable villains in the closing chapters who lead oppressive armies against apostate Israelites and are slaughtered by Yahweh's heroic judge-deliverers. All characters in chs. 17 and 18, named and unnamed, behave just as badly as we have come to expect of Israelites. The stories can be read as part of the early conquest traditions of the individual tribes and we may imagine their relocation to ch. 1 (perhaps after v. 34) to explain what the ruthless Danites do in order to find an alternative home when they are forced into the hills by the Amorites who occupy the lowlands.

When a Thief is Sponsored by his Mother as a Shrine Proprietor (vv. 1-6)

The storyteller introduces an Ephraimite whose name in Hebrew is Micayehu which is shortened to Micah as his story progresses. We anticipate an honourable story to be forthcoming about a character whose name means 'Who is like Yahweh?' who hires a Levite-priest whose name is revealed in the following chapter also to have a promising meaning: Jonathan's name (18.30) means 'Yahweh has given'. Will these two characters, who both bear the name of Yahweh, lead wayward Israelites back to covenant loyalty? However, we have come to expect bad things of Ephraimites (cf. 5.14; 8.1; 12.1-6) and sadly we are about to be unimpressed yet again as the story unfolds.

Micayehu is not a devout character. He is a thief who steals 1,100 silver pieces from his mother. Micayehu's mother is a crafty character who, like Israel's other women in Judges, gives the beginning of the story pace and momentum. She is a savvy woman who is not one to allow an unknown thief to prosper or herself to become a victim. Micayehu has a sudden change of heart when he overhears her curse the thief and the stolen cash. Curses carry fear-evoking purposes and even though we are not informed about her specific words, what her son overhears is enough to cause his change of heart. The curse is made in order to contaminate the stolen cash and Micayehu is aware that unpleasant consequences could come upon him for the theft (Num. 5.21, 23; cf. Zech. 5.3-4). He decides to own up. He does not go quite so far as to admit his crime; his admission is simply, 'I took it' and he reassures his mother that her silver is in his safe keeping.

Micayehu's mother is delighted. But she now has to deal with the consequences of her curse because both the cash and the thief are contaminated. She thinks quickly and devises a plan that she hopes will not only protect her son but is designed to retain the value of the recovered cash within the family. Micayehu's mother becomes proactive. She makes all the moves. First, she blesses her 'repentant' son in the name of Yahweh. Second, she makes a big religious gesture when designating the 1,100 pieces of silver to be set aside as Yahweh's sacred property. Third, she returns the silver back to her son. And fourth, she says that an idol can be made with the silver. She continues to act in the role of a project manager when she commissions a silversmith—to whom she gives 200 of the silver pieces—to make an idol which is installed in her son's own shrine. Micayehu's mother sets him up in business in the profession of a shrine proprietor. The cunning scheme that she devises appears to neutralize her curse with a blessing on her son and the consecration of the silver to Yahweh which is made into an idol of unspecified shape or form for his shrine. Strangely, the remaining 900 silver pieces are not mentioned; perhaps we are to understand that the 200 silver pieces are the silversmith's fee and that the idol is made of the larger portion.

When the storyteller drops the divine part of Micayehu's name he becomes Micah (v. 5), the Ephraimite entrepreneur, who fills a gap in the religious market with the provision the means for Israelites to consult, not only Yahweh, but also a collection of idols in his shrine about matters of concern and about what is unknown. The silver idol is installed in Micah's 'house of gods' with his homemade ephod, which is a vest or tunic associated with priest's clothing (8.27) and is worn by a priest when petitioning Yahweh. The ephod may also contain the Urim and Thummim by which a priest makes known the will of Yahweh (cf. Exod. 28.30). The silver idol and the ephod are accompanied by 'teraphim', which are a collection of pagan idols and regarded by Micah as 'my gods' (Judg. 18.24). If Micah's 'teraphim' are amulets or charms which are to provide protection from evil, their assumed properties may soon be required. The items will become significant as the story unfolds. When he formally installs one of his sons as priest-in-residence, 'Micah & Son'—religious entrepreneur and priest—is in business.

By sponsoring her son and grandson's religious business venture as the proprietor and priest of a local shrine with their collection of idols—no doubt available for a consultation fee—the mother and the men in her family demonstrate their disregard for Israel's exclusive covenant with Yahweh. They break Yahweh's fundamental commandments. First, the installation of the teraphim—portable images of local gods which are thought to provide oracles (cf. Gen. 31.19)—breaks the first commandment (Exod. 20.3). Second, the provision of funds for a silver idol to represent Yahweh breaks the second commandment (Exod. 20.4). And third, the commission of a silversmith to make an idol will attract the consequences of more formidable curses (Deut. 27.15). Furthermore, by setting up their own shrine, mother, son and grandson show contempt for the local Israelite shrines at Shiloh (Judg. 18.31) and Bethel where Phinehas is priest-in-residence with the ark of the covenant (20.26-28).

The Appointment of a Levite as Priest (vv. 7-13)

Having a 'house of gods' in which one's son is installed as priest does not quite have the same mystique as having a Levite in residence as priest. As it happens, a young Levite, who is looking for a vacancy and has been living in Bethlehem among the Judahites, turns up on Micah's doorstep. Levites possess status. As the keepers of Israel's sanctuaries, they have a range of prestigious religious tasks. They are assistants to priests and responsible for the religious instruction of Israelites. They are also the 'blue collar' workers—porters, removal men and 'security guards' for Israel at worship. Their high status duties include the maintenance, furnishing, transport and construction of the tabernacle and the guarding of the ark (Lev. 3–4). It appears that the Levite is looking for a vacancy with prospects now that Israelites are settled in the land and showing an active interest in the gods of Canaan rather than in Yahweh.

Micah considers himself fortunate to have the opportunity of employing a Levite (even a young Levite) and following the briefest of interviews he is hired with the respectful title of 'father' (or teacher) and priest for an annual salary of 10 pieces of silver plus the perks of suitable clothing, food and board. The Levite unwisely usurps the exclusive holy work of a priest combined with service to Micah's collection of cultic objects which may attract the consequences of curses made by Moses and other Levites (Deut. 27.15).

In just a few sentences of storytelling, readers and listeners have seen the devoutly named Micayehu transformed from cursed family thief into Micah the entrepreneur-businessman proprietor of 'Micah & Sons', who in his home-made shrine combines diverse and opposing religious systems in which Yahweh shares a shrine with idols. His son officiates as priest with a Levite also appointed as priest who is regarded like a second son. Micah anticipates that Yahweh will provide them with a prosperous future. Such are the confused religious expectations of these characters who favour a diverse collection of religious practices. We have come to expect as much from Ephraimites.

What is the Significance of the Phrases about the Absence of a King and for People who do 'What is Right in their Own Eyes'?

Two versions of the refrain appear in the closing chapters, 'in those days there was no king in Israel; all the people did what was right in their own eyes' (v. 6; 21.25, NRSV) and a shorter refrain, 'in those days there was no king in Israel' (18.1; 19.1, NRSV).

The refrains, which do not appear elsewhere in Judges, give chs. 17–21 a structural unity. However, they do not point to particular characters who appear in the earlier chapters such as judge-deliverers and their collaborators as is often supposed. In these closing chapters (17–21) Israelites do as they see fit. The storyteller is not so overtly critical of Israel as in the former chapters. The refrains—which are generally assumed to have been inserted later by an editor—are theological statements which explain that before the monarchy, Israelites are left to themselves. Yahweh says little and does little and Israelites decide their own affairs. In the early days—before there is a higher earthly authority in the land for consultation and leadership—Israelites make their own decisions. However, when the monarchy is established, it is to be acknowledged that their religious and moral conduct shows little sign of improvement.

If the first refrain (v. 6) is a storyteller's negative evaluation as is generally supposed, it refers to the characters who inhabit chs. 17 and 18 such as Micayehu (Micah), his mother and her grandson, a Levite employee and the unscrupulous Danites to whom readers and listeners are about to be introduced. The repeated refrain (19.1) may also refer to events in the following chapters, including the abandonment, rape and murder of another Levite's concubine followed by civil war, the acquisition of 400 unmarried girls—who are the selected survivors of an attack on a city's indifferent inhabitants (21.10-12)—and 200 women taken from their dance in the Shiloh vineyards (vv. 19-23). The refrains have the narrative purpose of informing us that these dire events take place before the monarchy when—particularly in chs. 17 and 18—Israelites follow a confused pattern of consulting both Yahweh and idols. The repeated refrains may also be read as affirmations, not of the Judahite monarchy as is sometimes supposed, but of Yahweh's kingship—as Gideon says, 'Yahweh rules' (8.23)—even though his presence is less obvious than in the earlier chapters. We have also come to expect mixed things of the tribe of Judah whose military power is initially favoured by Yahweh (1.2; cf. 20.18); however, the tribe is not mentioned in Deborah's exuberant song for 'Victory in Israel Day' and Judahites prefer to live under Philistine rule when they betray Yahweh's judge-deliverer (15.9-13).

In the meantime, 'Micah & Sons'—a religious entrepreneur and his two priests—are in business and awaiting clients.

Judges 18:
The Desperate Tribe of Dan

We are taken back to the time of Israel's initial attempts at the conquest of the land and the unsuccessful attempt of the Danites to take possession of their allocated land (1.34; cf. Josh. 19.40-48). Even though their militia is substantial (Num. 1.39) and they have some tough or mean characters in their company, the Danites are unable to evict the Amorite inhabitants and they settle for living in the hills where they reside in a temporary encampment near Zorah and Eshtaol (18.2, 8, 11; cf. 13.1, 25). Danites decide to look for a home elsewhere.

The story of a Danite expedition is placed in a later position in Judges because of its associations with the Samson story: the Danites live in 'a camp of Dan' in the south (13.25) and it is interesting to note that the 1,100 stolen silver pieces from Micah's mother (17.2) are also the five units of Delilah's betrayal payment. However, such associations may be no more than coincidences.

The story of how the Danites acquire their new home is an epic tribal tale—in contrast to the brief listings in ch. 1—in which characters interact with one another over a wide geographical area from Laish (Leshem, cf. Josh. 19.47) in the north to Ephraim in the midlands and Bethlehem in the south. The storyteller provides the geographical extremities of the land: 'from Dan to Beer-sheba' (Judg. 20.1). We are again reminded that events take place before the monarchy (18.1) when the Danites are on the move and looking for land in which to settle without harassment.

The Expedition of the 'Danite Five' (vv. 1-10)

Five able men of proven ability are selected by the Danites from among their tribe and sent to reconnoitre the land. The sending out of trustworthy spies prior to invasion and settlement is a common strategy used by Israel's tribes; (cf. Num. 13–14 and Deut. 1.22-25, twelve spies; Josh. 2, two spies; Judg. 1.23, an unspecified number). The 'Danite five' are not sent in any specific direction; their mission is to make a careful investigation; to discover a home for the tribe and report back.

When they arrive in the Ephraimite hills it turns out to be Micah—the shrine proprietor of 'Micah & Sons'—who provides the 'five' with hospitality. However, it is the Levite-priest who attracts their attention. He may have a distinct accent that is recognized by 'the five' or they may have met before. A brisk interrogation follows in which questions tumble over one another: 'Who brought you here? What are you doing in this place? Why are you here?' It appears that a Levite is unexpected in such a venue. Danites are suspicious; answers are demanded. The Levite stumbles over his words; he is under pressure, embarrassed, uncertain: 'Micah has looked after me. He hired me. I am his priest.'

When the Danite visitors hear the Levite-priest's explanation of his appointment they realize they have an opportunity to ask God if their expedition will have a successful outcome. An answer is immediately forthcoming. By implication the answer can only comprise the alternatives of approval or disapproval. The young Levite makes no elaborate show with a religious formula such as 'thus says Yahweh'. He evidently wants to see the back of the Danites and an answer is pronounced in haste. As he says, their journey meets with Yahweh's approval and they may go in peace.

The Danite expedition and reconnaissance of the land is resumed and they travel north. They discover that their expedition is worthwhile when they chance upon a desirable city with peaceful inhabitants who are secure and complacent (perhaps living within strong defences). What is most appealing about Laish is that the city is not threatened by others like the Amorites in the south who do not allow Danites to occupy the fertile lowlands (1.34). Laish is a Sidonian city with an autonomous population situated in a remote location far away from allies who may come to their defence. The 'Danite five' form the opinion that the city presents a soft target. They return south. When they report their discovery they urge their tribe that a military expedition must leave immediately, because the northern land presents them with an opportunity that is too good to miss. Laish is vulnerable and theirs for the taking. The spies press their point with some urgency, adding that the land is fertile (situated at a source of the river Jordan with an abundant water supply from Mount Hermon). The inhabitants will offer little resistance;

Laish will be a push-over. Moreover, an expedition will be well worthwhile because the territory is open and spacious with everything the Danites require. Laish is perceived as a gift from God.

The Looting of Micah's Shrine (vv. 11-26)

Six hundred warriors armed and equipped for battle leave Zorah and Eshtaol and establish a base camp in Kiriath-jearim. The 600 retrace the steps of 'the five' and, they also happen to pause at Micah's house in the Ephraim hills.

The contents of Micah's shrine presents the Danites with another timely opportunity. The Levite-priest has already served them well with a favourable oracle and now that they are returned in force they can acquire their own idols and the means of being religiously self-sufficient in the north. The 600 armed Danites position themselves menacingly at the entrance to Micah's shrine. While the young Levite-priest is detained in conversation, the spies take his idol, ephod and teraphim. When he raises objection, the Levite-priest is told in no uncertain terms to keep quiet because he is also being detained. The Danites offer him a prestigious career move: he is no longer to be a priest in a single household but is promoted to the position of father and priest to a whole tribe. He is glad of the opportunity and takes the idols in hand himself for safe keeping. The Danites continue on their way north.

For the first time the storyteller mentions the Danite order of march. We may think that children, cattle and provisions are placed in front of the advancing army as a safety precaution against the event of pursuit and attack from the rear. However, the Danites' strategic methods are more subtle. They anticipate meeting no enemies apart from the unsuspecting citizens of Laish who have no need to fear the advance of children, cattle and women behind whom the 600 advance. As in the Exodus story there is no special reference to women, who may also be included among the company that travelled ahead of the main army (cf. Exod. 10.10, 24; 12.37). Progress is slow and Micah, with his neighbourhood militia, is able to catch up. He demands a halt:

Micah:	*Stop!*
Danites:	*Why are you shouting at us? Why are you following us?*
Micah:	*You thieves! You have stolen my idols! You have kidnapped my priest! My shrine is empty and you*

> *have the cheek to ask me why I am following you?*
> *Return my property.*

Danites: *Shut up! Be quiet! You had better not let everyone hear your accusations. We've got some stroppy individuals with us who do not suffer fools like you gladly! Be careful or they will get upset.*

Micah is outraged. He protests that the Danites' questions are absurd. They know very well what they have done: they have abused his hospitality, they are thieves, they have taken his idols and his priest; his shrine is empty. The Danites square up and intimidate him with their superior strength. Micah is to be quiet or he and his militia will be attacked and killed by the unpleasant characters in their army (Judg. 18.25). Micah and his company are intimidated; they have no alternative but to back down and return home empty-handed. His 'teraphim' give him no protection.

The entrepreneur-businessman of an independent Ephraimite religious establishment has lost everything: his mother's investment, his means of livelihood and the opportunity for a prosperous future. Does Micah and his shrine suffer the consequences of the curses of Deut. 27.15 for making an idol or may his mother's curse on her stolen silver and the thief still hold good? 'Micah & Sons' is out of business.

The Destruction of Laish and the Slaughter of the Inhabitants (vv. 27-31)

The Danite army arrive at a remote city whose citizens have no reason to fear the slow approach of families. The Danites are subtle. Their children, who are no doubt weary from their journey, are followed by their 600 warriors among whom are some unpleasant characters. Even though the land is spacious there are no negotiations for peaceful co-existence—the Danites have wholesale slaughter in mind. The inhabitants are attacked and slaughtered and the city is burnt; no ally comes to their rescue. As expected, Laish is a push-over. The peaceful unsuspecting inhabitants are 'ethnically cleansed' in order to provide Danites with a home.

With the assistance of a Yahweh oracle from Micah's priest, the Danites have taken their own land by force in a remote location. The city is rebuilt and given the tribal name.

The stolen cultic objects are set in a place of honour in the rebuilt and re-named city by the Levite-priest who until now has

been unnamed. He is none other than Jonathan the son of
Gershom who is the son, grandson or descendant of Moses! We
are shocked to discover that a descendant of Moses presides at a
tribal shrine that houses an idol (Exod. 20.4). Later scribes who
were uncomfortable with the name of Moses being associated
with idolatry in the story of Micah and the Danite migration
inserted a suspended Hebrew letter *nûn* after the first consonant in the printed name of Moses (MT, Judg. 18.30) in order to
change the name of Moses to 'Manasseh' (the tribe of Moses).
The insertion shows that the idolatrous Jonathan is a descendant
of an idolatrous tribe rather than a specific descendant of Moses
himself. The descendants of Moses (or Manasseh) supervise the
northern Danite shrine until the 'deportation' which refers to the
forced depopulations of the land in 734 BCE (2 Kgs 15.29) and
722 BCE (2 Kgs 17.6).

The Desperate Tribe of Dan: A Summary

Everyone behaves badly in the stories of Micah, his mother and
the Danite migration. Even though Yahweh is petitioned, no one
is loyal to Israel's deity. Just two characters are named and both
names possess meanings which suggest character potential:
Micayehu, 'Who is like Yahweh' and the Levite Jonathan, 'Yahweh has given'. However, as the story unfolds, neither character
fulfils the religious significance of their names. All characters,
named and unnamed, are religious opportunists who live off the
fortunes of others by theft, deception and genocide. Micah steals
from his mother and only admits to the theft when he overhears
her curse uttered upon the thief and stolen silver. Furthermore,
by owning up to the theft, Micah anticipates a reward and his
mother sets him up as a religious businessman. The Danites are
interested in a quiet life away from Amorite harassment (Judg.
1.34). They rob Micah of his idols and make his young resident
priest a prestigious offer. When the Danite army arrives in the
remote north and discovers the soft target of Laish as reported
by their spies, they are merciless—all the inhabitants are slaughtered and the city is destroyed. The storyteller emphasizes their
callousness by twice describing the inhabitants as 'peaceful and
unsuspecting' (18.7, 27). We may consider that the Danites
behave badly because:

- they do not stand and fight but run away from Amorite
  opposition in the south.

- Danites fail to join Barak's militia against Sisera's iron chariots and receive a humiliating reprimand from a prophetess for their laziness (5.17).
- Danites fail to support Samson their judge-deliverer (13.2) against the Philistines.
- Danites are thieves—they steal Micah's property from his 'house of gods'.
- Danites are kidnappers—they take Jonathan the Levite from Micah's shrine.
- Danites are cowards—their army destroys a soft target, a peaceful city and slaughters all its unsuspecting inhabitants.

The tribe that steals, cheats and murders its way to a secure future fulfils the prophecies of Jacob their ancestor and patriarch:

> Dan shall be a snake by the roadside, a viper along the path, that bites the horse's heels so that its rider falls backward (Gen. 49.17, NRSV).

We may be shocked at the behaviour of the desperate tribe of Dan but the storyteller is not so concerned and is not as negative about their conduct as he is with the Israelites in the previous chapters, apart from framing their story within comments (Judg. 17.6 and 19.1) which may be later editorial signals for hearers and readers to think negatively of the tribe. However, the story-teller also implies that Yahweh and the Danites work together. When they make an inquiry at Micah's shrine if their mission will meet with success they are told that Yahweh is going ahead of them. Is this a valid oracle? Are we to accept the Levite-priest as a reliable character? Moreover, when the spies return to Zorah and Eshtaol, the discovery of Laish is reported as 'God's gift' (18.10). Is it? Do they simply assume a suitable discovery to be God's provision because it is suitable? Furthermore, after the slaughter of the Laish inhabitants, the Danites successfully establish a secure tribal home in the north and install their own shrine—with Micah's confused collection of idols—attended by a priest with a prestigious ancestry. Does Yahweh approve of being associated with idols? Is it possible that Yahweh approves of the Danites' conduct? We do not know; he does not say.

We may be dismayed at what we have just read but there is worse to come in the concluding stories.

Judges 19:
A Quaint Rambling Tale of Innocence and Hospitality

Have you ever been led along by a storyteller with a quaint tale that includes limited movement and easy conversation in which characters say and do little of any significance, only to become alarmed by what a turn of the page reveals?

In the closing chapters we are cleverly drawn into a storyteller's shock-horror-fest accompanied by a unique appeal to respond to the bad behaviour of wayward Israelites. Like the stories of 'Micah & Sons' and the Danite quest for a new home, events take place before the monarchy (v. 1).

A Levite and his Concubine (vv. 1-3a)

The story concerns an unnamed Levite, who may be the same character as in the previous story, also with Bethlehem associations and residing temporarily in the Ephraimite hills. The Levite has acquired a concubine from Bethlehem. 'Concubine' is the word that English translators use for the Hebrew word *pilegeš*. The Levite does not appear to have a wife or wives with whom her status may be compared. The storyteller refers to the concubine as the Levite's 'woman' or 'wife' (vv. 1, 26, 27; 20.4); he is also referred to as her 'man' or 'husband' (v. 3; 20.4) and the concubine's father is the Levite's 'father-in-law' (vv. 4, 7, 9). The storyteller makes an earlier reference to a *pilegeš* which may indicate the woman's role and status and her relationship to the Levite. When Jotham rages at Abimelech, the murderer of his brothers, he refers to him with contempt as the 'son of a slave' (9.18). Such a reference may be a term of contempt or may describe the status of Abimelech's mother as a slave. Abimelech's mother, who resides in Shechem—but does not make an appearance—is identified, not as one of Gideon's seventy wives, but as his *pilegeš* (8.31). The appearance of the word *pilegeš* in the Gideon-Abimelech story suggests that a concubine may not be a free woman but a slave. The Levite also refers to his concubine as his 'slave' (19.19) when informing his Gibeahite host that he has sufficient food for the members of his party. The Levite is also 'lord' or 'master' of both his young male servant and of his concubine (vv. 11, 12, 26).

Concubines in Israel may, therefore, be female slaves who have been taken as spoil in Israel's conquest battles or spoil from oppressors who are defeated in the judge-deliverer stories. Concubines may also be acquired from Canaanites who enter Israelite households for 'duties' which may be domestic or sexual or both (cf. 1.28, 30, 33, 35). Other characters also acquire concubines and have children by them: Abraham (Gen. 25.6; 1 Chron. 1.32), Caleb (1 Chron. 2.46), Saul (2 Sam. 3.7); David's wives and concubines are distinguished from each other (2 Sam. 5.13), but Solomon's 300 concubines are numbered among his many wives (1 Kgs 11.3). Even though the precise meaning of *pilegeš* remains uncertain, the reading will continue to use the word 'concubine' which appears in modern translations.

Some English translations follow ancient versions and say of the concubine that 'in a fit of anger she left him' (Judg. 19.2, NEB) or she 'became angry with him, and she went away from him to her father's house' (NRSV), which suggests that the Levite gives her cause to run away and signals to us that we are to be sympathetic towards the offended party. According to the MT the concubine is 'unfaithful' and running away is her act of unfaithfulness. The concubine is characterized by the storyteller, like other female characters, as an independent woman when she takes the initiative and absconds. She does not leave the Levite in order to co-habit with another man but returns to a place of safety, to her father's house in Bethlehem. When she does not return after a reasonable length of time (four months), the Levite pursues her.

The storyteller informs us that the Levite's intentions are honourable; he intends to win the runaway back by reasonable negotiation which is suggested in the MT as the purpose for his visit, 'to speak tenderly to her heart' (v. 3). However, this Hebrew phrase may not be the kindly romantic gesture that commentators would wish it to be but a reprimand and, if necessary, she will be brought back by force.

Generous Hospitality in Bethlehem and Gibeah (vv. 3b-21)

When the Levite arrives at his concubine's father's home, accompanied by his young male servant and two donkeys, he is met by the cheerful man of the house. No 'tender' reconciliation takes place between the Levite and the woman; the meeting is between the male host and his male guest. Generous hospitality is offered and received. Levites possess status and the host is honoured to receive his guest. Like the Levite and his servant, the host is unnamed but is referred to as 'the girl's father' (vv. 3, 4, 5, 6, 8). He is an admirable host who welcomes the Levite upon whom he prevails to stay for the customary three days of ancient hospitality. However, the Levite does not want to overstay his welcome and he is ready early in the morning of the fourth day to leave with his concubine. The host prevails upon his guest further and will not allow him to leave without breakfast. The Levite agrees. The host is even more generous and appeals to his guest to be kind to himself by staying another night which he does. The Levite is up early on the morning of the fifth day ready to leave, but again he is pressurized with further offers of generous hospitality. Again the two linger over a good breakfast. When the Levite rises to leave the host points out that the day is advanced and his guests can stay on yet another night and make an early start the following day. The Levite—who no doubt has enjoyed too much of a good thing—makes up his mind and leaves accompanied by his servant and his concubine. We are not told if she is consulted or if she willingly accompanies her 'master'.

After a late start the Levite discovers he has made a traveller's misjudgment when he finds himself in hostile territory at nightfall. As the night draws in the party is within sight of Jebus (the ancient name for Jerusalem), which is still occupied by the Canaanites whom the Benjaminites are unable to expel (1.21). The Levite is understandably reluctant to accept his servant's suggestion to spend the night among foreigners who may be hostile. They continue on their way and arrive in Gibeah when it is almost dark, where they sit in the town square to await an offer of hospitality. In an informative aside the storyteller provides readers with the information that they are now in Benjaminite territory (19.14), which implies they are within Israel and in a place of safety where hospitality will be forthcoming. An old man enters the town from working in his field, and it happens that he too, like the Levite, is from the Ephraimite hills. For a second time we are informed that the travellers are within Benjaminite territory (v. 16). The old man takes the initiative and asks where they are from and where they are going. In reply the Levite simply states that they are going 'home' (English versions) or to the 'house of Yahweh' (MT, v. 18) and they are in need of hospitality for the night. The Levite assures the old man that they require little because they are well provisioned with wine and food for themselves and feed for their donkeys. The old man takes them to his house where the donkeys are fed. The travellers wash their feet and enjoy a meal (v. 21). The Levite has been fortunate with the hospitality he has received, first from his concubine's jolly father in Bethlehem, now from a kindly old Ephraimite in Gibeah.

A Storyteller's Tactics

A question arises. Why does the storyteller detain us with a quaint tale about generous hospitality? The rambling story about a jolly host who tries to delay his guest tells us little of interest about the characters and adds little to the story. Some characters act badly in Judges but here we are presented with two hosts who are fully aware of their obligation to be hospitable to travellers. We are informed about the generosity in Bethlehem of the girl's father who does not appear again in the story once his guests have departed. We learn little about the Levite apart from his eagerness to return home. We are not informed why the girl's father delays the Levite's departure. Is he merely a lonely chap who likes company? Is he embarrassed about his daughter's conduct and attempts to make amends with generous provision for the Levite who has been inconvenienced? Might his attempts to delay the Levite's departure also be an attempt to keep his daughter at home because he fears she may be mistreated? Hebrew storytellers generally tell their stories with a minimum of detail; however, not only does it seem that unnecessary details are provided, it also appears that an unnecessary story is told. The offer of generous hospitality to a guest who wants to leave appears to be a storyteller's indulgence. If the storyteller is trying to tell us something, his method is too subtle. We have come to accept that pace, momentum and resolution are the usual methods of Judges storytelling.

The stories may have two minor functions that could have been briefly told rather than with a rambling tale. They account for the late arrival in the day of the Levite and his party in Gibeah, in Benjaminite territory. They may also contrast the generous hospitality in Bethlehem with what we are about to be told occurs in Gibeah.

The storyteller may also have an unusual hidden agenda. We are led along and set up with quaint tales of innocence and hospitality which do not prepare us for the different type of story that follows. We are cleverly made to feel at ease and are ill prepared for the shock of what happens next.

Interruption (vv. 22-28)

As the travellers enjoy an evening meal provided by their Gibeahite host in his home, the house is surrounded by a group of yobs. The storyteller calls them 'sons of belial' (v. 22; cf. 20.13) which indicates they are 'worthless' and 'wicked', or 'yobs' as I choose to call them. They bang on the old man's door demanding that his male guest be brought out to them for the purpose of sexual abuse. The old man emerges and engages them in conversation; he begs them twice not to abuse his guest with such a disgraceful demand (vv. 23-24). He offers the predators an alternative of—not himself in the place of his male guest, but— the two women who are in his house, his own young daughter and the Levite's concubine. As the old man says, the yobs can do as they like with the women, but they may not abuse his male visitor; male guests are to be respected. When the yobs make it clear that the alternatives are unacceptable, the concubine is seized and put out of the house (v. 25).

A further question arises. Who takes hold of the concubine and puts her out into the night? Is it the old man or the Levite? The text could be read that either party takes the initiative. However, in the way the story unfolds it is the owner of the house who opens his door; it is he who talks to the intruders, he who objects to their demand and he who makes the initial offer of the two women. It is, therefore, the old man (the host) who also seizes the concubine and puts her out of his house into the night. The Levite does not appear. He does not stand beside (or behind) his host offering support when the door is opened. He does not engage the predatory yobs in conversation. It is the old man who makes all the moves at his doorstep.

The woman is raped and abused by the Gibeahite yobs through the night and in the morning; when discarded (v. 25), she makes her way to the host's doorway where she falls. It appears that the Levite sleeps soundly; he rises in the morning and no doubt takes his time over another good breakfast. When he opens the door, there lies his concubine where she has died with her hands upon the doorstep reaching for sanctuary and protection. He tells her to 'get up' because 'we are going'. When no answer is forthcoming—not even a cry of pain or despair—we assume she is dead. The Greek translations of Judges (LXX A&B) both add the detail that she does not answer the Levite's call to get up 'because she was dead' (LXX, v. 28). The Levite puts her on one of his donkeys and resumes his journey. Neither the Levite's servant, the host or his daughter make an appearance.

We might pause to ask if we have read the events correctly:

- A group of yobs knock at the door and demand that the owner of the house send out to them his male guest for their sexual amusement.
- The host is dismayed at their evil intent which he calls a disgrace. He offers the two women who are in the house, his own young daughter and his guest's concubine who is also his guest. The yobs may have their way with them (rape them) and do with them as they like ('what is good in their eyes', MT, v. 24), a phrase which evokes the framing statements of the whole story (cf. 19.1; 21.25).
- According to the owner of the house, the sexual abuse of women is preferable to the sexual abuse of a male guest which will be a despicable act (19.24).
- When the offer of the two women is refused, the house owner seizes the Levite's concubine and puts her out of his house into the night to the predators by whom she is gang-raped. When they are finished with her, she is discarded.
- The honour of the Levite's concubine is not defended. She is not pulled back into the house by the Levite or by his servant. The Levite and his servant do not appear at the doorstep.
- It appears that the abuse of a women guest is preferable to the abuse of a male guest.
- When the door is closed we can only assume that all occupants—the owner of the house, his daughter, the Levite and his servant—go to their beds and sleep soundly.
- No discussion takes place in the morning over breakfast. No argument; no protest; no explanation or expression of regret is forthcoming from the host. The Levite demands neither explanation or apology. The Levite's servant, who

has not been slow to make a suggestion about hospitality (v. 11), does not reappear in order to ask his master about his concubine.

This is a Levite from the Ephraimite hills who emerges as a terrifying character.

The Grim Processional Tour of the Land (vv. 29-30)

When he arrives home, the Levite 'seizes' his concubine's body (v. 29; cf. v. 25), takes a knife (*the* knife, MT) and butchers her into twelve pieces without breaking her bones. The twelve pieces are sent throughout the whole territory of Israel.

We are not informed whether the woman's body parts are sent in different directions to specific individuals who are representatives of Israel's twelve tribes, to twelve cities in tribal areas or to twelve cultic centres. I imagine that all twelve items are carried in a bizarre processional tour of the land by twelve porters in order for Israelites to view the exhibits, to demand their meaning and to summon an assembly where an explanation will be demanded (cf. 1 Sam. 11.7). Interest is aroused; the land is in shock and alarm; everyone agrees:

'Such a thing has not happened nor been seen since the Israelites came up from the land of Egypt until today.'

The porters are to make an urgent appeal:

'Consider her! Discuss the matter! Speak up!' (v. 30, my translation).

The Levite anticipates that viewers will be scandalized, but we may ask: what is it that has 'not been seen before in the land'? Certainly a procession of butchered female body parts is something new! It is anticipated that Israelites will want to know how the woman has died and to bring whoever is responsible to account. The three concluding imperatives: 'consider', 'discuss', 'speak up' are the storyteller's appeals to those who view the macabre procession and to us; we too are to consider for ourselves what has taken place. The storyteller demands a reaction from everyone who will hear the story read, or read for themselves. Israelites do not yet know the circumstances of the concubine's death, but we know. He asks *us* what *we* think. He does not want his story to be ignored. He wants what he writes to be talked about. The story is morally outrageous and the horrific events speak for themselves. We are not to be indifferent about what we read. What do you think?

There is no concern with the logistics of the procession. No details are provided about how the butchered body parts are transported, whether they are carried ceremonially on trays, in baskets or unceremonially over the porter's shoulders. Those who see the dismembered procession will agree that such a sight has not been seen before in Israel. Demands will be made about the significance of the tour; however, no explanation accompanies the procession. No details are provided for viewers about the events prior to the victim's butchering or what has taken place and where. The procession is a bizarre performance of dark travelling theatre sent on its way to shock and summon the inhabitants of 'the territory of Israel' to a meeting where questions will be asked and an explanation will be forthcoming.

A Parallel Story in Genesis 19

The inhabitants of Sodom are described as 'very evil' (Gen. 13.13); Yahweh is aware that their sin is great and that the matter requires investigation (Gen. 18.20-22). However, the specific nature of their sins and evil conduct are not disclosed.

One evening while Lot sits at the gate of Sodom, two messengers or angels approach (Gen. 19.1); they are referred to again as messengers (v. 15) but they are also called 'the men' (vv. 10, 12, 16) but they are not identified as Yahweh's messengers. Even though Lot is a visitor to the city he rises, greets them with respect and offers hospitality. They decline; they will not trouble him but will spend the night in the open. Lot insists and when his offer is accepted he prepares a meal. Before the host and his guests turn in for the night, 'men of Sodom' surround his house and demand that the visitors be brought out for the purpose of sexual abuse. Lot is more courageous than the old man of Gibeah; he goes out to the men, closes the door behind himself and challenges the predators face to face. He begs them not to do anything evil to those who are his guests and offers an alternative—his two virgin daughters. The men of Sodom will not accept the alternative from someone who has the low status of a mere foreign resident in their city; they attempt to overpower him and to break into his house. It is the messengers inside who rescue Lot when they open the door and pull their host back inside. Those who threaten Lot and make the evil demand are struck with sudden blindness. The messengers reveal that their mission is to destroy the city (v. 13) and their association with Yahweh. The stories are strikingly similar but dependence and priority are uncertain:

- Travellers arrive at night.
- An open space within the city is featured.
- Hospitality is offered, not by an indigenous inhabitant, but by a host who is a temporary resident in the city.
- Men surround the house.
- A meal is interrupted.
- There are knocks at the door. Demands are made. The doorway is significant as the way *in* to security and *out* to danger.
- The hosts protest at 'evil' proposals.
- Two women are offered with whom the intruders may behave as they please.
- Attempts are made to save the male guests.
- The Sodom story almost ends in tragedy for the occupants of the house; the Gibeah story does.

For What Purpose do the Gibeahite Yobs Demand the Male Visitor?

The MT uses the verb 'to know' him (*yāda'* Judg. 19.22; cf. Gen. 19.5) which in both stories is understood as a Hebrew euphemism for sexual intercourse or, on these occasions, for the sexual abuse of a male by males. The verb generally means 'to know, perceive, understand' in the sense of meet, converse, gain knowledge and of making an acquaintance. The different use of the verb may be seen in the primeval story in which Adam and Eve discover the difference between good and evil, and Adam has sex with Eve (Gen. 3.5, 7, 22; cf. Gen. 4.1). The Judges storyteller has already used the verb 'to know' in a sexual context when a daughter agrees to be sacrificed and to die a virgin (Judg. 11.39). We are about to be informed in ch. 21 about the selection of girls because they also are virgins (vv. 11 and 12). None of the females in these stories have 'known' (*yāda'*) a man. However, there is also a difference in the storyteller's use of the word that is first applied to the rising Israelite generation who 'do not know Yahweh' (2.10) but is now used in a demanding atmosphere of threat, abuse and sexual violence of males against another male (19.22) and males against a woman (v. 25).

It is not necessary to identify the Gibeah yobs (or 'all the men of Sodom') as predatory homosexuals who lust after a male stranger as is generally supposed. Their intent is to abuse the male stranger by male rape in order to shame him because he is a newly arrived outsider. They refuse the young daughter who belongs to the old man's household but they are content to abuse the Levite's concubine in the place of the Levite because this is an act that directly dishonours him. What the intruders demand is identified by the host as being disgraceful (vv. 23 and 24), which indicates that they are intent on inflicting a degrading sexual act of gross humiliation on a visitor who is a brother Israelite with the status of a Levite.

When the Israelites see the grim procession of female body parts it is clear that something dark and dreadful has taken place. The Israelites will have to *do* something.

Judges 20:
The Three Battles of Gibeah

A macabre procession of butchered female body parts, which are paraded around Israel on the orders of a Levite, attract attention. The procession becomes the talk of the land. Everyone agrees that nothing like this has occurred or even been seen since the Israelites left Egypt. The exhibits produce a result when all the tribes meet in an assembly at Mizpah, a tribal unity that has not been seen before in Israel.

Israelites Assemble at Mizpah (vv. 1-10)

Representatives of all Israel's tribes from within the geographical extremities of the land, from Dan in the north to Beer-sheba in the south and as far inland as Gilead (apart from the city of Jabesh-gilead, cf. 21.8), meet in a united assembly before Yahweh at Mizpah. The leaders of the tribes are present, accompanied by 400,000 armed men. Mizpah is located in the middle of Benjaminite territory; the Benjaminites are aware of the assembly but are also conspicuous by their absence. Assembly members are outraged by the procession of body parts throughout the land and just one item is on the assembly's agenda: 'how did this evil act occur?'

The Levite is identified as the husband or 'the man' of the murdered woman and until now all the people of Israel have been unaware of the reason for the grim procession that has toured the land. The assembly is silent; all Israel is focused and united; assembly members lean forward to hear everything, to miss nothing as the Levite rises to speak:

> 'I arrived in Gibeah in Benjaminite territory with my concubine to lodge for the night. During the night citizens of Gibeah rose up against me and surrounded the house where I was staying. They wanted to kill me but they raped my concubine and she died. I cut her body into pieces and sent her throughout the whole territory of Israel because they have done a violation and an outrage

in Israel. People of Israel, all of you! Give your advice
and counsel' (vv. 4-7, my translation).

The Levite is an orator who presents a plausible account. He
claims the moral high ground when he says he is the victim of a
disgraceful crime that has violated Israel's customs of hospitality
and brought disgrace to the land. The assembly is horrified that
Israelite travellers have been abused by other Israelites.

The Levite makes an impressive case. He is given a hearing
and his evidence is accepted because he possesses status. His
listeners cannot mistake that an evil act has been committed or
that justice is demanded. However, the assembly is of course
unaware that the Levite is selective with his evidence. He accuses
the general citizens (cf. 9.2) of Gibeah but the yobs (the 'sons of
belial', 19.20; 20.13) are not yet mentioned. He does not say that
his host initially offered two women in his place or that he failed
to defend the honour of his concubine. He does not say what he
was doing while the outrage took place. He is not specific about
what happened to the woman; his information is ambiguous
when he informs the assembly that she was raped and died. He
does not say that she was seized, put out of the house, ruthlessly
gang-raped through the night and, as a result, died on their
host's doorstep. His evidence is selectively presented from his
own point of view. The Levite is only concerned with *his* honour
and safety when claiming that a disgraceful act has been
committed against himself. Furthermore, he presents himself as
the victim when he exonerates himself of all blame; he is fortunate to have escaped with his life. The Levite concludes with the
same words that accompany his procession of body parts.
Assembly members are to speak up and give their verdict on the
matter.

It is fortunate for the Levite that no Benjaminites are present
in the assembly to make a cross-examination and that no
assembly member requests clarification. No one asks the Levite
if he did anything to protect the woman. No one asks what he
was doing while she was being abused. No one asks for the
corroborating evidence from the witnesses who were also present
in the house at the time.

The Levite wins the sympathy of the assembly; it is enough
that Israelite guests—when away from home—are abused by
other Israelites. The exhibits have been viewed; the assembly

are united in accepting the Levite's testimony and no one is going home until the matter is resolved (v. 8). No voices are raised in dissent. No provision is made for a defence hearing before Israel's elders at the Gibeahite gate. The matter has been heard to the assembly's satisfaction. Even though we are aware that the Levite has been selective in the telling of his story, an outrage has been committed—let's call it what it is and not hide behind metaphor—a woman has been gang-raped and those responsible will be brought to account. All Israel is united and a strategy is decided. A tenth of Israel's militia will supply provisions for the remainder who will march to Gibeah with the task of punishing those responsible for the disgrace that they have brought upon Israel. When Israel's militia is in position before Gibeah, messengers are sent throughout the territory of Benjamin, announcing:

> 'What is this evil that you have committed? Give up the men, the Gibeahite sons of belial, so that we may execute them and purge the evil from Israel' (vv. 12-13, my translation).

A sharp question is asked in order to make the Benjaminites feel their guilt. They refuse to listen and respond by making preparations to defend themselves. Their response is a declaration of solidarity with the yobs who they will not give up to the assembly's demands. They muster a militia of 26,000 armed men from their cities, plus, as the MT says, 700 men chosen from Gibeah. They also muster their secret weapon: 700 hand-picked marksmen who possess a left-handed skill with a sling (Ehud possessed the same skill, 3.15). They are so skilled with their slings that they can aim a stone at a single strand of hair without missing (20.16). The Benjaminites do not petition Yahweh.

The opponents face each other at Gibeah. On one side are 400,000 armed warriors from the assembly's united eleven tribes of Israel who consider they have right on their side. On the other are the Benjaminites with 26,700 armed warriors, including those chosen from Gibeah, among whom are 700 skilled with a sling in their left hands. The Benjaminites do not listen to the demand of Israel's assembly and the whole tribe is held responsible for the evil act because the yobs are not given up for justice but are protected.

Israelites 'go up' to Bethel to consult God about the conflict solution to which they are now committed. As at the beginning of Judges (cf. 1.1)—when engaging with Canaanites—the Israelites want to know who among them is to begin the hostilities, not on this occasion to expel the inhabitants, but to bring their own to justice. Judah is identified but no assurance is given that their cause is just, or that the Benjaminites are 'given into your hand'. The following morning the Israelites assemble before Gibeah ready for battle. The Israelites, fronted by Judah, who have been reluctant to follow Yahweh's judge-deliverers and engage with oppressors (cf. 5.16-18, 23; 15.11), prepare to fight among themselves.

The First Battle of Gibeah (vv. 19-21)

The battle is a humiliating defeat for Israel's assembly. The Benjaminites take the initiative when their left-handed marksmen emerge from Gibeah and knock 22,000 Israelites to the ground (v. 21). No losses are reported among the Benjaminites.

The Second Battle of Gibeah (vv. 22, 24-25)

The defeated Israelites lick their wounds and prepare to do battle again. As part of their preparations, they 'ascend', which suggests a return to Bethel where they cry all day to Yahweh. This time they are not so presumptuous and request permission to do battle 'with our brothers' (v. 23). Yahweh's 'permission' is granted, but—as before—without any assurance that the Benjaminites are 'given into your hand'.

Again Israelites line up for battle. Again the Benjaminites emerge from the city. Again the left-handed marksmen take the initiative and this time knock 18,000 of Israel's armed men to the ground (v. 25). Again no losses are reported among the Benjaminites.

Preparations for the Third Battle of Gibeah (vv. 26-28)

Israel's crisis intensifies. The Israelite assembly still consider right to be on their side because a Levite has been abused by Israelites. His testimony has been heard and accepted. Exhibits have been received in evidence. All agree that the execution of those who are responsible for a disgraceful and evil act will rid the land of a stain. Yahweh has identified the Judahites as the tribe to attack and has given Israel permission for a second offensive. But they have been defeated twice by the Benjaminite secret weapon: the 700 left-handed marksmen have knocked a total of 40,000 armed Israelites to the ground.

Israel's situation is dire. Their whole army retreats back to Bethel where they sit, fast and weep in Yahweh's company all day (v. 23). A day of serious religious intent concludes with animal sacrifices (v. 26) which are designed to atone for their sins and to restore harmony between themselves and Yahweh in order to prevent further disaster. First, they offer ascending burnt offerings which provide Yahweh with a soothing aroma with the aim of winning his approval (cf. Lev. 1.9, 13, 17) in which the whole animal is completely consumed by fire on an altar. Second, peace offerings are presented to Yahweh which also have a soothing aroma (cf. Lev. 3.5; 7.11-36). The peace offering includes a covenant meal that is shared between the priest and the worshippers which affirms the relationship between Israel as a community of believers and Yahweh. Is Israel coming home to Yahweh?

Mention of Phinehas and his patronym 'son of Eleazer, the son of Aaron' as the officiating priest before 'the ark of the covenant of God' at Bethel has the narrative purpose of demonstrating that the Israelites are making a big religious gesture in order to win Yahweh's approval and an assurance of victory. Not only do the Israelites spend a day weeping, fasting and making evening offerings, they go further by appealing to Yahweh through none other than the grandson of Aaron, the priest of the conquest generation. The assembly of the eleven united tribes is facing a crisis and they participate in the biggest cultic act that is available in order to win Yahweh's support. The only sacrifices that have been offered to Yahweh in the book of Judges so far are those presented individually and under duress by Gideon (Judg. 6.26), Jephthah (11.39) and Manoah (13.16-23). This is the first occasion in Judges when offerings of a public tribal nature are made. Is Israel merely desperate when facing a crisis or may it be that the prospect of a further defeat at Gibeah, combined with the urgency to remove the reproach of evil from the land, points Israel back to Yahweh and to covenant loyalty? Are Israel's two defeats in battle examples of the misfortune from Yahweh (cf. 2.15) that comes upon Israelites for their apostasy?

Hints of doubt and hesitancy emerge when they ask: 'shall we go to battle again against our brothers the Benjaminites or shall we stop?' Israelites allow that they have the option of halting hostilities against their own. Yahweh could command Israel to return home and bring the Gibeahite yobs to account by a further appeal to the Benjaminites. Nevertheless, Israel is committed to a conflict solution and has suffered 40,000 casualties. A wayward tribe is to be punished. Yahweh's answer is unequivocal: 'tomorrow I will give them into your hand' (20.28).

The Third Battle of Gibeah (vv. 29-48)

When the Israelite army returns to Gibeah, they decide upon a military strategy which includes ambush and deception in a coordinated attack on two fronts—upon the city as before, but this time combined with a retreat, and a running battle out in the open.

10,000 Israelites are selected to hide near Gibeah ready to attack the city when the Benjaminites are drawn away (v. 29). Israel's main army line up in front of the city ready for battle as on two previous occasions (v. 30). When the Benjaminites (with weary resignation?) emerge from the city, the Israelites do not give the marksmen a third opportunity; they run away and their retreat lures the slingers from the city. Retreating Israelites are pursued along the roads and into open fields where they receive just thirty casualties. The battle begins for the Benjaminites much the same as on two previous occasions and they are confident (over confident?) that the militia of the eleven united tribes will be defeated yet again. However, the Benjaminites are unaware that a trap is set. Gibeah is undefended and the 10,000 selected Israelites charge out into the open from their hiding places, take the city and slaughter the inhabitants (v. 37). The retreating Israelites turn to face the pursuing Benjaminites and stand their ground when they see smoke rising from the burning city which is the prearranged signal to Israel's army (vv. 39, 41). When the pursuing but unsuspecting Benjaminites also see that their city is burning, they are dismayed that they have been taken in by an ambush planned by an army that they have twice defeated. Benjaminites themselves now retreat into the desert but are unable to shake off the pursuing Israelites supported by their comrades who emerge from sacking and burning the city and join the chase. They are ruthlessly pursued and trodden down (v. 43). 18,000 Benjaminites are slaughtered. They are pursued to a desert feature known as Pomegranate Rock and a further 5,000 are cut down along the way. Others are prevented from escaping and are chased to Gidom where 2,000 are slaughtered. The pursuit of the Benjaminites is ruthless, relentless, breathless and thorough. Israel's aim is total annihilation. A mere 600 survive at the inaccessible Pomegranate Rock caves where they remain for four months (v. 47). The Benjaminite cities that supplied warriors for their army are burned (v. 48; cf. vv. 14, 15).

There is some discrepancy in the number of Benjaminite losses. They are able to muster 26,000 from their cities plus 700 chosen men from Gibeah (MT, v. 15). Among the 26,700 are 700 marksmen (v. 16). No Benjaminite losses are reported in the first two battles. The third battle records 25,100 Benjaminite losses (v. 35); however, a second counting records 18,000 who are killed in the battle (v. 44) plus 5,000 at Pomegranate Rock and a further 2,000 on their retreat to Gidom (v. 45), making a total of 25,000 (v. 46). 600 survivors are besieged at Pomegranate Rock (v. 47). All the Benjaminites who are killed are 'brave men' (vv. 44, 46) and 'brother' Israelites (vv. 13, 23, 28). 1,100 Benjaminites are unaccounted for.

Even though a total of 65,130 Israelites are killed in three battles, plus the unrecorded numbers of Benjaminites who are slaughtered in the cities (v. 48), we are not specifically informed that the Gibeahite yobs—the 'sons of belial' who committed what the Levite and the assembly of Israelites regard as an evil disgraceful act—are brought to account.

Why does Yahweh Send Israelites out on Two Occasions to be Defeated in Battle? (vv. 18, 23)

In the central narratives we are informed that Israelites are not only unable but are unwilling to expel the inhabitants from the land and that Yahweh is abandoned in favour of Canaanite gods. Israelites settle for co-existence with the Canaanite inhabitants and are content to live under the rule of others. They only cry out to Yahweh when they are oppressed by invaders and even then they are unwilling to do battle for the land. Deborah reprimands the tribes who fail to muster (ch. 5); Ephraimites do not support Gideon (ch. 8) or Jephthah (ch. 12); Danites fail to support Samson (chs. 14-16); and Judahites are content to be ruled by Philistines (15.11).

At Bethel Yahweh uses different methods to win wayward Israelites back to covenant loyalty when he does little and says little. Yahweh tells self-confident Israelites at Bethel what self-confident Israelites want to hear, and they are twice abandoned to the costly consequences of their own independent folly. After two attempts to bring the Benjaminites to account when they suffer 40,000 casualties, the Israelites come to themselves and return to Yahweh with appropriate sacrifices accompanied by tears and fasting.

The assembly's problem with the Benjaminites is not over. A further crisis has arisen: an Israelite tribe is almost extinct. How is Benjamin's future to be assured when only 600 males survive and all their women have been slaughtered?

Judges 21:
The Survivors of Jabesh-Gilead
and the Dancers of Shiloh

Israel's assembly of eleven tribes at Mizaph agree that the Gibeahite yobs must be brought to account for the abuse and murder
of the Levite's concubine which is regarded by all as a disgrace
that has been brought upon Israel. However, the Benjaminites
refuse to hand them over and the two battles that follow are
both humiliating disasters for the eleven tribes. The progress of
the war changes when the third battle ends in defeat for the
Benjaminites and a mere 600 of their men survive.

Even though we are not informed specifically that the Gibeahite
yobs are punished, the Israelites regret that the victory and the
relentless slaughter in the aftermath of the third battle threatens
the existence of one of their tribes. The 600 males are alone; they
lack women in their company with whom they can establish new
families and secure their land inheritance and tribal future.

The storyteller provides background detail for the problem now
facing the Israelites after their civil war: the survival of the
Benjaminites after the women of the tribe have been slaughtered
(v. 16). Israelites were so shocked at the sight of the Levite's grim
procession of butchered female body parts, and when hearing his
evidence at Mizpah, that an oath of an extreme nature was made
and reinforced with a curse. The far-reaching implications of both
are considered in this final chapter. Both are extreme, but together,
when considered with a second oath, they are understood by Israel's assembly to provide a horrific solution to Israel's new dilemma,
an act which in the modern world is called genocide—the attempted
annihilation of an identified group of people. Like Jephthah's vow
(11.10) and the curse uttered by Micah's mother (17.2), oaths and
curses that are made with serious intent are irreversible.

Two Oaths and a Curse (vv. 1-7)

At Mizpah, Israelites made an oath that none of their daughters
will ever again be given in marriage to a Benjaminite (v. 1); the

oath was made in the name of Yahweh (v. 7) and reinforced with a curse on anyone who did give a daughter in marriage to a Benjaminite (v. 18). Israel's dilemma is this: how will the 600 Benjaminite male survivors recover as a tribe if none of Israel's women can be made available to them as marriage partners? It is interesting to note that intermarriage with the Canaanites, Hittites, Amorites, Perizzites, Hivites and Jebusites, which in the past has led to Israel abandoning Yahweh and serving their gods, is not considered as an option (cf. 3.5-6).

Israel's tribes return to Bethel in tears and ask Yahweh, the God of Israel, how it has come about that one of their number is almost extinct. No answer is forthcoming. The next day a new altar is constructed and for a second time burnt offerings and peace offerings are made which suggests that Israel has serious religious intent with Yahweh.

Israel's further problem is to discover how to live with the outcome of an oath and a curse that threaten the existence of one of their tribes. Now that hostilities are concluded, Israelites feel compassion for the Benjaminite survivors who they do not want to become extinct as a tribe (21.6, 15). The 'compassion' that is felt by Israel could indicate a range of emotions from repentance and deep regret for their actions to feeling sorry and responsible for their plight. Israelites express corporate responsibility and want to do something for the matrimonial future of the survivors (v. 7).

The Fate of the Child Survivors of the Slaughter at Jabesh-Gilead (vv. 8-14)

A solution to Benjamin's matrimonial problem presents itself with an interpretation of the precise wording of a second oath that was also made earlier by Israelites at Mizpah. The Israelites swore that any tribe who did not attend the assembly would be put to death (v. 5). When they make an investigation among themselves in order to determine if any failed to turn up, it is discovered that the inhabitants of Jabesh-Gilead are absent (vv. 8, 9). A decision is taken that the absentees are to be the victims of the assembly's second oath. Non-appearance decides guilt. Oaths and curses are irrevocable. The city is not granted an opportunity to account for their absence or to present a defence before the assembly's elders. Moreover, Jabesh-Gilead is situated in Manasseh tribal territory and their tribal militia do not muster to their defence in the way that the Benjaminites defended the yobs of Gibeah. 12,000 experienced warriors are sent by the assembly to Jabesh-Gilead with precise orders to slaughter all the men, married women and children (v. 10). We have seen that Israel's war strategy is sometimes accompanied, at Yahweh's behest, by the total annihilation of a city's inhabitants which in Hebrew is called *ḥērem*, a ritual in which the Canaanites are designated for destruction (v. 11; 1.17; Num. 21.2-3). However, a radical change takes place: Israelites carry out the *ḥērem* ritual at the specific order of the assembly—not upon the Canaanites, but upon their own, upon Israelites who have dared to ignore the summons to Mizpah. Moses slaughtered Midianites (Num. 31.15-18); Joshua slaughtered the Canaanite inhabitants of Jericho (Josh. 6); a leaderless Israel slaughters Israelites in an act of genocide.

The solution to the threatened extinction of the tribe of Benjamin is provided when 400 virgins are 'found' among the inhabitants of Jabesh-Gilead (Judg. 21.12), selected for survival and taken to Shiloh. How are the 400 'found'? How does the selection take place? Are parents, who are about to be killed, first interrogated about the status of their daughters? Are the girls questioned themselves? Are they subjected to a crude physical examination? It is probable that, as marriage took place at puberty or just after, many of the 400 are infants and children of various ages.

Israel's assembly makes peace with the Benjaminite survivors, who leave the security of Pomegranate Rock and at Shiloh are presented with the 400 selected child survivors. Benjaminite males will have to wait until their potential 'marriage partners' are old enough for marriage. However, the Benjaminite men are 200 females short.

The 200 Dancers of Shiloh (vv. 15-23)

Not only have Benjaminite women and children been exterminated but the males of the tribe have been slaughtered (apart from the 600) as have many thousands of Israelites in the three battles of Gibeah. Israel is broken, ruptured and breached. As a result of this massive overkill by the disproportionate use of maximum force the storyteller seems to voice the opinion of the assembly: Israelites have used force of arms but Yahweh is responsible for their new condition (v. 15).

The assembly elders are imaginative and propose a further solution to the Benjaminite female shortfall. It so happens that an annual 'Yahweh festival' is taking place in Shiloh which includes the girls of the city joyfully dancing in the vineyards. The 200 Benjaminites are instructed to lie in wait and each to snatch a girl—as a lion seizes its prey (cf. Ps. 10.9)—and to take her home. The precise nature of the festival is not disclosed. It could be Shiloh's annual joyous end-of-year harvest (Exod. 23.16; 34.22) and vintage festival which is associated with bride-choosing dances. It is interesting to note that the Hebrew word that is translated 'festival' (*ḥag*) in English versions is not necessarily a solemn occasion but includes dancing in a ring or circle or procession. It is possible, therefore, that the elders may not be suggesting anything that is improper, such as kidnap or rape. The 'lying in wait' and the 'seizing' of girls (21.21) may be no more than a local custom that unmarried men follow at Israel's festivals in order to choose and pounce upon a bride.

The suggestion that the purpose of the Shiloh vineyard dance is for local males to choose marriage partners is reinforced when the elders are ready with a defence should their instruction to the Benjaiminites be challenged. If the fathers and brothers of the female dancers object to the seizure of their girls they will be asked to be reasonable, to be generous, to share their daughters and sisters with those who have not taken females as spoil in battle. It is not anticipated that the men of Shiloh's families will object to their girls being taken, but they may protest when they are taken as marriage partners by male survivors of a cursed tribe. The fathers and brothers are to be assured that they will not be liable to the consequences of the assembly's oath and curse because they have not willingly given their daughters and sisters. The Benjaminites are given precise directions to the Shiloh dance venue and they do as they are instructed.

In seven brisk verbs the storyteller describes the 200 survivors doing the bidding of the assembly elders as they make provision for their own futures: 'they do as they are told', 'they carry off the women', 'who they seize' (or robbed from their families), 'they go on their way', 'they return to their land' where 'they rebuild their cities' in which 'they live' (v. 23). No objections are made to the assembly by the men of Shiloh to the abduction of their daughters and sisters. Now that the business of the assembly is complete, Israelites return to their land (v. 24).

The land is not said to rest, but—when we are informed that the Israelites return to their homes (their inheritance)—the storyteller indicates that harmony between Yahweh and Israel is restored. Israel's problems are evidently solved to the storyteller's satisfaction which implies that everyone is content and lives happily ever after in a time before kings reigned when Israelites made the best of things—and the worst of things (v. 25). We may consider the storyteller's presentation of a 'happy ending' for this violent horror-fest to be a deeply disturbing conclusion.

How are We to Evaluate Israel's Conduct in chs. 19–21?

These are hard-hearted merciless episodes of storytelling. Trying to make sense of what we read in the closing chapters is a deeply problematic task. We may be inclined to close the book here and not reflect further because what we read makes for harsh reading and there are so many similar episodes that already trouble us in the modern world. If the book of Judges is to be considered a sacred text, we are entitled to ask: what is God doing in these closing chapters? There may, however, be an alternative way of understanding Israel's actions to what is often referred to as Israel's disintegration into religious, moral and social chaos. The phrases about Israelites 'doing what is right in their own eyes' (18.1 and 19.1) need not be understood as the storyteller's negative evaluation, as is generally supposed, but may indicate that they simply make their own decisions about complex matters.

No one is excused here. Israel's problem-solving methods—which include the loss of thousands of warriors in battle plus the mass murder of unknown numbers of women and children—are brutal and outrageous. The body count is high and we may wonder if there could be a less ruthless way of punishing those responsible for the taking of one life in Gibeah during the night. Can it be argued that Israel's solutions are more barbaric than the rape of the Levite's concubine? Or might the assembly consider that if the disgraceful act committed by the Benjaminite yobs is ignored, Israelites will disintegrate into religious, moral and social chaos?

We need to marvel at the result of the Levite's macabre travelling theatre and the presentation of his evidence, which have a profound result: the unity of the tribes of Israel (apart from the Benjaminites) who assemble 'as one man' (20.1) which was not achieved by the judge-deliverers when engaging oppressors. Israelites are not indifferent to the abuse of the Levite and the rape and the murder of his concubine. The matter is regarded as so serious that an assembly is called to which everyone is to attend.

All agree that a disgraceful act has been committed, the land is polluted and it is to be purged from the land by the execution of those responsible who are referred to by the assembly as 'sons of belial' (20.13). The gathering of the tribes at Mizpah is a sacred assembly 'before Yahweh' and not a presumptuous meeting before a miscellaneous collection of gods and idols like those assembled by Micah at his shrine (ch. 17; 18.24). It appears that Israelites no longer serve the local gods of Canaan because only Yahweh is petitioned at approved cultic centres. Had the assembly ignored the Levite's grim procession and his evidence (even though selective), Israel would be in a state of religious, moral and social chaos.

Israelites attempt to avoid conflict with the Benjaminites by negotiation when they request that the 'sons of belial' are handed over for execution. Even though the Gibeah yobs are not assured of a fair trial or hearing before the elders in the gate, everyone agrees that a disgraceful act has been committed and those responsible are to be apprehended and punished. The disgrace is then compounded by the Benjaminite call to arms. If an act of solidarity with those who commit rape and murder had been ignored, Israel would be in a state of religious, moral and social chaos.

Israelites petition Yahweh on three occasions at Bethel (20.18, 23, 26-28)—twice with tears and fasting (vv. 23, 26)—which suggests they engage in acts of repentance. Israelites twice make burnt offerings and peace offerings (20.26 and 21.4). Neither offering has been made before in the book of Judges and together they form the prescribed methods for approaching Yahweh (Lev. 1–3).

The members of the Israelite assembly take the evil and disgraceful act as described by the Levite seriously when making two oaths and reinforcing the first with a curse. No Israelite is to marry a Benjaminite (Judg. 21.1, 7); a curse is announced on anyone who does (v. 18), and a 'big' or a 'substantial' oath is made against those who fail to attend the Mizpah assembly (v. 5). Two groups are absent: the Benjaminites show no concern about the behaviour of their citizens, and the inhabitants of Jabesh-Gilead indicate their indifference when they ignore the assembly's summons. Both are held accountable.

Oaths are made with serious intent and both are kept. It is discovered that the precise wording of the two oaths and the curse provide solutions for the survival of the threatened tribe. Assembly members grieve for the 600 Benjaminite survivors when it is realized that their land inheritance is threatened because their women and children have been exterminated in the aftermath of the third battle. It is to be noted that the assembly elders do not tell the Benjaminites to take wives from among the Canaanites (cf. 3.5-6). However, the inhabitants of Jabesh-Gilead suffer the consequences of the second irrevocable oath due to their failure to attend the assembly which indicates their indifference to the disgrace that comes upon Israel (21.1, 7) which the assembly has taken so seriously. The inhabitants are ritually annihilated but not before 400 of their children are selected for survival as a living sacrifice of sorts to the cause of Benjaminite survival. The 200 dancing girls who are chosen from the Shiloh vineyards; like the 400, all marry within Israel. When their fathers and brothers do not raise objection, we assume the storyteller indicates their approval of their daughters and sisters being requisitioned for the worthy task of helping the Benjaminites to survive in Israel as a tribe.

It may be argued further that a result of the Mizpah assembly is the restoration of the covenant between Israel and Yahweh by the application of appropriate sacrifices even though the word 'covenant' is not mentioned by the storyteller. However, we may protest that the 'restoration' is at the high cost of the ruthless taking of so many lives. It is to be noted, therefore, that in these closing chapters it is the character of Yahweh that is most problematic. Yahweh says little apart from giving Israelites permission to fight among themselves. The storyteller—who is not slow elsewhere in Judges to criticize wayward Israelites for their apostasy—does not employ any of the negative evaluations used in the theological introduction or in the central narratives and is not overtly critical of Israel. For example, Israelites are not said to do evil; they do not abandon, forsake or forget Yahweh; they do not follow after, whore after, bow down to or serve other gods. Israelites are not said to behave worse than their ancestors; moreover, Yahweh is not said to become angry. The storyteller appears to be untroubled about such matters.

Why does the Storyteller Conclude Judges with Stories in which Yahweh, the God of Israel, Says Little and Does Little?

Yahweh, the God of Israel, does not become angry in the closing chapters of Judges as the storyteller says he does in the theological introduction and in the introduction to the deliverance stories. Yahweh does not send an oppressor to oppress those who decide to solve an injustice by civil war. Yahweh does not send a messenger to rebuke (2.1-3) or a prophet to reprimand (6.8-10). Yahweh takes no other initiatives than hostility to the Benjaminites when he is said to strike them down, thereby creating a gap among Israel's tribes (20.35; 21.15). Yahweh is one of the storyteller's minor players and his reaction is not recorded while his people slaughter one another. Yahweh is referred to from time to time, but he only speaks when he is spoken to and his replies are brief (20.18, 23, 28). Yahweh makes no comment about the annihilation that is ordered by Israel's elders upon the inhabitants of Jabesh-Gilead. Yahweh does nothing to avenge the slaughtered inhabitants. Yahweh does nothing to protect the young female dancers in the Shiloh vineyards. This is not the first story in Judges in which Yahweh has been absent or silent and aloof. We may ask: what sort of God takes the initiative to empower a judge-deliverer (ch. 11) and awards a great victory but is silent as a daughter is sacrificed in his name by her father? How may we account for the presentation of Yahweh in Judges as the silent bystander to carnage?

The storyteller is well aware of what is happening in the world around him. He, like us, is only too aware of the unfairness of life for the world's vulnerable victims who are generally women and children and the elderly. The storyteller is aware, when, in the actual world, no god comes to the aid of victims. Yahweh is as inactive and silent in the events in the closing chapters as are the non-existent Canaanite Baals. Our storyteller writes about what he observes in the world around him—he tells it as he sees it—which makes the ancient book of Judges essential reading in the modern world. As well as a collection of hero stories, Judges is also a collection of oppressor stories. National groups are called upon by Yahweh to oppress wayward Israelites which makes him the initiator or first cause of their oppressions. When Israel is 'given away' or 'sold', Yahweh is characterized as an oppressor who will employ any means to win his people back to covenant loyalty. But there is more. In the concluding chapters the storyteller shows that Yahweh is an oppressor by another means, by silence and inactivity. Evil triumphs when God does nothing. God acts in history—in Creation and Exodus—but in the closing chapters he is silent and still. Yahweh, the God of Israel, does nothing while thousands of his people are slaughtered and while many thousands more are bereaved. God does nothing in these chapters except to give permission for Israelites to fight among themselves and to slaughter Benjaminite women and children.

The ancient storyteller—who is too cautious to criticize Yahweh openly—puts perplexing matters into story-form in order to connect with ancient hearers and modern readers who are well aware that life can be like this when the God who we think should be outraged at injustice says little and does nothing. The book of Judges concludes as ancient protest literature. Modern readers may observe much the same in the world around them when they and so many others have cause to rage and demand, 'where is God in all this?'

Afterword

What's so Special about Judges?

The book of Judges is not an example of comfortable storytelling; the prose and poetry are neither beige nor bland. The style is robust and tabloid; detail is sparse. Judges-stories take place in hard-hat areas (literally, 9.53). Characters interact with each other in a harsh distant story-world in which conflicts are resolved in acts of violence and brutality. But these are not stories of casual violence. Judges has none of the spurious glamour which is generally attached to the telling and retelling of macho manly exploits. Rather, there is work to be done. Israel is more interested in the gods of the land than in Yahweh. Yahweh wants Israel to return to covenant loyalty and summons oppressors who are powerful and formidable. When Israelites cry out for help, Yahweh sends judge-deliverers who—although disadvantaged—are able to soundly defeat the oppressors; survivors (if there are any) are expelled from the land. We are to think highly of the judge-deliverers who bring peace and independence. Their stories are also told with humour and we are to laugh along with the storyteller at the pantomime ethnic characterization of oppressors and gasp at how they are dispatched. The book of Judges also contains women's stories. There is no need here for feminist interpreters to give female characters voices; they are more than able to speak up and act for themselves.

You may think you are confronted with a collection of offensive and repugnant stories in which bad people do bad things to other bad people. It is natural therefore that questions arise about the place of Judges in sacred literature. Old Testament writers have a consistent philosophy of history: Yahweh, the God of Israel, not only controls world history but everything that Israel experiences is an act of Yahweh (von Rad 1962: II, 327-47; Wolff 1975: 83-100). Judges therefore forms part of Israel's salvation history in which Yahweh acts on Israel's behalf. It appears that Yahweh will use any means—including intimidation and violence, and silence and inactivity when necessary—in order to win his apostate people back to covenant loyalty from serving the gods of the land. Judges characters are ordinary people who get caught up in extraordinary times. The stories are about little people, about victims who fight back and survive against the odds. You can read about such people in today's newspapers and they live in the many troubled margins of the modern world. Judges is, therefore, a book with which to be emotionally involved; the storyteller does not write for indifferent readers. We are to engage with the printed page, to argue, complain, disagree, agree, be angry, be pleased, be appalled; we are to be *something*! We are to do more than just sit there! This ancient storyteller is anxious to make an impression, to make a difference. Your close attention is required. Judges is a great read. Enjoy!

Written by Whom and When?

The reading assumes that the Judges scroll was written by an ancient scribe to be read aloud to assembled groups in an age when few could read or write and all were fascinated by the new communication technology of symbols scratched on a leather scroll which explained the ways of Yahweh to the people of Yahweh. Biblical scribes who possessed the new skills were brothers Baruch and Seraiah sons of Neriah the son of Mahseiah who wrote at Jeremiah's dictation and read aloud from what Jeremiah himself had written (Jer. 36.4; 51.59-64). As Ezra the scribe read from the Torah, the Levites gave interpretation so that all the assembled listeners understood (Neh. 8.1-8). We cannot think here in terms of ancient readers purchasing a bestseller from a book shop or of a newspaper purchased at a street corner. In this essay I refer to two groups that engage with the text of Judges: to ancient 'listeners' who assemble for public readings and to you and me the modern readers.

A difficulty for biblical interpreters is to determine the historical and social context of the ancient society in which biblical literature was written and edited and to identify those whom the author addressed. I suggest that it is plausible for the formation of Judges in its final form to be located among the dispersed Israelite communities living outside the land, for example: those who were compulsorily transported or deported to Assyria by Tiglath-Pileser in 733–32 BCE and Shalmaneser 722–21 BCE (2

Kgs 15.29; 17.6-23; to which 'the captivity' in Judg. 18.30 may refer); the 200,150 'people, young and old, male and female' who Sennacherib 'drove out' of the land in 701 BCE (2 Kgs 18.13–19.37); the deported communities forcibly settled in Babylon by Nebuchadrezzar in 597 BCE (2 Kgs 24.10-17; cf. 2 Chron. 36.18-21), 587 BCE (2 Kgs 25.11) after the destruction of Jerusalem and the temple (2 Kgs 25.9) and 582 BCE (Jer. 52.30); and those who fled to Egypt to escape unfavourable political situations and invading imperial powers (2 Kgs 25.26; cf. Jer. 41.16-18).

Such a hypothesis, which includes the book of Judges in the literature of exile, is suggested by the deuteronomic view that crisis is Yahweh's judgment on Israel's religious and moral failure and by the repeated pattern of apostasy and divine grace in the judge-deliverer stories.

A New Reading

The reading uniquely presents the view that the characters who are raised up to deliver Israel from oppressors neither participate in, nor contribute to, what scholars refer to as Israel's moral and religious decline. The focus of the reading is therefore to give positive evaluations for judge-deliverers who 'are the pride of their countrymen' (Wellhausen 1885: 234).

Judges is read here as the work of a 'storyteller' or an 'implied storyteller' which is the collective name I give to the many tellers, writers, redactors and editors who contributed to the book in what may have been a long pre-life.

The reading suggests a modified but valid coherent interpretation of Judges in contrast to the scholarly consensus which claims that the book records Israel's gradual moral and religious decline, hits bottom in the final chapters and 'disintegrates into religious and social chaos' (Olson 1998: 726). I propose that Israel's behaviour is consistently and evenly bad, apart from those interludes when judge-deliverers and their collaborators bring peace to the land. A narrative change is to be discerned in the closing chapters (19–21). I suggest that the change is not with Israel but with Yahweh and his methods of interaction with his people. Yahweh takes initiatives in the opening chapters and in the central narratives when he is abandoned in favour of the gods of the land. Israelites are 'sold' or 'given' into the hands of oppressors, a course of action which in time drives them back to Yahweh. However, in the closing chapters Yahweh barely makes an appearance and is rarely mentioned; he no longer appears to be concerned with Israel's conduct and only speaks to give permission for Israelites to fight among themselves. Even though these chapters contain harsh and brutal episodes, Israelites may be thought of more positively because they are not negatively evaluated by the storyteller with any of the blunt criticisms used in the theological introduction and the central narratives. I therefore suggest that even here—in what is generally referred to as final 'disintegration' and 'chaos'—there may be an alternative way of understanding Israel when the storyteller indicates that the covenant between Yahweh and Israel is restored and secured when Israelites twice offer appropriate sacrifices (cf. 20.26; 21.4).

The book of Judges is read as the literature of hope written by a refugee storyteller for refugee Israelites in exile in Assyria, Babylon and Egypt in the sixth century BCE.

The reading proposes that the storyteller has three aims. First, Israelites in exile are presented with reasons to be ashamed of their moral and religious behaviour. Second, they have cause to feel cautiously hopeful for the future because Yahweh repeatedly responds to Israel's cries for help by raising up deliverers who defeat those who have overrun the land at Yahweh's behest; Yahweh will respond again in the future. Exilic listeners are to be impressed with the performances of those who are raised up by Yahweh. Third, Israelites in exile are warned not to assimilate with the inhabitants of the land; they are reminded of their monotheistic religion and of their obligation of covenant loyalty to Yahweh.

Even though Judges is read here in its final form as a book in its own right, acknowledgment is made that it is considered in scholarship to be part of a deuteronomistic history—Joshua–2 Kings—in which the influence of the language and theology of the book of Deuteronomy may be discerned.

I acknowledge the hypothesis that the book may include sources that were available to the storyteller such as the cyclical deliverer stories, the lists of 'consecutive' judges and the 'song' of Deborah. Such sources may have been preserved in written or oral form.

Judges is read as a story-world in which biblical Israel is constructed. This is not to imply that Judges is a work of fiction because the hero stories may record events that took place and originated in the first person by 'participants or survivors, or possibly in the third person by observers' (Parker 1997: 9).

Judges is understood to be among the first examples in the ancient world of the literary genre of heroism told by means of the new technology of writing which records for posterity heroic epic struggles of good against evil when central characters—who are placed in jeopardy—win the day.

Judges is read in English translation (NRSV), sometimes in my own translation, with some reference to the Hebrew text (MT) and the two Greek translations (LXX A & B).

Put briefly, the reading assumes that the storyteller's 'big ideas' and 'take-home messages' for exiled Israelite listeners who listen and lean-in when the ancient scroll is read aloud in public readings, are: if you want to return home, stay loyal to Yahweh; do not lose your national and religious identity; do not assimilate with the inhabitants of the land; and be warned, Yahweh will go to any means to retain your covenant loyalty, even to the extent of summoning oppressors and not answering when you call.

I also draw attention to what is not addressed in the reading. I am not concerned with the rehabilitation of characters by suggesting a softer reading that smoothes their rough edges in order to make them and their methods acceptable for sensitive readers. As Israel's oppression and deliverance involve ordeals of physical and emotional trauma for characters, the stories they inhabit claim our respect. A disservice is done when stories are dismissed with a cursory selective reading. It is not my purpose to sanitize the text; I allow that characters are dark, that they inhabit a harsh story-world in which listeners are led into dark places at the edge of the abyss and into places where risks are taken and conflicts are resolved. The reading is literary and does not attempt a historical-archeological reconstruction in order to place characters within a history of ancient Israel or ancient Palestine. This is not a historical-critical study in which I engage with sources or a piecemeal dissection of the text in order to suggest how creative redactors may have selected, reworked and edited earlier material. Even though the reading is not a study of Old Testament ethics, some ethical discussion of character and event is inevitable when evaluating how characters act and react in the complex story-world of land invasion and oppression and characters are sponsored by Yahweh to participate in the brutality of war.

It is not my purpose to propose a Christian theological interpretation of Judges; such a task may be attempted in a further study. Before the application of a Christian interpretation, Old Testament narrative is to be understood in its historical and literary

context accompanied by reflection on the history of the text's interpretation followed by proposals for the plain meaning. I acknowledge that my reading is influenced by the person that I am.

How Judges is Generally Read

Even though Judges attracts a regular harvest of commentaries
and scholarly articles, the book is not among the popular well-
thumbed reading matter in church, chapel or synagogue. Judges
is pessimistically referred to as Israel's 'dark ages' marked by an
absence of peace, security and justice (Cundall 1968: 178; Boling
1975: 11). Trends in recent commentaries seem to highlight the
negatives, cautiously acknowledge anything positive and exoner-
ate Yahweh, the God of Israel.

Judges is understood in scholarship to be part of a longer
'deuteronomistic history', an hypothesis formulated by Martin
Noth as a way of understanding and reading Joshua–2 Kings
which is thought to be a unified and self-contained compilation
of oral and written traditions with additional connecting
narrative resembling the language and style of the book of
Deuteronomy. According to Noth, the anonymous author, who
is referred to by the abbreviation 'Dtr', has a recognizable style
and he identified what he called 'the real theme' of the work as
'the conduct and fate of the people once they have settled in
Palestine' (Noth 1981: 91). The theological themes of the deuteronomistic history appear in the conclusion of the first section of
the prologue (2.1-5), in the second section (2.6–3.6) and in original material that connects the core narratives. The prologue
shows that Yahweh is at work in Israel's history. Israel's
moral and religious decline is met with warnings, rebukes and
punishments, and Israel is reminded of being freed from slavery
in Egypt and is under covenant obligation to remain exclusively
loyal to Yahweh (Noth 1981: 89; Campbell and O'Brien 2000).

The hypothesis of an anonymous Dtr and a deuteronomistic
history is generally accepted in scholarship though not without
discussion about whether there was one creative exilic author or
multiple redactions; whether sources were oral or written and
are preserved intact; whether there was some shaping of sources
before Dtr and reshaping of Dtr's work by other hands over time;
whether there was a pre-exilic composition that was expanded to
include the destruction of Jerusalem.

A range of issues are proposed by scholars which the author of
Judges may have addressed. For example, J.P.U. Lilley proposes

the hypothesis of the 'author' as a mature historian who 'cast the book in its present structure, having conceived in his own mind the general idea and plan' (Lilley 1967: 95). The book is a single piece of historical writing of literary initiative with a unity of purpose that can be read as an integrated whole. Lilley saw a coherence in the traditional subdivision of 1.1–2.5 and 2.6–3.6 and with what follows, such as the prophet in 2.1-5 whose speech is similar to other confrontations between Yahweh and Israel (6.8-10 and 10.11). The characteristic formulaic phrases of the episodes, which also appear in the introduction, are not merely repetitive but have a marked progression of deterioration which suggests the author is not bound by a pattern but is 'giving precedence to historic actually' (1967: 98). The book concludes with two episodes of 'special horrors' and civil war which show the moral and religious state of the nation without a central government. Lilley proposes a 'general theme' of increasing deterioration.

In his literary study of the Deuteronomic History, Robert Polzin also regards Judges as a distinct unified literary work within the larger whole. Making sense of this chaotic period is the main task facing the 'implied author'. That Israel not only survives, but more often than not thrives in spite of continual disobedience, strains the Deuteronomist's two ideological voices which are those of God's retributive justice and God's mercy. Polzin identifies unifying themes such as the emphases on Israel's continual disobedience which confirms the bleak picture of 2.17; Yahweh's repeated demonstrations of compassion are one of the mysteries of the book; and it is the stories themselves that deepen the mystery of Israel's continual existence. According to Polzin, 'in all fairness and honesty, Israel should not have survived' (Polzin 1980: 175).

Judges is understood by J. Alberto Soggin to be the work of an editor who creates a history about the remote past with lessons for readers of the exile about their times and is a deuteronominist's explanation for the fall of the kingdoms of Israel and Judah. Soggin understands the exile as a deserved punishment, the consequence of divine judgment on Israel's sin (Soggin 1987: 7, 43).

It all begins to go wrong, according to D.W. Gooding, in the latter part of the Gideon story: from Gideon on, the judges 'engage in strife against sections of Israel' (Gooding 1982: 75); not only does the people's behaviour deteriorate, but there is also a decline among the judges themselves. Deliverer stories are not set in a simple repetitive pattern but Israel becomes worse as each story is told. The stories are arranged in symmetry: the first (Othniel) is the best; the last (Samson) is the worst. The latter part of Gideon's career—which is the centre piece of the symmetry arrangement—shows a decline in the judges themselves. J. Cheryl Exum says that the cycle framing device begins well but becomes unsustainable because after Gideon the unlikely deliverers exhibit 'highly questionable behavior' (Exum 1990: 412). The cycle breaks down altogether with Samson. Gooding's symmetry hypothesis is followed by J. Paul Tanner who also says that 'the cycles reflect a progressive degeneration' (Tanner 1992: 161). Gideon's flawed character is placed at the 'focal point' of the book because 'he represents a significant shift in the "quality" of the judges that served Israel' which, according to Tanner, is a 'progressive deterioration': Othniel is 'idealized' but Samson is 'debauched' (1992: 152).

In an integrated reading, Barry Webb considers *The Book of the Judges* as a literary unit in its own right when he demonstrates that in its final form it is a far more coherent and meaningful work than has hitherto been recognized (Webb 1987: 39; cf. 1994: 261-86; 1995: 110-20). Webb's purpose is to reopen the question in a thematic sense of what the book is about when he asks two questions: how is the text structured, and what does it mean as a complex whole? Webb ably demonstrates the text's coherence and also includes character evaluations, some positive, others negative. Webb's principal findings are: first, the book addresses the fundamental issue of the non-fulfilment of Yahweh's oath sworn to the patriarchs to give Israel the whole land; second, Israel's persistent apostasy and the freedom of Yahweh to act against Israel's presumption are developed in the body of the book receiving a climax in Samson; and third, the final chapters contain the same themes with elements from the introduction and form the work into a rounded literary unit. The contrasting perspectives in which the judges are set 'do not allow us the luxury of simple moral judgments' (1987: 209).

Lillian R. Klein's basic premise is that Judges is a *tour de force* of irony which 'is expressed in moments of ambiguous knowledge, generated by incompatibility between opposites' (Klein 1989: 199) and its ironic structure—of opposing and contrasting perceptions—is illustrated in the central episodes. For example: Ehud is the left-handed deliverer who deliverers Israel single-handedly; he has a 'word' for the king which is really a 'thing' (a pun allowed by the same Hebrew word for both). Eglon expects a secret divine revelation but receives a secret of human origin. Klein evaluates Ehud's actions as successful but dishonourable.

In a feminist reading, Adrien Bledstein suggests the possibility of Judges being written by a 'deeply religious woman', one Huldah, the prophetess who lived in Jerusalem in Josiah's day (cf. 2 Kgs 22.14-20; 2 Chron. 34.22-28). Huldah's aim as narrator is to satirize and censure men for their excesses in a world where 'women bear the brunt of their extravagance' (Bledstein 1993: 52). Men are seriously criticized and parodied for their rash actions and pitiful preconceptions which make them 'hem and haw' (1993: 42); in short, men have made a tragic mess of things. Bledstein rejects what she calls the 'common assumption' that Judges is a story in which heroes are honoured; she asks readers to shift their assumptions and hear a woman's voice condemning the violence of men. According to Bledstein's reading, all judge-deliverers receive sharp censure: Othniel nags his wife; Ehud is deceptive; Shamgar is a snide; Barak is surly; Gideon is panic-stricken; Abimelech is puffed-up with arrogance (here, surely, Bledstein is correct even though Abimelech is neither judge nor deliverer); Jephthah is a ruffian; minor judges are either petty potentates or jackasses and Samson is the greatest jackass in the Bible. Predictably, women shine: Deborah is a woman of faith who unequivocally trusts in Yahweh despite the odds, Jael is courageous and Jephthah's daughter possesses both presence of mind and self assurance. Strangely, Bledstein omits to commend Delilah for ridding Israel of Samson, a judge for whom she expresses only contempt.

In an unfinished commentary Barnabas Lindars presents the view that Judges is a deuteronomist's interpretation of Israel's history constructed from the artificial compilation of the tales of heroes and other incidents presented in a scheme of successive episodes to show how the ideal state of affairs left by Joshua was ruined by the disobedience of successive generations (Lindars 1995: 91, 94).

According to Robert H. O'Connell (1996), the overall purpose of the compiler/redactor is revealed in the repeated monarchical phrase in the dénouement chapters (Judg. 17.6; 18.1; 19.1; 21.25) which endorses a Judahite king who will exemplify loyalty to deuteronomic ideals of expelling foreigners from the land and maintaining intertribal loyalty to Yahweh's covenant, cult and social order as the solution to Israel's problems. The author's purpose is to demonstrate why Israel needs a king. All the non-Judahite deliverers after the Judahite Othniel—who is the only judge without fault—evince flaws of character.

Dennis T. Olson says that Israel lives in continuous moral and religious decay described as a negative collection of stories about Israel's 'downward slide', 'gradual decline', 'downward spiral' and 'descent into failure, unfaithfulness and disintegration' (1998: II, 726, 729, 742). The individual judges themselves exhibit a similar gradual decline towards ineffectiveness and unfaithfulness. Israel is allowed to hit rock bottom in the final chapters.

In the *Woman's Bible Commentary* Danna Nolan Fewell says that the stories illustrate a downward spiral for Israel; Othniel is an ideal hero of noble lineage; those who follow are more unlikely candidates; Samson begins with promise but his story is characterized by violation and vengeance showing that 'Israel's leadership sinks a long way from Moses to Samson' (Fewell 1998: 74). The chaos of the closing chapters is an appropriate conclusion to the story of Israel's decline.

Yairah Amit proposes the hypothesis that the book of Judges in its completed form carries the message not only of an author but also that of successive editors who worked on the text in stages and sub-stages. The editing of Judges is intended to convince the reader that monarchy is a preferable alternative to the rule of judges; moreover, when looking back, the reader is to be convinced that 'all the acts of deliverance of the judges had extremely limited value' (Amit 1999: 336). The function of chs. 17–21 is to arouse discussion about the failure of the judges as leaders and to recommend monarchy (1999: 314-15).

According to Daniel Block, Judges has a literary integrity and is 'written in the light of the authentically Moasic theology of Deuteronomy', material has been selected and arranged by one mind into a coherent literary work with the theme of the 'Canaanization of Israelite society', a familiar term also used by Johannes. Pedersen and Noth (Block 1999: 58, 543; cf. Pedersen 1926: 25; Noth 1958: 144). Block says that Israelites are given a wake-up call in Judges to return to Yahweh and the covenant and to abandon paganism; however, the deliverers emerge as 'antiehroes' and are part of Israel's problem rather than Israel's solution (Block 1999: 40, 58).

In an ethical reading Gordon Wenham (2000) proposes that the main issue in Judges is one of leadership. The structure of the book reveals a progressive deterioration in the behaviour of the nation and that of the judges who deliver them. If Israel is to survive, a different kind of leadership is required and the closing chapters suggest a king.

In the *IVP Women's Bible Commentary*, Ailish Ferguson Eves claims that Judges is about violent and sadistic men and women who inhabit accounts of Israel's 'downward spiral of accelerating decadence, corruption and defeat in which the judges themselves participate' (Eves 2002: 129), showing that trusting in human heroes is an illusory hope. Yahweh is gracious and patient and uses the unexpected and the inadequate in the Gideon story to show that no human is able to claim glory. Criticism is heaped upon Samson, who is a 'maverick fighter', has 'childish tantrums', is sadistic, misuses grace and power, is a disgrace and is 'driven by his hormones', is gullible and a 'paranoid manic-depressive' who dies for his own cause rather than God's. According to Eves, Samson's story is included as an example of God's patience with perverted humans who fail to cooperate with his divine purposes.

In the introduction to his commentary, J. Clinton McCann (2002) justifies reading and studying Judges—which he says is considered to be an embarrassment—rather than just ignoring it by suggesting that the book is both timely and relevant when considering the parallels between the problems of the period of the judges and our own times. Answering those who object to the violence of Judges, McCann reminds readers that the twentieth century was the most violent in the history of humankind. Editors or compilers used older materials that were available to show Israel's progressive deterioration and that of the judges themselves whose leadership is increasingly questionable and ineffective. Israel's God is gracious and merciful; Israelites are idolatrous and disobedient.

Victor H. Matthews says that hero stories are drawn from oral tradition and edited by a deuteronomistic historian into a theological framework for exiles in Babylon to describe the difficulties of Israelites who lack strong leadership as they settle in Canaan (2004: 6). The editorial agenda could support Josiah's administration in Judah or to demonstrate that Yahweh is Israel's true king. Even though Othniel is a 'paragon of virtue', the judges are not good role models. Ehud is a bloody-handed assassin. Gideon is uncertain. Jephthah is a bandit who attempts to blackmail God. Samson engages in a lustful romp. Male characters like Barak are shamed when they act as little boys who are dependent on their mothers (2004: 66).

In a substantial summary of a negative evaluation of Barak, John Petersen begins with him falling short of Deborah's 'natural charisma' and concludes that 'he doubts her prophecy because she is a woman' (Petersen 2004: 197 n. 55).

What is required for a retelling of Israel's legendary frontier adventure stories of heroes, according to Gregory Mobley, is a temporary suspension of moralistic voices because the entire tradition of Israelite heroic storytelling has often been lost in the moralistic matrix of biblical interpretation (Mobley 2005: 15). The heroic performance of the 'empty men' who lack land is measured by: keeping a score of enemy kills; killing an elite adversary; fighting alone; using inferior weapons; having the support of Yahweh and his 'breath'; panicking the enemy and courage which is the supreme martial virtue.

In summary, there has been a change in the methods used by scholars in the twentieth century to interpret Judges from the historical-critical dissection of the text in an attempt to identify sources as part of a larger history of Israel (for example, see the earlier commentaries by George Moore [1895] and C.F. Burney [1918]), to reading the text as a literary, coherent, integrated whole held together in its final form by themes, generalizing statements and rhetorical purpose. It is a feature of those who address the book in its final form as a coherent narrative with its own literary integrity that they share similar conclusions: first, the book of Judges is the story of Israel's religious and moral decline; second, even though judge-deliverers—to whom Yahweh's spirit is made available and Yahweh delivers Israel by their hand—are generally thought of as heroic, all, apart from Othniel, the 'exemplary' and 'model' judge (Boling 1975: 81, 205, 240), are said to possess flaws and shortcomings of character; and third, the issues of leadership and the monarchy are in the forefront and the tribe of Judah is preeminent.

It is generally agreed by scholarly consensus that judge-deliverers are 'anti-heroes' rather than noblemen or great men of God (Brettler 1989: 407; Block 1994: 236; 1999: 40, 58; Matthews 2004: 8). It is said that they fail to provide a solution to Israel's apostasy and are considered to be part of Israel's problem. After 'Othniel the good', judge-deliverers are understood to be characterized by diminishing faithfulness, shortcomings and serious faults that contribute to Israel's decline:

- Ehud is a treacherous brutal villain and a bloody-handed assassin.
- Barak is a wimp who is weak, indecisive and unmanly.
- Gideon is a cynical coward who is vindictive and brutal to his own countrymen.
- Jephthah is a self-centred bandit who manipulates Yahweh with a vow and the murder of his daughter is the ultimate in child abuse.
- A great deliverer is anticipated by Samson's birth narrative but he proves to be the worst of the judges, a foolish love-struck playboy who ignores his nazirite status, fritters away his high calling by chasing pagan women and does nothing in anyone's interest but his own. Webb admires as 'pure genius' a line in John Milton's imaginative poem 'Samson Agonistes' describing Israelites visiting the blinded Samson in Gaza and saying of him, 'O mirror of our fickle state' (Milton [undated]: 435). Webb's understanding is that Samson 'epitomizes' or 'recapitulates' Israel (Webb 1994: 279; 1995: 116). I argue in the reading that Samson is no 'mirror' of *this* Israel whom the storyteller characterizes as cowardly betrayers.

The focus of the reading and of this essay is to challenge the naysayers and to suggest the possibility of positive evaluations for courageous judge-deliverers and their equally courageous collaborators.

The Author of Judges as a Storyteller

The author of Judges may be identified in four plausible roles. First, the author could be a historian who presents a chronological history of Israel's past. Second, the author's role could be as a theologian who makes the case for Israel's religious and moral deterioration in the introductions, in the cyclical framework and in the speeches of Yahweh's messenger and Yahweh's prophet and in Yahweh's momentary rejection of Israel. Third, a strong case can be made for the author as a lawyer who acts like Yahweh's counsel for the prosecution when marshalling evidence against Israel for breaking the covenant. For example, Israelites are to be ashamed when hearing the accusation of Yahweh's messenger, 'what is this you have done?' (2.2). And fourth, my own preference is to consider the author as a storyteller. Everything in the text is the creation of the implied author, including the mediation of an omniscient third-party narrator who has the predominant 'voice' of a storyteller creating a story-world in which a story unfolds, or in the case of the book of Judges, a collection of stories. The identification of stories as the primary mode of communication and of a 'story-world' focuses the reader's attention on the creator of this 'world' as a 'storyteller'.

Rather than a bland prose work of ancient legislation, Judges is resplendent with examples of ancient storytelling. A literary analysis identifies genres which, as well as stories, include lists, speeches, riddles, songs, fables and other traditional materials that have been selected, edited, organized and incorporated into the whole. A literary analysis also identifies the story-genre to be predominant which in Judges is the art of storytelling in its purest form. Plots are set in motion, events unfold, characters are placed in a structure with a beginning, a middle and an end. Each story unfolds with suspense and tension in order to hold the reader's attention until its resolution. The hero stories follow a conventional plot-form of action and resolution which stirs up interest and curiosity. Listeners want to know how a dire 'situation' will be resolved which generally comes in the climax of a decisive meeting of two parties in which only the hero survives.

Momentum is carried along in lean plots by sparse yet intriguing narrative details with the gaps and ambiguities heightening the tension. For example, the Ehud story may be an oral storyteller's brief notes for a fuller telling. The descriptions of Ehud as left-handed and Eglon, the Moabite king, as very fat, are going to be important to the *how* of Israel's deliverance. Detail is sparse. What matters to the storyteller is the telling of a story about the intriguing means of Israel's deliverance.

The imaginative creativity of the story-genre as 'narrative art' focuses the reader's attention on the author as an 'implied storyteller' who is the sum of the many unknown 'tellers', oral storymakers, oral storytellers, oral collectors, singers of tales and others who may have contributed to the 'book' in its constituent parts. The storyteller creates character and characterization with an economy of attributes and description. Judges is a work of extraordinary frugality. Characterization in Judges, like other biblical narrative, is laconic, a sketch rather than a portrait. Our storyteller only reveals details about characters which will be important to the development of the plot and its dénouement. Reading Judges is not an easy matter because we have ambiguity on our hands. There are gaps between what is told and what may only be inferred by prying into the text. Our response to the storyteller's ambiguities could be like that of R. Christopher Heard whose method is to decide whether an ambiguity is resolvable from the narrator's clues or whether 'readerly intervention is required for such resolution' (Heard 2001: 22-23). For example, have I attempted in the reading to close the gaps in the story of Jephthah and his daughter or have I simply read what is in the text? There are sufficient ambiguities in Judg. 11 for many possibilities to be considered. Even though care is required to avoid multiple and contradictory readings so as not to violate the text, it is inevitable that ambiguity in texts leads to discussions and proposals. My method is to read the text, to stay on the page and to simply offer a reading for consideration. Will my reading be regarded as plausible?

The storyteller does not provide us with sufficient information in order to visualize characters. Neither clothing nor appearance are described. Artists may have painted Samson as a giant; however, the text does not say that he is a big man, unless the comment 'when they [the Philistines] saw him, they brought thirty companions to be with him' (14.11) is an indication that his enemies are intimidated by his appearance, that is his size as well as his uncut hair. For example, in an exhibition report about Rembrandt's *The Blinding of Samson* (1636), on loan to the National Gallery, London for public display from the Stadelsches Kunstinstitut in Frankfurt, art critic Richard Cork says, 'the most thrusting element is the weapon held by the halberdier. He stands astride the foreground, pushing his thick, ugly blade towards the Jewish giant...' (cf. Richard Cork, 'The Blinding of Samson', *The Times*, London, 30 September 1997, p. 16). Characterization is conveyed by speech and actions, by what characters say and do. Heroic deeds are reported in uncluttered narratives that contain raw acts of violence. The story rests in action. Much of the power of Judges-storytelling is generated by the matter-of-factness and abruptness of violent and emotional events. The storyteller in ch. 5 (with the voice of a poet) expresses the heightened emotions of characters which we are to share. Characters in Israel's narrative life participate in a perilous business; they require hardness and determination, focus and passion, drive and control as the storyteller drives their stories forward with restless narrative energy. Events are carefully selected and organized in a structure in order to arouse the reader's attention.

What the storyteller lacks in the provision of characterization is compensated for by action as charismatic deliverers deliver in a series of heroic deeds. We are to notice the storyteller's method which is to signal to the reader when very rarely providing detail about characters and events.

In sum, the omniscient narrator is the construct of the implied author who exists in the narrative like a character. In Judges, the author has the predominant 'voice' of a storyteller. Sometimes the implied storyteller takes the role of a chronological historian when accounts are linked with 'after him' (cf. 3.31; 10.1, 3; 12.8, 11, 13) and characters are placed in geographical locations: Barak at Mount Tabor, Gideon in Jezreel, Samson in Gaza. The implied storyteller may also take the role of a theologian when making a theological comment such as the explanation for Abimelech's demise (cf. 9.24, 56) and Israel's repeated apostasy as the reason for Yahweh's anger in the repeated formulaic phrases of the framework in which heroic stories are set. The role of Yahweh's covenant lawyer may also be assumed when Israel is called to account (cf. 2.2). Rather than the work of an editor or redactor, the reading regards Judges as the literary creation of a 'storyteller' who uses the genre of hero stories in the creative setting of a story-world in order to make an account of Israel's past.

The Storyteller's Three Aims

It is necessary that literature that addresses those who encounter the hopelessness and powerlessness of exile is perceived as having an empowering and hope-giving function—rather than a message of final judgment—in a situation that would otherwise cultivate despair. As exilic listeners contend with deportation and refugee status combined with the loss of Yahweh's gift of land, the loss of their homes, the destruction of Jerusalem and the temple and living as a dominated minority among the formidable emerging powers of the ancient world, they are assured that Yahweh will again be merciful and answer Israel's cries for deliverance and homecoming.

In what can be understood as a rather dismissive statement of the book, Ailish Eves may have alighted upon a possibility for the author's unique rhetorical stance when she suggests that Judges could be advertised as a modern blockbuster novel because it is often presented as 'exciting fodder for youngsters' (Eves 2002: 128). It is therefore plausible, in my opinion, that the storyteller writes in a suitably terse and urgent style for young Israelites in exile who are weary of the restrictions of their overlords and want to break away in a bid for independence. Stories are graphically told in a style that may attract idealistic young listeners in order to warn them not to follow the examples of their ancestors but to be loyal to Yahweh and his covenant. However, Eves does not appear to be concerned with a possible rhetorical function; her comments are securely 'within the box' when she is highly critical of Israel's heroes. I propose that the storyteller has three aims.

The Storyteller's First Aim: Exilic Listeners are to Feel Ashamed of Themselves

Exiles and refugees are cautiously presented with reasons to be ashamed of themselves and of their past because successive invasions and final expulsion from the land are due to their own repeated apostasy. The storyteller is personal; this is *their* story. 'Exile' in the Hebrew Bible is the crisis of invasion followed by the further crisis of forced deportation and resettlement as a dominated conquered minority which represented a loss of status and a threat to community identity. It is difficult to describe the situation for exiles with any precision but it is reasonable to assume that the concerns of deportees themselves went beyond individual self-preservation to the maintenance of a collective sense of identity and solidarity as a powerless minority living in a powerful foreign environment. For background to Israel and the exile, see Ackroyd 1968; Klein 1979; Smith 1989; Brueggemann 1997; Smith-Christopher 1997; Mein 2001: 40-75; Holdsworth 2003.

Deportees were also groups under stress who had good reasons to be angry and disorientated due to what they had lost. Their social world had disintegrated: the nobility lost their status; priests and Levites lost the cult; community leaders lost their places in the gate; craftsmen lost their contracts; merchants lost their trade; their houses were no longer lived in and the fruit of their vineyards was consumed by others (cf. Deut. 28.30, 49-51). The prophets reminded exiles that mass deportation and their powerlessness among foreigners was a punishment for their apostasy and disobedience (Ezek. 1–12; 2 Isa., cf. Deut. 28.32, 43). Israel's apostasy occurs when giving way to the seductions of Canaanite religion.

The author is relentlessly critical of Israel and writes in the theological introduction like a prosecutor marshaling evidence to prove Israel's guilt. As the Bochim messenger says, Yahweh will not break the covenant (Judg. 2.1) and Israel is not to make a covenant with others, but Israel is forcefully accused, 'what is this you have done?' (v. 2): Israel has done evil and served the Baals and Astartes (vv. 11, 13). Israel has abandoned Yahweh (vv. 12, 13) and provoked Yahweh to anger (v. 12). Israel has not listened to their judges but lusted after other gods. Israelites have not followed what their ancestors were told (v. 17); intermarriage follows which leads to worship of their gods (3.6) and they forget Yahweh (3.7). As Aaron Wildavsky says of the Joseph stories, the great theme in Judges is fidelity: 'Hebrews are not only contaminated by foreigners, the Hebrews contaminate themselves by violating their moral law' (Wildavsky 2002: 4).

Israelites therefore live with the consequences of their own consistent apostasy (2.3): adversaries and snares keep them on their toes; they are 'given' to plunderers (spoilers) (v. 3) and 'sold' to surrounding enemies who could not be overcome (v. 14). They lose their battles (v. 15; 20.19-22, 24-25). The inhabitants remain (2.21) and are left in the land as a test and to give Israel opportunity to practise self-defence (v. 22; 3.2).

A summary charge is included: Israelites have not given up their practices or stubborn ways (2.19) but are charged with ignoring the covenant and disobeying Yahweh's voice (v. 20). It is possible that the consequences that befall Israel for covenant-breaking are not to be understood as punishments but are to be read as Yahweh's measures to win a wayward Israel back to covenant loyalty from the threat of assimilation into the inhabitants of the land.

Accusation and judgment, however, are not the final words. It is also possible that stories about heroes who fight wars of independence and bring peace are told to assist deported and refugee listeners to make sense of their past and of their present social situation by demonstrating that they have a future destiny. Such literature thrives among exiles.

The Storyteller's Second Aim: To Impress Exilic Listeners with the Honour and Ability of Judge-Deliverers

Judge-deliverers—and their collaborators—secure the means of Israel's independence. Such stories demonstrate that Yahweh will not give up on his people but will respond to Israel's cries again and again. Such literature is of necessity outrageous, bawdy and humourous in order to capture the imagination and inspire listeners of all ages as characters act with courage and panache against those who are powerful and oppressive, but are also lacking in intelligence. The storyteller writes like a historical novelist who imaginatively uses heroic stories from the past about characters who overcome oppressors—and are beckoned by Yahweh to threaten their communities—in a new creative literary structure in order to cultivate hope among those who have lost their status at home and are now exiles in a foreign land. I have noted that the narrative is relentlessly critical of Israel but the storyteller is not concerned with the alleged character faults and flaws of Israel's heroes. The narrative informs listeners about the honour of judge-deliverers and the independence they achieve for an oppressed Israel. Judge-deliverers are Yahweh's gifts to his oppressed people; they secure the means of Israel's liberation and hold out the hope of future restoration. All are characterized as robust, focused (once they are confident that Yahweh will deliver by their hand) and ruthless. Does an oppressed Israel expect their deliverers to be any different? Deliverers do not deliver the land from oppression by being considerate to Israel's enemies. It is my judgment that those who worked and reworked traditional material, whom I collectively refer to as a 'storyteller', have created a collection in which the characters of Yahweh's judge-deliverers impressed exilic listeners. Their stories are jubilantly told.

The Storyteller's Third Aim: To Remind Exilic Listeners of their Monotheistic Religion

The storyteller's third aim is not only to remind exiled Israelites of their monotheistic religion, but they are to resist the gods of the dominant imperial powers and to be aware of the new threat of assimilation into the foreign Babylonian state. Exiles are reminded of their covenant obligations to Yahweh.

As well as disintegration and the loss of independence, exile in Babylon is also understood to have been a time that was both positive and creative in which Israel's national spirit survived with a new understanding of the past. Their ancient records were collected and preserved in what is described as a 'phenomenal outburst of literary activity' (Thomas 1961: 35). The narrative is not a disinterested account but contains powerful messages and specific rhetorical purposes in order to persuade readers and listeners, form opinion, make judgments and exert change in the social world they inhabit. The storyteller cultivates exilic hope for a return home to the land.

In summary, in its final form the book provides a coherent message for powerless deported and refugee communities who are aware of the devastation of their land. Even though the religious and moral conduct of Israel is consistently abysmal, Yahweh does not give up on Israel but responds again and again in mercy to his apostate people. When Yahweh answers Israel's repeated cries as recorded in the formulaic introductions, the 'book' may be understood as the literature of hope and that final divine judgment is not the last word; Israel has a future. It is therefore plausible that listeners had mixed feelings. First, they had reason to be ashamed of how they behaved. Second, they had cause to feel cautiously hopeful for the future when Yahweh responds again and again in mercy to Israel's cries for help with the provision of deliverers who defeat those who have overrun the land at Yahweh's behest; Yahweh will respond yet again. And third, exiled Israelites are reminded of their monotheistic religion and of their covenant with Yahweh.

I understand the 'book' of Judges in its final form to be an exilic voice of hope addressed to marginalized readers/listeners who—even though they have brought oppression upon themselves—ache for a better world and cry out for their home (Ps. 137).

Evidence for the Storyteller's Three Reasons for Writing as Observed in the Stories of Jephthah and Samson

Jephthah

Jephthah's story informs exilic listeners that those who are expelled from home and live among foreigners may prosper in their country of exile and acquire honour; moreover, they may return home to take up a more desirable position to that from which they were expelled. The matter of renewing trust in Yahweh may also be an issue for exiles who feel abandoned when they are removed from the land that Yahweh has promised. Jephthah's story reminds exiles that such a return may not happen without anxiety and they may not know who they can trust, even from among their own families, elders and tribes. Exiles are not to lose heart when those who invade their land ignore their attempts at negotiation and they are to resist the temptation to give way under duress by attempting to secure the future by making vows. Furthermore, Jephthah's encounter with the Ephraimites cautions Israelites in exile to maintain their unity.

Samson

It is plausible that a major concern for exiles is the maintenance of a collective sense of identity and solidarity. It is possible that the Samson story addresses those Israelites who no longer entertain longings about the past or about a return home to the land.

The Samson story features a judge-deliverer who possesses everything required in order to deliver Israel from the Philistines. What Samson lacks is support from his own Danite tribe, the majority of whom may have moved north or are engaged elsewhere, and from the Judahites who are content to live in co-existence with the Philistines under their rule. The story warns exiles to remain loyal to Yahweh and not to be content to remain under the rule of their overlords. The story assumes that Israelites in exile may have already succumbed to the advantages (as exiles perceive them) of living in peaceful coexistence and cultural assimilation among a powerful majority and have given up any claim to the land, or the storyteller may assume that succumbing to such a temptation is a likely prospect. The proposed aims imply that a sense of shame may be an appropriate response for readers who have succumbed to such a temptation:

First, Israelites may feel ashamed when Israel yet again does evil but does not cry out to Yahweh as on other occasions.

Second, Israelites may feel ashamed that a deliverer who is commissioned and equipped with Yahweh's spirit is unsupported by Israel's tribes and, of necessity, creates his own conflict opportunities.

Third, Israelites may feel ashamed that Samson's own tribe fails to give support.

Fourth, Israelites may feel ashamed that the Judahites, who in the first chapter expel the inhabitants, now appear in force at Etam with two new ropes to betray a judge-deliverer rather than equipped with weapons to do battle under his leadership.

Fifth, Israelites may feel ashamed when Samson allows himself to be 'bound' (Judg. 15.10, 12, 13) with new ropes by the Judahites and is 'bound' again with metal chains and 'imprisoned' (vv. 21 and 25) by the Philistines which D.L. Smith-Christopher refers to as 'the harsh vocabulary of defeat' which is 'frequently associated with the Babylonian conquest' (Smith-Christopher 1997: 28-29).

Sixth, Israelites may feel ashamed that the Samson story can be no more than a 'beginning' as foretold by Yahweh's messenger (13.5) and, unlike other deliverers who are supported by Israel's militia, he is unable to go beyond his beginning when he dies alone among the 'uncircumcised'.

Seventh, Israelites may feel ashamed when they read about Samson's family collecting his body from the rubble of Dagon's house, which is not left to be shamefully buried with the 'uncircumcised', but is honourably buried in the tomb of Manoah his father (unlike the bodies of Jeroboam, king of Israel [1 Kgs 13.22], and Jehoiakim, king of Judah [Jer. 22.19; 36.30]).

Eighth, listeners may feel ashamed when they compare the cyclical stories and consider how former judge-deliverers are able to bring peace to the land with tribal support but the Samson story concludes with the Philistines, though weakened, still occupying the land that is not said to be at rest.

Ninth, listeners may feel ashamed when reading in the theological conclusion that Samson does not give up or petition Dagon, but slaughters the followers of one of the gods to whom Israelites give preference (Judg. 10.6). Exilic listeners are to resist the religion of their conquerors.

The Samson story may be unpleasant storytelling for listeners in exile who have succumbed to the temptation of living under the rule of their overlords. However, fault does not lie with Yahweh's judge-deliverer who fights Philistines at the cost of his life, but with Israelites who are content to live in peaceful co-existence with those for whom the storyteller has only contempt. Yahweh would have it otherwise.

From Oral Stories to Final Written Form

The hypothesis of the development of independent tribal hero stories and the purposes for which they are used may be traced in a discussion of stages from a proposed primitive context of oral telling, to their interim inclusions in a hero-collection followed by being placed in a history of Israel, to the final form where they are used by editors in the service of specific purposes (cf. Burney 1919: 6-11; Niditch 1997).

The narrative may be composed of raw materials which are the oral prototypes suggested by Hermann Gunkel for Genesis (1964: 41), by Robert Boling for Judges (1975: 32) and by Edward

Campbell for Ruth (1975: 18-23). Stories may have been sung or recited by 'singers of tales'—a role that Deborah beckons herself perform (5.12)—moreover, a rhythmic patterned utterance may lie beneath the surface of the Samson story which has been the subject of studies of the 'oral poet's feeling for sounds' (Fox 1978) and the 'poetic flavor' of the narrative (Kim 1993). Singers or reciters of poetic narratives may have been like the ballad singers who gloat over defeated Moabites (Num. 21.27) and those who recite mocking taunts (cf. Judg. 5.16-17, 28-30; Isa. 14.4; Mic. 2.4).

It is not my purpose to engage with sources but there are ancient settings in which stories may have been recited and thrived such as places where people met together within families, among workers in fields, at threshing floors, at court, at the well and oasis, at religious gatherings and at city gates. The purposes of such tellings by reciters, Levites and the 'wise' may have been to edify and entertain, to teach, to interpret law, customs and institutions and to tell heroic stories in which Israel's heroes, empowered by Israel's God, were able to defeat rival tribal societies, city-states and their deities.

This hypothesis of a development from ancient traditions to final form as the work of many hands is also challenged by the further hypothesis that the 'book' is the coherent work of one creative exilic writer. For example, the narratives are said to cohere so well 'because they derive solely from the hand of one writer who produced a well-crafted work...for a specific purpose— that of creating a "period of the judges"' (Guest 1998: 60). As the stories do not appear in any other form with which they may be compared, it is uncertain if (or how) they have been adapted, edited or shaped. The presence of 'gaps' may suggest omissions; editorial asides may represent inclusions; the absence of distinctive framework language in the stories may indicate their careful preservation.

What is interesting to note for the focus of my reading is that both theories of 'composition' support a positive reading of the characters of judge-deliverers. If the final form is the result of many hands working during a long pre-life, then it is to be noted that the text has not 'collected' along the way negative character evaluations. If the text is written by one creative scribe, later than is generally supposed, the scribe considered the 'book' to be complete without negative character evaluations.

The Tasks and Functions of Judge-Deliverers

Judges are not learned men and women in wigs; they do not sit in the gate and settle disputes (cf. Deut. 17.8; Ruth 4.1; 1 Sam. 4.18; 9.18); they do not decide legal cases or make general legal pronouncements. Only Deborah the prophetess, a non-combatant, resides in office. The combatant judges are neither prophets nor priests; they are not reformers, holy men or exponents of the Torah. Judge-deliverers have neither a religious nor a moral agenda. It is inappropriate to suggest that judges 'ultimately failed as religious leaders' (Olson 1998: 732); religious leadership is not their task. Dominic Crossan would appear to be correct when he identifies their limited and specific function as 'to deliver God's people from their pagan oppressors' (Crossan 1968: 149). To judge (*šāpaṭ*) in the Pentateuch is to decide matters and to dispense justice (i.e. Exod. 18), a term that could also be applied to an administrator and a governor. Judges in the book of Judges are warriors or leaders who deliver (*yāša'*) Israel from oppressors. They are little people who are called upon to accomplish great things. In just one situation (Judg. 11.27) it is Yahweh who is said to judge between two causes. The 'minor' or consecutive judges may also be office holders.

According to Max Weber, the judges of the book of Judges were charismatic warlords who fought feuds, killed oppressors, successfully led armies and were 'saviors in grave war emergencies' (Weber 1952: 18, 40, 84-85). Charismatic warriors respond in moments of national distress; they possess gifts of body and mind combined with personal strength. As the charismatic is not elected and lacks a 'divine right', his authority is retained by performing heroic deeds and establishing well-being for followers (Weber 1978: 1111-17). According to Abraham Malamat, the time was not right to give what he calls 'the charismatic attitude' a permanent form (Malamat 1976: 164; Armerding 1991).

It is Yahweh who raises up 'judges' to do acts of justice in order to restore peace to the land by delivering Israel from oppressors. Judges are therefore raised up to be 'bringers' and 'providers', 'doers' and 'restorers' of justice. Listeners are not told the form that the 'raising up' takes; they are, however, informed about their functions, which are delivering, subduing and bringing peace. The record of the number of years until their death suggests that their reputation and prestige maintains peace in the land.

Ancient listeners are informed specifically how judge-deliverers function and why Yahweh raises them up. Some are designated judge, some are deliverer, some are both, some are 'raised up', but not all. We are not told what form the 'raising up' takes. An alternative view of 'charismatic military "judges"' is that they already hold office: Ehud heads the tribute bearers like a civil servant, Deborah is a prophetess and Samson a nazirite. Other charismatic judges respond to the calls of sanctioned office holders: Barak is summoned by Deborah, Jephthah is appointed by the Gilead elders. Full stories and brief listings follow the introduction: 'then Yahweh raised up judges, who delivered them from the hand of those who plundered them' (2.16).

Yahweh's judge-deliverers function as his own judicial representatives who decide for a marginalized vulnerable Israel by restoring justice, order, right and rest to the land when they 'subdue' and 'slaughter' oppressors. Judge-deliverers are Yahweh's answers to the songs of exilic listeners in a foreign land which are uttered as cries 'of protest and longing for right and justice' to put matters right and restore peace (Zenger 1996: 64, 71, 93). They are chosen to participate in Yahweh's messy wars in the valleys of the shadow of death in response to Israel's appeal to the God who is at work in history and society to intervene and restore everything as it should be.

Success in the ancient world was measured by the accumulation of honour. Even though Shane Kirkpatrick says that the characters of 'the judges themselves are less and less appealing' (Kirkpatrick 1998: 37), his analysis of 'honour', which he says helps to shape the narratives of 'these ancient Israelite tales' (1998: 21), makes judge-deliverers look good. Honour in the ancient world was a social commodity, 'a claim to worth and the social acknowledgment of that worth' (Malina 1993: 32; Miller 1996: 105) which, as well as behaviours, includes ascribed and acquired prestige and status acquired through military conquest, accumulation of wealth from spoils and (as in the case of the judge-deliverers) divine favour. For example, Jephthah's honour is lost when he is expelled by his siblings from the family home but he is given a positive characterization when he acquires honour in a 'good land' as a mighty warrior. He is also given honour (status) by the leaders of Gilead who—when they are threatened by the Ammonites—'head-hunt' him as their 'ruler' and 'head'. Jephthah acquires more honour with his military victory over the Ammonites and takes their spoil by right and enjoys divine favour (11.29, 32).

The narrative recalls the triumphs and heroism of Israel's leaders against overwhelming odds which are 'often achieved by daring, bizarre and comic means' making exciting reading to 'enthrall and encourage the reader' (Wenham 2000: 58). Yahweh's judge-deliverers take the assertive risks that are required for task-orientated achievement.

Yahweh's spirit is mentioned seven times as a positive and task-affirming provision that prepares and equips judge-deliverers for their tasks. Judge-deliverers do not misuse Yahweh's spirit to their own ends. Yahweh's spirit is also an initiator of conflict between his judge-deliverers and Israel's oppressors. The spirit *comes upon* Othniel and Jephthah (3.10; 11.29), *clothes* Gideon (6.34), and is *available* to Samson (14.6, 19; 15.14). All three verbs suggest the spirit's irresistible energy which in each case appears to be accommodated to the tasks faced by each deliverer.

A Consideration of Criteria for the Evaluation of Judge-Deliverers

Evaluation in a narrative is a complex matter which may be broadly defined as the writer's attitude, or stance towards, and viewpoint on, what and who is being written about. The function of evaluation in texts is to inform the reader what the writer thinks or feels about something and to disclose the author's point of view (Thompson and Hunston 2000: 5).

The storyteller provides no explicit moral condemnation of judge-deliverers and it may be argued that listeners are expected to recognize their morally problematic nature. However, it may also be argued that the storyteller is not a morally indifferent writer when employing a wide vocabulary of strong verbs in sentences of unequivocal moral disapproval of apostate Israelites who serve, bow down to and follow after other gods. Moreover, they forget, abandon and provoke Yahweh to anger; they behave worse than their ancestors and do not stop their stubborn ways. None of the storyteller's verbs of disapproval that are applied to Israelites are applied to judge-deliverers and their collaborators.

Narratives provide information for listeners which signal how the narrative may be interpreted. The reader is not appealed to directly in Judges—apart from when directed to respond to the Levite's grim procession (19.30)—but the reader's acceptance of the text's evaluation is assumed. For example, when the story-teller repeatedly provides the information in the framework formulaic phrases that Israel 'does evil', it is assumed that listeners will, with the text, form a negative opinion of Israel-ites. Furthermore, when the storyteller says that Yahweh is forgotten as Israel 'whores after' other gods, listeners are being signalled with unequivocal evaluations that they are to share the text's ideology and disapprove of the conduct of Israelites as they rebel against Yahweh. Biblical authors use evaluations as a means of conveying powerful messages in order to persuade their readers and listeners, whether ancient or modern, to see things in a particular way.

The purpose of my reading is to read the text again, to inspect the stories inhabited by characters, to understand why they act as they do, to explore their reality and their choices with integr-ity and to suggest the possibilities of positive evaluations for those who deliver an oppressed Israel based on the following criteria:

1. Does the character accept Yahweh's commission or is Israel abandoned to the mercy of oppressors? Gideon is wisely cautious before engaging with those who are repeatedly characterized as formidable oppressors. The characterization of Jephthah suggests that making a vow may be read as an understandable option. A positive char-acter evaluation could not be made of a judge-deliverer who flatly refused to be raised up by Yahweh. It is, however, to be acknowledged that judge-deliverers are not presented by their storyteller as 'eager warriors' or selfish exhibitionists who are hungry for conflict opportu-nities in the pursuit of fame and recognition (Hastings 2005: xx). Judge-deliverers are cautious and careful as they do their duty.

2. Do characters risk their lives for the community? Judge-deliverers possess a 'popular morality' and a social bond of loyalty and solidarity to their oppressed tribe and fulfil a moral duty to the community to fight for independence, 'in times of war, fighting men are suddenly cherished and become celebrities' (Hastings 2005: xi). For example, Jotham reminds the Shechemites that his father, Gideon-Jerubbaal,

not only fought for them but risked his life to deliver them
(9.17), as do other judge-deliverers.

3. Does the character go beyond 'popular morality' and
   natural impulse to serve a 'higher purpose'? Judge-deliverers are raised up or commissioned by Yahweh, sometimes by others, to fulfil Yahweh's purpose which elevates
   the level of their heroism above that of many other ancient
   heroes of myth and fable. Judge-deliverers have the
   approval of their storyteller—and the approval of listeners
   sympathetic to Israel's cause—when they respond to the
   divine call, defeat oppressors and bring peace to the
   land.

4. Is the character successful? The purpose for which judge-
   deliverers are raised up is to fulfil Yahweh's agenda to deliver
   Israel from plunderers and enemies (2.16, 18); success is
   therefore measured by achieving this goal. When Gideon is
   certain, he leads his small militia. When Jephthah's negotiations fail, he acts. Samson begins or becomes the first to
   commence the deliverance of Israel from the Philistines as
   foretold by Yahweh's messenger (13.5; cf. 10.18). A positive
   character evaluation by this criterion could not be made of an
   unsuccessful judge-deliverer.

5. Does the character act in his own self-interest? A positive
   evaluation could not be made of a character who acts like
   Abimelech in his ruthless pursuit to become Shechem's
   king (9.1-2).

6. Does the character attack other Israelite tribes without
   cause? Gideon is careful to avoid conflict as he responds to
   the Ephraimites' complaint. Jephthah goes to war against
   the Ephraimites because he holds them responsible for the
   circumstances of his vow and, on their late appearance,
   they threaten to burn him and his house, apparently
   because they are deprived of Ammonite spoil. Samson,
   who may have just cause to attack those of his own people
   who betray him to the Philistines, does not harm the
   Judahites.

7. Does the character raise himself up and act independ-
   ently? Yahweh promises his presence and support; Yahweh
   gives his spirit and strength; Yahweh goes before them
   with manifestations of nature and gives their foes into
   their hands. A positive character evaluation could not be

made of a judge-deliverer who ruthlessly usurps his position as does Abimelech when he murders his rival half-brothers (9.1-6).

8. Does the character contribute to Israel's apostasy? Gideon is not to know that making an ephod will ensnare his family. A positive character evaluation could not be made of a judge-deliverer who deliberately leads Israel into apostasy which none do.

9. Is the character a tyrant? Judge-deliverers do not take advantage of Israelites when weakened by oppression, nor do they demand tribute from those they liberate. A positive character evaluation could not be made of a judge-deliverer who misuses position, power and prestige as does Abimelech who not only murders his half-brothers but also tyrannizes the inhabitants of Shechem and Thebez.

Judge-deliverers and their exploits are not referred to in the wider canonical context with either regret or criticism. For example, on the occasion when Saul is made king, Samuel says that he disapproves of Israelites in the past when they 'forgot' Yahweh who 'sold' (1 Sam. 12.9) them into the hands of enemies. However, it is with approval that Samuel reminds 'all Israel' assembled for Saul's coronation that Yahweh delivered them from their enemies by sending Jerubbaal and Bedan (an unknown character who is translated as 'Barak' in LXX and NRSV) and Jephthah and Samuel (translated as 'Samson' in NRSV; cf. 1 Sam. 12.11). When Nathan reminds King David about Yahweh's appointment of judges in the past, he does not express regret about their conduct as he does for Israel's king (2 Sam. 7.11). In anxious times, Gideon's victory over Midian is recalled to mind in Israel's liturgy without embarrassment; for example, when the author of Ps. 83 complains to Yahweh that 'those whom he treasures' (v. 4) are threatened by enemies who have 'raised their heads' (vv. 1-2), encouragement is found by recalling the stories of Yahweh's destruction of former enemies (vv. 9-12). The psalmist wants enemies to be removed by the wind, like Sisera and Jabin, like the Midianites and their nobles, Oreb, Zeeb, Zebah and Zalmunna, whose corpses rotted into the ground like dung (v. 10) because they attempted to seize the 'pastures of God' (v. 12). Israel's conduct also receives disapproval in a review of Israel's past but without negative evaluations of judge-deliverers: Israel whored after other gods (Ps. 106.39), Yahweh became angry, Yahweh gave them into the hands of other nations and they were oppressed but Yahweh delivered (vv. 40-43) Israel many times. No regret is expressed in the Levites' review of Israel's past of the conduct and methods of the 'deliverers' who Yahweh gave 'many times' to Israel to deliver them from their enemies (Neh. 9.27-28). The removal of a burden, bar and rod from 'people who walk in darkness' is said by the prophet to be as significant as Israel's deliverance 'on the day of Midian' (Isa. 9.4). Moreover, enemies will be defeated as soundly as when Gideon executed a Midianite leader at Oreb rock (cf. Isa. 10.26).

Some judge-deliverers are listed without embarrassment by the writer of the Epistle to the Hebrews in the New Testament where they are commended for their faith and daring deeds which are illustrations of their faith. The writer is obviously impressed with their stories and makes no reference to so-called 'flaws' or 'moral and religious failings'. The author applies specific positive criteria to characters which may be rendered here (as above) in the form of questions: do they conquer kingdoms? Do they administer justice? Do they receive what is promised? Do they stop the mouth of lions? Do they quench raging fire? Do they escape the edge of the sword? Are they empowered? Are they mighty in war? Do they put foreign armies to flight? According to the author, characters fulfil the criteria and more besides (Heb. 11.32-34, NRSV).

I allow that stories are wild and crude, which is part of their appeal—a sword is pushed up inside a king's stomach, a hammered tent peg secures an enemy commander's head to the floor, flesh is flayed and the dead are piled high, an upper millstone thrown from a great height finds its target—however, the storyteller does not shy away from informing us what is necessary for Israel's survival and well-being when judge-deliverers bring rest to the land by violent means. Lindars concludes that the writer of Hebrews is impressed with stories of faith, that is, faith in the sense of 'firmness, fidelity and moral perseverance' (Lindars 1983: 12). In the reading I understand 'firmness' to describe a character as steadfast, solid and determined, like Ehud when he acts with purpose with an end in view. 'Fidelity' is focused dedication, loyalty and faithfulness to a course of action and to the initiator of that course of action, such as when negotiations for peace with the Ammonites fail and Jephthah commits his future to Yahweh who will judge between them. 'Moral perseverance' describes actions that are just carried out by those whom Yahweh raises up.

Later biblical storytellers, poets, prophets and correspondents do not distance themselves from the means and methods Yahweh takes to deliver Israel. Biblical authors are not concerned with so-called 'flaws' but with character successes which are listed to inspire readers and listeners. Judge-deliverers and their collaborators are not negatively evaluated, criticized or regretted but are honoured in biblical tradition. Characters are also admired in Ben Sira's triumphant hymn:

> The judges also, with their respective names, whose hearts did not fall into idolatry and who did not turn away from the Lord, may their memory be blessed! May their bones send forth new life from where they lie, and may the names of those who have been honoured live again in their children! (Sir. 46.11-12, NRSV)

One of the difficulties with making character evaluations in Judges is that many of their actions fall outside what modern readers might expect of those who follow moral norms. A further difficulty is the silence of Yahweh, which may imply the storyteller's intention to present Yahweh's approval (or disapproval) of actions that we might consider to be amoral. For example, Yahweh does not intervene or utter disapproval when arguably morally questionable conduct is used to achieve his will, such as when Ehud deceives the Moabite king, Jael deceives an oppressor on the run, Gideon responds to the taunts from the inhabitants of two wayward cities, Jephthah sacrifices his daughter and Samson visits a prostitute. On all these occasions, Yahweh is silent. What can be said in response to these difficulties is that judge-deliverer stories are not set in biblical Israel's restful periods, characters inhabit a world of conflict resolution, their stories are set in war zones where they are pitched against those who are characterized as formidable oppressors. Bad things happen in war for the common good. Notions of right and wrong are less clear-cut when Israelites wait to be delivered, when a hero has to survive and when dominated exilic listeners have a need for heroes. Judge-deliverers function in a raw world of pain as they square up to oppressors who possess overwhelming numbers and military advantage. They engage in battles against those who are depicted as cruel and inhumane. Negotiation does not bring resolution (Judg. 11.12ff). Judge-deliverers live in an uncomfortable untidy story-world of conflict, battles and slaughter without remorse. Warfare in this story-world is about winning, not about humanity. All Israel's oppressors are villainized. Judges-stories are not the 'politically correct' accounts of the wars of gentlemen pitched against gallant enemies.

I argue for my reading that the conduct of judge-deliverers need not be viewed as 'flawed' or as 'moral and religious failings'—as the scholarly consensus maintains—in the circumstances in which they are placed, because this is what hero stories evidently regard as necessary for the removal of oppressors and to allow the land to rest.

Judge-deliverers are to be understood and evaluated like any other characters to whom tasks are given: by what they are raised up to accomplish, which is the limited military objective of bringing an end to Israel's oppression. Characters in stories who have a task-orientated agenda are to be primarily evaluated according to their success—or failure—to accomplish their tasks in the stories they inhabit. It seems to continue to be a matter of regret for scholars that judge-deliverers are not characters of genuine piety. However, it is unnecessary for them, and for those who collaborate with them, to be pious men and women. The characters in these stories do not appear to be raised up for the task of solving Israel's religious and moral problems or to bring solutions to the covenant breakdown between Yahweh and Israel. It is arguably inappropriate to evaluate them negatively on the grounds that they do not halt Israel's religious and moral decline. Even though Israelites do not 'listen' to their judges (2.17), the task of calling apostate Israelites to repentance is not their work but that of messengers (2.1-5), prophets (6.7-10) and Yahweh (10.10-14). Judge-deliverers are therefore evaluated in the reading by whether they act in Yahweh's higher purpose and in the national interest of Israel's welfare by delivering Israel and bringing peace to the land. Their stories do not unfold with regret. None act in their own self-interests like David who arranges for the demise of one of his loyal warriors in order to acquire that warrior's wife. The narrative does not seem to be concerned with a display of character faults and flaws but is focused on the honour, heroism and success of those who deliver an oppressed Israel. Their successes are jubilantly celebrated (5.11) and left raw on the page for the imagination of readers and listeners.

In sum: the storyteller employs a large vocabulary of unequivo-cally strong verbs and adjectives to convey a moral vision of Israel to readers and listeners in sentences of disapproval, none of which are applied in the narrative to judge-deliverers. A posi-tive reading of their characters therefore emerges as a credible reading and would seem to be strengthened when judge-deliv-erers are considered in the broad literary context of the canon.

Formidable Oppressors

Effective narrative use is made of contrasts as evaluation sig-nals when characterizing each invading oppressor—who oppress apostate Israelites at Yahweh's behest—as possessing fearful and powerful strategic military advantages which make them formidable foes. They oppress a marginal Israel in turn for eight (3.8), eighteen (3.14), twenty (4.3), seven (6.1), eighteen (10.8) and forty (13.1) years. Such oppressions are described as over-whelming and Yahweh's judge-deliverers are unevenly matched when raised up to engage oppressor-invaders. For example, Oth-niel faces 'Cushan the double wicked king of the "Land of Two Rivers"' (characterized like a pantomime villain). Ehud faces Moabites who are well-fed robust warriors (characterized like rugby prop-forwards). King Jabin of Canaan has 900 iron chari-ots (not unlike modern tanks in the desert). Midianites are accompanied by the Amalekites and 'Easterners'; their numbers, livestock and tents are like locusts and their camels are too many to count (a coalition of overwhelming numbers). Ammonites have the ability to crush and restrict Israelites for eighteen years, make war on Israel and intimidate the Gileadite chieftains who lack the services of a skilled commander and head-hunt an exile from the 'Goodlands'. Philistines—the storyteller's archetypal villains—who are referred to in Egyptians records as the 'Sea Peoples', intimidate the tribe of Judah and may already possess the monopoly of metal-working (cf. 1 Sam. 13.19-22).

Israelites are at a military disadvantage when facing such a formidable collection of well-equipped invaders. Israelites use primitive weapons, which, when not homemade, include farm tools and domestic implements. A theme emerges. When Israel-ites engage in conflict with formidable oppressors, they impro-vise. Ehud makes his own blade. Shamgar adapts an agricultural tool used for prodding wayward oxen. Jael uses a hammer and a tent peg. Gideon uses pots, torches and trumpets. Samson uses a dog's dinner, a bone! Israelites are clever. Formidable oppressors are a pushover. They can be easily defeated. When exiles sit down by the rivers of Babylon, they may weep tears of laughter as they hear how easy it is to defeat oppressors and how easy it will be to defeat future oppressors when they return to the land (Ps. 137).

Although I am uncertain what made ancient Israelites laugh, stories seem to contain wit, satire, humour and comedic input which mocks formidable oppressors who are to be laughed at rather than feared (cf. Exod. 10.2). The technical term is *ethnocentrism*, which nourishes the superiority of one's own group with stories and boasts while viewing others with contempt as outsiders (Sumner 1907: 13; Davies 1990: 308). One such epithet is reference to Philistines as the 'uncircumcised' (Judg. 14.3; 15.18). Judge-deliverers are clever; Israel's enemies are daft. Even though a nasty reputation is suggested by his fearsome name, Cushan is easily defeated by Othniel, the hero of Debir. Moabites are characterized as fat, overweight simpletons; they are well fed like their king who is closeted at the top of their national food chain (3.17, 29); Moabites also need to be 'strengthened' by Yahweh with the assistance of Ammonites and Amalekites in order to take just one Israelite city (3.12-13) and their king is no more than a fatted calf awaiting slaughter. For example, Lowell Handy says that the story of Ehud and Eglon is 'gruesome' and 'grotesquely comic' and is told in the genre of an 'ethnic joke' which is insulting to Moabites and incites laughter or at least 'a smile of superiority' from readers and listeners (Handy 1992: 233-34). Moreover, 'the Ehud story was intended to leave the hearers laughing and slapping their thighs' (Lindars 1983: 11). According to Ferdinand Deist, the Ehud story is not included with the 'aim of rationally convincing the opponent, but with the express aim of publicly shaming him out of his socks, that is, by making him the laughing stock of bystanders' (Deist 1996: 269). Ehud is the clever Israelite who outwits stupid Moabites (1996: 243). Philistines are characterized as a 'goofy group of partying fools' (Handy 1992: 243) who are unable to answer Samson's riddle without resort to threat; they are killed by Samson the lone Israelite armed with a mandible (15.15); Gaza's city gates are picked up and carried away like a bundle of fire wood (16.3). When Philistines attempt to humiliate Samson their tormentor by disabling him, blnding him and giving him the work of women and prisoners of war, they foolishly release him into their own crowded temple where he is able to take his vengeance (16.23-30).

There does not appear to be any concern in the text that ethnic humour may be considered unsuitable humour. In certain contexts ethnic humour in rhyme, song or story is a release for those who live with threat of imminent invasion and others who subsist in exile. In war, those who are perceived as the enemy are caricatured, especially plunderers who plunder (2.14, 16), who press and shove (2.18), who enslave (3.14), press with force of arms (4.3); invaders whose strength prevails so that Israelites are forced to hide in highland caves (6.2), who ruin the land and its produce (vv. 4, 5), who destroy (10.8; cf. Exod. 15.6 describing Yahweh's destruction of the Egyptians), crush (10.8) and squeeze (2.15; 10.9).

In summary, judges in the book of Judges do not appear to have a judicial task. The association of 'judge' (*šāpaṭ*) with deliverance (*yāša*) shows that they have the task of ridding the land of those to whom Israel has been 'given' or 'sold' by Yahweh as Yahweh's means to win his wayward people back to covenant loyalty from apostasy. A consideration of the formidable characterization of oppressors demonstrates the honour and heroism of judge-deliverers, and of Barak and Jael who are their collaborators. Characters who inhabit stories that may have originated in a distant oral past—where certain moral standards may have been in view—are not corrected; their stories have not acquired negative comments and their methods are not reported with the addition of regret or apology. Actions that may be evaluated as reprehensible in peacetime may be evaluated by the criteria above as appropriate in war; in these stories, judge-deliverers are at war. Characters are to be evaluated in their practical situations rather than by the application of a morality appropriate to a later non-threatened comfortable readership.

Women and Children in Judges

Countless unnamed women and children are treated badly in Judges, very badly. Women become victims in the closing chapters: a Levite's unnamed concubine is pushed out into the night to be gang-raped and murdered. The identity of 'the man' who seizes the concubine (19.25) is unclear. He may be either the Levite or the host; his identity may also be ambiguous. My reading of ch. 19 identifies the host as the one who seizes her and puts her out into the night because it is he who opens his door and reprimands those who I refer to as 'yobs' (cf. Stuart 2001: 51-52). Her body is butchered into pieces and paraded around the land; we are not told if she receives an honourable burial. 600 females are required for the surviving Benjaminite males in order to secure the tribe's future: 400 girls are selected from Jabesh-Gilead after their families are slaughtered (which I consider to be genocide) and 200 female dancers are pounced upon and seized from the Shiloh vineyards. There are also, as implied in other biblical narratives, countless bereaved voiceless women in the shadows mourning their men (sons, husbands and fathers) who are killed when Israel goes to war.

Some of Israel's women (and women who act in Israel's interests) are proactive; their actions are robust and their stories are driven forward with narrative pace and energy. Israel's women are in the right place at the right time; they fight back, their sleeves are rolled up, they are ready. They have power, they have a voice, they assert themselves, they are formidable, they demand our attention. Israel's women are given voices and most are named. For example, Achsah—who has been used by her father and presented to his warriors as a possible trophy wife—demands a dowry of two choice water supplies. Deborah commissions a militia commander and informs him when the time is right to attack. Jael seizes her opportunity. An unnamed woman—who is careful not to leave her upper millstone at home when she runs for safety to a tower—has only a small walk-on–walk-off part but she has fifteen minutes of fame when she makes an accurate throw and rids Israel of a tyrant. Jephthah's daughter controls her own future. Mrs Manoah (Samson's mother) calms her husband about the visit of Yahweh's messenger and the news he brings. Micah's mother—who, in just four verses, is called six times 'his mother'—sponsors her son and grandson in business as shrine proprietor and priest.

In contrast to Israel's women who enter the fray, Canaanite women are high maintenance delicate females with fluffy temperaments who stay at home. You may object and think of me as an insecure male who makes an insensitive sexist comment, but let's be real, these women are Canaanites and Canaanites—when reading from the storyteller's point of view—are the enemy. Moreover, no self-respecting ancient storyteller would say anything 'politically correct' about women who belong among Israel's oppressors. Consider, for example, Sisera's mother—the anxious curtain twitcher—who waits safely at home and longs for the return of her son with spoils of clothing for her wardrobe, but not before he and his men have raped a few Israelite women. Consider Samson's wife and the woman he loves (if Delilah is a Philistine) who whine, nag and pester the poor man for information. Canaanite females lack honour.

The Structure of Judges

Judges may be divided into the following main sections:

1. Prelude (ch. 1): episodes about Israel's limited success and failure to take the land, concluding with Israelites living in co-existence with the inhabitants. Like the account in Joshua, the conquest is only partial when Israelites fail to occupy all the land.
2. Theology (2.1–3.6): a theological introduction and a description of Israel's apostasy which is told against Israel from Yahweh's point of view. Following a severe reprimand from Yahweh's messenger, Israel's behaviour is described and evaluated as 'evil' when Israelites fail to keep their oath of loyalty to Yahweh and to the covenant (Josh. 24). Israelites abandon Yahweh in favour of local Canaanite deities. Yahweh 'sees' everything, burns with anger and becomes threatening, intimidating and violent towards Israel. Powerful nations are not merely 'allowed'—in the natural order of things—to oppress an apostate Israel. Oppressive nations have the status of commissioned agents when the storyteller explains that Yahweh 'sells' and 'gives' Israel into the hands of others. Israel's oppressions are Yahweh-sponsored.
3. The central narratives (3.7–16.31): an account of Yahweh's methods to win wayward Israelites back from apostasy by a combination of oppression followed by deliverance by judge-deliverers. The stories of Israel's heroes appear in a new context enclosed in a 'framework' of 'formulaic phrases': Israel sins; Israel is handed over to an oppressor; Israel cries to Yahweh; Yahweh raises up a deliverer; the oppressor is defeated; the land rests. Hero stories are set in a cyclical theological context: Israel's apostasy brings the response of oppression at Yahweh's behest in order to win his wayward people back to covenant loyalty; Yahweh responds to Israel's cries for deliverance by raising up 'judges' who rescue Israel. A second category are the

'consecutive judges'—officials who decide disputes between individual Israelites (cf. Exod. 18.13-26), and appear in two short listings in (Judg. 10.1-5) and 12.7-15 and are linked by the phrase 'after him'. Jephthah features in both categories, in a brief listing, 'Jephthah judged Israel for six years, then Jephthah the Gileadite died and was buried in the town(s) of Gilead' (12.7) and in his own deliverer story (10.6–12.6) which begins with the familiar framework of the longer stories and the words, 'Israel again did what was evil' (10.6).

4. The story of 'Micah & Sons' and the relocation of the desperate tribe of Dan (chs. 17–18).

5. Hospitality in Bethlehem and Gibeah (ch. 19), followed by civil war between Israel's united tribes and wayward Benjaminites (chs. 20–21).

The stories in chs. 17–18 appear to be part of the earlier conquest traditions of the individual tribes and may be relocated in ch. 1 (perhaps after v. 34) to explain what the Danites do to secure a safe home when they are forced into the hills by the Amorites. The Micah stories combined with the Danite discovery of Laish, the slaughter of its inhabitants and its burning, rebuilding and renaming as 'Dan' completes this tribe's settlement activities and gives the land its geographical northern extent (Dan to Beer-sheba, 20.1; 1 Sam. 3.20). Even though it is uncertain how the stories in the concluding chapters (19–21) may also fit into Israel's conquest traditions, the loss of 25,000 Benjaminite warriors in a civil war from which just 600 survive may account for this tribe's inability to expel the Jebusites from Jerusalem (1.21).

It is reasonable to suppose that the longer stories of the conquest account are placed in an epilogue or appendix so that they do not detract from the brief listings of partial success and failure of Israelites to settle in their allotted tribal areas or from the two stories of Othniel who represents the older conquest generation.

The main structural concern for chs. 17–21 is not about chronology as with the central narratives but becomes thematic when the stories of the Danite settlement are placed after the story of the judge from Dan who judges Israel for twenty years. The repeated monarchical refrain—in its longer form: 'In those days there was no king in Israel; all the people did what was right in their own eyes' (17:6; 21.25); and in its shorter form, 'In those days there was no king in Israel' (18:1; 19.1)—gives chs. 17–21 a unified structure that contrasts with the formulaic structure of the central narratives. Two characters in the closing chapters associate events at the beginning (rather than at the end) of Judges with the third generation of Israelites after the exodus (Amit 1999: 311-12): Jonathan (the grandson of Moses, 18.30) and Phinehas (the grandson of Aaron, 20.27). Chs. 17–18 and 19–21 feature unnamed Levites as central characters (may they be the same character?) who are both associated with Bethlehem. It is also interesting to note—or it may just be a coincidence— that Delilah receives 1,100 pieces of silver from each of the five Philistine lords and that Micah's mother also has savings of 1,100 pieces of silver. Furthermore, it is claimed by those who see decline and deterioration as a theme of the final form of Judges that chs. 19-21 demonstrate that Israel's 'deterioration is complete' and 'terror reigns on all sides' (McCann 2002: 117); the lack of a king in the closing chapters 'sums up the continual slide of the people into social and political anarchy' (Matthews 2004: 202).

Reading Strategies and Proposals for the Modern Relevance of Judges

My proposal that the storyteller wrote initially for exiles does not imply that Judges is only relevant for ancient fifth century (BCE) readers and listeners. Judges is timeless and may speak powerfully to modern readers who face the daunting tasks and problems that are thrown up in the modern world. In order to understand what is happening in the story—who is doing what to whom and why—I have adopted reading strategies that are similar to those of Jacqueline Lapsley in order to be drawn 'into the story as a participant, as opposed to occupying a position outside the story' (Lapsley 2005: 12). A reading strategy is a means of assisting a reader's engagement with narrative in order to go beyond merely understanding and to consider the text's relevance in the modern world.

The first reading strategy is to *accept the text*. I put to one side objections to what may be considered offensive and I attempt to read without prejudice.

Rather than reading from a 'safe distance' and impose on the text a morality of disapproval from modern times, my second reading strategy is to allow my imagination to *step into* what I read and to *enter* this dangerous ancient story-world. My method here is to take a reader's risk, to be less suspicious and to trust the storyteller. I acknowledge that such a risk may carry consequences: will the storyteller always be trustworthy? Will I always agree? Might I face the dilemma of disagreeing with what I consider to be the plain meaning of the text?

A third proposed reading strategy is to read alongside the characters of judge-deliverers, their collaborators and others in order to *sympathize* and *empathize* with them as they accept and carry through formidable challenges. This is a strategy that encounters characters in order to consider with the eye of readerly imagination (from within the story-world) the personal cost of what they achieve in the storyteller's harsh story-world of conflict resolution. I hope that I am cautious here and that I do not abuse the text with the addition of my own prejudicial interpretation.

My fourth reading strategy is to read with *caution*. Judges may appropriately be described as a threatening text in which Yahweh, the God of Israel, solves problems by violent means. As I have read, reread and translated the text from Hebrew I have continued to ask myself: what does this text have to say to me and to modern readers who face the tasks, problems and threats of the modern world? A discussion of modern relevance needs, in my view, to focus principally on the matter of conflict resolution by the use of force. As a biblical interpreter, I struggle with texts which—whether regarded by scholars as history or as later ideological constructions of the past—contain divine approval of the slaughter of individuals and families as a means to an end. I am not a pacifist, but in my opinion it is immoral for the use of force to be considered a justifiable means of furthering a cause, unless it is used nobly—by liberators or by the oppressed themselves— in a bid for freedom, liberation, independence and peace or as basic elements of our lives for the eternal purposes of 'defence and security' (Smith 2006: 9). Cautious readers of the Old Testament will be aware that the storyteller does not encourage *us* to resolve *our* conflicts by violent means. Moreover, Yahweh's instructions to take land, which is already occupied by others, by force of arms and to annihilate the inhabitants by *ḥērem*, were only applied at a specific time and in a specific situation in the distant past. The 'weapons' of conflict resolution in the modern world are those of 'analysis' (Smith 2006: 373-77), negotiation, diplomacy, personal courage, political will and risky peace processes which take 'time to engage local communities and to build bridges' (McTernan 2003: 157-64). The meanings of stories change and become subversive if powerful people appropriate the methods of violent biblical characters to 'justify their own aggression' (Dyksta 2002: 144). However, while it may be tempting for modern readers who live in comfortable situations to dismiss the methods of judge-deliverers as raw and harsh, it is to be acknowledged that Judges is also read in situations where readers face the stark oppressors and oppressions of the modern world, and conflict resolution by violent means may have an appeal as the option of last resort.

My proposal for the relevance of the text for modern readers is this: if judge-deliverers in their ancient biblical setting—acting alone and against the odds in a terrifying story-world—can overcome oppressors and oppression, then so too may you and I overcome the oppressions of the modern world that threaten to overwhelm, such as terrorism, prejudice, racism, poverty, homelessness, fear of crime (both real and imagined), abuse, debt, violence and much more. Consider, for example, the extraordinary account of the Balkan horrors of ethnic civil war in which journalist Anthony Loyd observes the power of the human will which is able to withstand and carry the final victory against the unequal and disproportionate might of armies equipped with machines (Loyd 2002: 260). Judge-deliverers—and their collaborators who participate in their cause—succeed, with Yahweh's help, against overwhelming odds. These are stories about ordinary people who cope and survive in extraordinary circumstances in a world that is not right; their mission is to make it so. Judge-deliverers are not infallible, but they do succeed; even Samson makes his 'beginning' (13.5). In Judges, we discover characters who have needs, emotions and frailties, as we do ourselves. They are people like us who also have to cope with the human condition and we may *empathize* with them. Their stories can feed our lives as we *encounter* them on the page. The storyteller demonstrates how judge-deliverers cope in crisis and trial and still remain human. Judges stories are crisis stories. Conflicts are raw and robust; they are neither clean nor antiseptic. Of course there is a wide gap between their time and ours, their culture and ours, their circumstances and ours, but we also share much in common. Consider the following:

- Some of our problems, though formidable, are reasonably straightforward to overcome, such as when Othniel dismisses a 'world-class oppressor'.
- Other problems you have to face alone because they are your responsibility; you cannot run away. You have to think carefully, decide strategy, make plans, prepare equipment, evaluate your strengths, identify your weaknesses and the weakness of the problem and then, like Ehud, make your move.
- You may wake up one morning to a threatening presence which was not there the day before. You are alone. You think quickly. Like Shamgar, you improvise with what little resources you have to hand. You win the day and you are celebrated in verse for your courage and ingenuity (3.31; cf. 5.6).
- Some problems and tasks may be so formidable and overwhelming that they cannot be handled alone. You are like Barak who needs the wise counsel and support of others. When you engage the problem, head on (as does Barak), it is only to find that what caused the problem in the first place is solved unexpectedly by another, by Jael, who possesses little in the way of resources when she happens to be in the right place at the right time and improvises with what is to hand. You are the member of a team and all team members play their part.
- Sometimes 'the buck stops' with you, and, like Gideon, you cannot run away; you have to face overwhelming opposition with your limited resources and experience. You are forced into absurd choices such as when Gideon subjects Yahweh to water tests and Yahweh responds (absurdly) by doing the same! Then you find that the solution is straightforward; you've cracked it, you are declared a hero and you have fifteen minutes of fame on your hands.
- At other times, an untidy mess is solved by the act of a lone anonymous individual which is as lucky as the throw from a great height of an upper millstone, the ancient domestic equivalent of a modern rolling pin! Victims are often heard to complain, with very good reason, outside our law courts that justice has not been done; protests are made to hungry news reporters because someone has got

away with it! Yet the Abimelech story (ch. 9) contains Yahweh's satisfying retribution to gladden a victim's heart. When retribution comes to this usurper-tyrant you realize that there is a God and that the world is not such a bad place after all.

- You may feel alone and isolated as you face the insurmountable; you do not know who your friends are, you do not know who you can trust and, like Jephthah, under duress you make promises that go against you. As a consequence, you are also faced with threats from jealous colleagues; you decide not to suffer fools gladly and you have no alternative but to act decisively.

- You may be like Samson and lack support and back-up of friends and colleagues like Dan and Judah. You have to engage with an overwhelming oppressive opposition on your own and in your own way as you see it. You have to make the best of it while spectators (3,000 Judahites)—who should know better and be supportive—watch, hoping you will fail.

When biblical characters are read, not as miracle workers who are *different* to us but as typical humans like ourselves, their stories speak powerfully into our own times.

Conclusion

We are in the hands of an ancient storyteller-raconteur who does not disown Israel's heroes but collects their stories from scattered folklore and carefully combines them with theological language into a chronological order to say something that is new and creative. The storyteller, who does not always show his hand, addresses Israelite exiles who have lost everything that gave them identity: the land, the city of David, the temple and their own homes. Judges is the cautious literature of hope which explains why all has been lost. Judges tells the story of wayward Israelites prior to the monarchy who are no longer able—or willing—to expel the inhabitants from the land; they have forgotten Yahweh who delivered them from Egypt and show a preference for local gods. Successive stories are told about how Yahweh uses oppressive methods to win Israelites back to covenant loyalty. The storyteller is not coy when presenting Yahweh as a God who uses the means of intimidation and violence to win his people from their devotion to foreign deities; moreover, the narratives 'are not embarrassed by what is necessary for survival and well-being' (Brueggemann 1986: 43). The storyteller warns ancient readers and listeners not to copy their ancestors but to remain faithful to Yahweh and to his covenant. Not only will they have a future in the land but they will be able to defeat their future enemies as easily as do these heroes in these stories. Readers and listeners are to be warned that just as Yahweh has acted as an initiator of oppression to win his wayward people back from apostasy to covenant loyalty, it may not be unknown in the future for Yahweh to be an oppressor by similar means.

The storyteller's aims for writing are proposed as follows. First, exiled Israelites are to be ashamed of themselves and of their past because their oppressions and expulsion from the land are due to Israel's repeated apostasy. Second, exiled Israelites may be impressed with the abilities and successes of judge-deliverers who secure the means of Israel's independence in hero stories which form a literature of hope and demonstrate that Yahweh will not give up on Israel. Third, exiled Israelites are reminded of their monotheistic religion; they are to be loyal to Yahweh and their covenant and are not to become assimilated into the people of the land. The focus of the reading is concerned with the second proposed aim.

Judge-deliverers (Othniel, Ehud, Shamgar, Deborah, Gideon, Jephthah and Samson) are Yahweh's gifts to oppressed Israelites. They are raised up by Yahweh to free them from oppressors to whom they have been 'sold' or 'given' by Yahweh. Moreover, they and those who collaborate with them (Barak and Jael) do not participate in, or contribute to, Israel's apostasy, but may be evaluated positively by the criteria listed above. It is to be noted that none of the negative evaluations that the storyteller applies to Israelites in general are applied to those individuals who deliver Israel. That heroes are thought 'problematic' is not due to a storyteller's characterization but due to the problems characters face as their stories unfold. All are heroic. All possess status and honour. Initial uncertainty or a judge-deliverer's hesitancy is due to the characterization of the formidable oppressors they encounter in a raw story-world of conflict resolution by violent means.

Bibliography

Ackerman, Susan, *Warrior, Dancer, Seductress, Queen: Women in Judges and Biblical Israel* (New York: Doubleday, 1998).

Ackroyd, Peter R., *Exile and Restoration: A Study of Hebrew Thought of the Sixth Century BC* (London: SCM Press, 1968).

Ahlström, Gösta W., *The History of Ancient Palestine from the Palaeolithic Period to Alexander's Conquest* (ed. Diana Edelman; JSOTSup, 146; Sheffield: Sheffield Academic Press, 1993).

Alter, Robert, *The Art of Biblical Narrative* (London: Allen & Unwin, 1981).

Amit, Yairah, *The Book of Judges: The Art of Editing* (trans. Jonathan Chipman; Leiden: Brill, 1999).

—, *Reading Biblical Narratives: Literary Criticism and the Hebrew Bible* (trans. Yael Lotan; Minneapolis, MN: Fortress Press, 2001).

Armerding, Carl Edwin, 'Judges', in *The New International Bible Commentary with the New International Bible* (ed. F.F. Bruce; Grand Rapids, MI: Zondervan, 1979), pp. 309-39.

—, 'A Charismatic Theology of the Judges', in *Gott lieben und Seine Gebote hatten: In Memoriam Klaus Bockmühl* (eds. Markus Bockmüehl and Helmut Burkhardt; Basel: Brunnen Verlag, 1991), pp. 9-20.

Auld, A., Graeme, *Joshua, Judges and Ruth,* (DSBS; Louisville, KY: Westminster John Knox Press, 1984).

Bar-Efrat, Shimon, *Narrative Art in the Bible* (trans. Dorothea Shefer-Vanson; Sheffield: Almond Press, 1989).

Barton, John, *Understanding Old Testament Ethics: Approaches and Explorations* (Louisville, KY: Westminster John Knox Press, 2003).

Bledstein, Adrien Janis, 'Is Judges a Woman's Satire on Men who Play God?', in *A Feminist Companion to Judges* (ed. Athalya Brenner; Sheffield: Sheffield Academic Press, 1993), pp. 34-54.

Block, Daniel I., 'Deborah among the Judges: The Perspective of the Hebrew Historian', in *Faith, Tradition and History: Old Testament Historiography in its Near Eastern Context* (eds. A.R. Millard *et al.*; Winona Lake, IN: Eisenbrauns, 1994), pp. 229-53.

—, *Judges, Ruth,* (NAC; Nashville, TN: Broadman & Holman, 1999).

Bluedorn, Wolfgang, *Yahweh versus Baalism: A Theological Reading of the Gideon-Abimelech Narrative* (JSOTSup, 329; Sheffield: Sheffield Academic Press, 2001).

Boling, Robert G., '"In Those Days There Was No King in Israel"', in *A Light Unto My Path: Old Testament Studies in Honor of Jacob M. Myers* (eds. Howard Bream *et al.*; Philadelphia, PA: Temple University, 1974), pp. 33-48.

—, *Judges: A New Translation with Introduction and Commentary* (AB; New York: Doubleday, 1975).

Brensinger, Terry L., *Judges* (Scottdale, PA: Herald Press, 1999).

Brettler, Marc, 'The Book of Judges: Literature as Politics', *JBL* (1989), 108: 395-418.

—, *The Book of Judges* (London: Routledge, 2002).

Brown, Cheryl A., 'Judges', in J. Gordon Harris, Cheryl A. Brown and Michael S. Moore, *Joshua, Judges, Ruth* (NIBC; Peabody, MA: Hendrickson, 2000), pp. 121-289.

Brueggemann, Walter, *Revelation and Violence: A Study in Contextualization* (The 1986 Père Marquette Theology Lecture; Milwaukee, WI: Marquette University Press, 1986).

—, *Cadences of Home: Preaching Among Exiles* (Louisville, KY: Westminster John Knox Press, 1997).

Burney, C.F., *The Book of Judges with Introduction and Notes* (London: Rivingtons, 1918).

—, *Israel's Settlement in Canaan: The Biblical Tradition and its Historical Background* (The Schweich Lectures 1917; London: British Academy, 1919).

Campbell, Antony F., and Mark A. O'Brien *Unfolding the Deuteronomistic History: Origins, Upgrades, Present Text* (Minneapolis, MN: Fortress Press, 2000).

Campbell, Edward F., *Ruth: A New Translation with Introduction and Commentary* (AB; New York: Doubleday, 1975).

Cartledge, Tony W., *Vows in the Hebrew Bible and the Ancient Near East* (JSOTSup, 147; Sheffield: Sheffield Academic Press, 1992).

Crossan, Dominic M., 'Judges' in *The Jerome Biblical Commentary* (eds. R.E. Brown *et al.*; London: Geoffrey Chapman, 1968), pp. 149-62.

Cundall, Arthur E., 'Judges: An Introduction and Commentary', in Arthur E. Cundall and Leon Morris, *Judges and Ruth* (London: Tyndale Press, 1968), pp. 7-215.

Davies, Christie, *Ethnic Humor Around the World: A Comparative Analysis* (Bloomington, IN: Indiana University Press, 1990).

Davis, Dale Ralph, *Judges: Such a Great Salvation* (Fearn, Ross-shire: Christian Focus, 2000).

Deist, Ferdinand, '"Murder in the Toilet" (Judges 3.12-30: Translation and Transformation), *Sc* 58 (1996): 263-72.

Dumbrell, W.J., '"In those Days there Was No King in Israel; Every Man Did what Was Right in his Own Eyes": The Purpose of the Book of Judges Reconsidered', in *The Historical Books: A Sheffield Reader* (ed. J. Cheryl Exum; Sheffield: Sheffield Academic Press, 1997), pp. 72-82.

Dykstra, Laurel A., *Set Them Free: The Other Side of Exodus* (Maryknoll, NY: Orbis, 2002).

Eves, Ailish Ferguson, 'Judges', in *The IVP Women's Bible Commentary* (eds. Catherine Clark Kroeger and Mary J. Evans; Downers Grove, IL: Inter Varsity Press, 2002), pp. 128-46.

Exum, J. Cheryl, *Signs and Wonders: Biblical Texts in Literary Form* (SBL Semeia Studies; Atlanta, GA: Scholars Press, 1989).

—, 'The Centre Cannot Hold: Thematic and Textual Instabilities in Judges', *CBQ* 52 (1990): 410-31.

—, *Fragmented Women: Feminist (Sub)versions of Biblical Narratives* (JSOTSup, 163; Sheffield: Sheffield Academic Press, 1993).

—, 'Feminist Criticism: Whose Interests are Being Served?' in *Judges and Method: New Approaches in Biblical Studies* (ed. Gale A. Yee; Minneapolis, MN: Fortress Press, 1995), pp. 65-90.

—, *Plotted, Shot, and Painted: Cultural Representations of Biblical Women* (JSOTSup, 215; Sheffield: Sheffield Academic Press, 1996).

—, *Tragedy and Biblical Narrative: Arrows of the Almighty* (Cambridge: Cambridge University Press, 1996).

Fausset, Andrew R., *A Critical and Expository Commentary on the Book of Judges* (London: James Nisbet, 1885).

Fewell, Danna Nolan, 'Judges', in *Woman's Bible Commentary: Expanded Edition* (eds. Carol A. Newsom and Sharon H. Ringe; Louisville, KY: Westminster/John Knox Press, 1998), pp. 73-83.

Fokkelman, Jan P., *Reading Biblical Narrative: An Introductory Narrative* (trans. Ineke Smit; Louisville, KY: Westminster John Knox, 1999).

Fox, Everett, 'The Samson Cycle in an Oral Setting', *AlEth* 72 (1978): 101-07.

Fretheim, Terence E., *Deuteronomic History* (Nashville, TN: Abingdon Press, 1983).

Gooding, D.W., 'The Composition of the Book of Judges', *ErIsr* 16 (1982): 70-79.

Goslinga, C.J., *Joshua, Judges, Ruth* (trans. Ray Togtman; BSC; Grand Rapids, MI: Zondervan, 1986).

Gray, John, *Joshua, Judges and Ruth* (NCB; London: Nelson, 1967).

Guest, P. Deryn, 'Can Judges Survive Sources?: Challenging the Consensus', *JSOT* 78 (1998): 43-61.

Gunkel, Hermann, *The Legends of Genesis: The Biblical Saga and History* (trans. W.H. Carruth; New York: Schocken, 1964).

Gunn, David M., *Judges* (BBC; Oxford: Blackwell, 2005).

Gunn, David M., and Danan Nolan Fewell, *Narrative in the Hebrew Bible* (Oxford: Oxford University Press, 1993).

Handy, Lowell K., 'Uneasy Laughter: Ehud and Eglon as Ethnic Humor', *SJT* 6 (1992): 233-46.

Hastings, Max, *Warriors: Extraordinary Tales from the Battlefield* (London: HarperCollins, 2005).

Heard, R., Christopher, *Dynamics of Diselection: Ambiguity in Genesis 12-36 and Ethnic Boundaries in Post-Exilic Judah* (Atlanta, GA: SBL, 2001).

Holdsworth, John, *Dwelling in a Strange Land: Exile in the Bible and in the Church* (Norwich: Canterbury Press, 2003).

Josipovici, Gabriel, *The Book of God: A Response to the Bible* (New Haven, CT: Yale University Press, 1988).

Kim, Jichan, *Structure of the Samson Cycle* (Kampen: Kok Pharos, 1993).

King, Philip J., and Lawrence E. Stager, *Life in Biblical Israel* (Louisville, KY: Westminster John Knox Press, 2001).

Kirkpatrick, Shane, 'Questions of Honour in the Book of Judges', *Ko* 10 (1998): 19-40.

Klein, Lillian R., *The Triumph of Irony in the Book of Judges* (JSOT-Sup, 68; Sheffield: Sheffield Academic Press, 1989).

Klein, Ralph W., *Israel in Exile: A Theological Interpretation* (Minneapolis, MN: Fortress Press, 1979).

Lapsley, Jacqueline E., *Whispering the Word: Hearing Women's Stories in the Old Testament* (Louisville, KY: Westminster John Knox Press, 2005).

Levenson, Jon D., *The Death and Resurrection of the Beloved Son: The Transformation of Child Sacrifice in Judaism and Christianity* (New Haven, CT: Yale University Press, 1993).

Lias, J.J., *The Book of Judges with Map, Notes and Introduction* (CBSC; Cambridge: Cambridge University Press, 1902).

Licht, Jacob, *Storytelling in the Bible* (Jerusalem: Magnes Press, Hebrew University, 1978).

Lilley, J.P.U., 'A Literary Appreciation of the Book of Judges', *TynBul* 18 (1967): 94-102.

Lindars, Barnabas, *Interpreting Judges Today* (The Ethel M. Wood Lecture; London: University of London, 1983).

—, *Judges, 1-5: A New Translation and Commentary* (ed. A.D.H. Mayes; Edinburgh: T. & T. Clark, 1995).

Loyd, Anthony, *My War Gone By, I Miss It So* (London: Black Swan, 2002).

Malamat, Abraham, 'Charismatic Leadership in the Book of Judges', in *Magnalia Dei, The Mighty Acts of God: Essays on the Bible and Archaeology in Memory of G. Ernest Wright* (eds. Frank Moore Cross *et al.*; New York: Doubleday, 1976), pp. 152-68.

Malina, Bruce J., *The New Testament World: Insights from Cultural Anthropology* (Louisville, KY: Westminster John Knox Press, 1993).

Martin, James D., *The Book of Judges* (CBC; Cambridge: Cambridge University Press, 1975).

Mayes, A.D.H., *Israel in the Period of the Judges* (London: SCM, 1974).

—, *The Story of Israel Between Settlement and Exile: A Redactional Study of the Deuteronomistic History* (London: SCM, 1983).

—, *Judges* (OTG; Sheffield: Sheffield Academic Press, 1989).

McCann, J., Clinton, *Judges* (Interpretation; Louisville, KY: John Knox Press, 2002).

McKenzie, John L., *The World of the Judges* (London: Geoffrey Chapman, 1966).

McTernan, Oliver, *Violence in God's Name: Religion in an Age of Conflict* (London: Darton, Longman & Todd, 2003).

Matthews, Victor H., *Judges & Ruth* (NCBC; Cambridge: Cambridge University Press, 2004).

Mein, Andrew, *Ezekiel and the Ethics of Exile* (Oxford: Oxford University Press, 2001), pp. 40-75.

Miller, Geoffrey P., 'Verbal Feud in the Hebrew Bible: Judges 3.12-30 and 19-21', *JNES* 55 (1996): 105-17.

Milton, John, [undated], 'Samson Agonistes: A Dramatic Poem', in *The Poetical Works of John Milton* (Lansdowne Poets; London: Frederick Warne), pp. 428-76.

Mobley, Gregory, *The Empty Men: The Heroic Tradition of Ancient Israel* (New York: Doubleday, 2005).

Moore, George F., *A Critical and Exegetical Commentary on Judges* (ICC; Edinburgh: T. & T. Clark, 1895).

Niditch, Susan, *Underdogs and Tricksters: A Prelude to Biblical Folklore* (San Francisco, CA: Harper & Row, 1987).

—, *War in the Hebrew Bible: A Study in the Ethics of Violence* (Oxford: Oxford University Press, 1993).

—, *Oral World and Written Word* (London: SPCK, 1997).

Noth, Martin, *The History of Israel* (trans. P.R. Ackroyd; London: A. & C. Black, 1958).

—, *The Deuteronomistic History* (trans. Jane Doull, revised by John Barton, Michael D. Rutter and D.R. Ap-Thomas; JSOTSup, 15; Sheffield: Sheffield Academic Press, 1981).

O'Connell, Robert H., *The Rhetoric of the Book of Judges* (Leiden: Brill, 1996).

Olson, Dennis T., 'The Book of Judges: Introduction, Commentary and Reflections', *NIB* II (1998), pp. 721-888.

Parker, Simon B., *Stories in Scripture and Inscriptions: Comparative Studies on Narratives in Northwest Semitic Inscriptions and the Hebrew Bible* (Oxford: Oxford University Press, 1997).

Pedersen, Johannes, *Israel: Its Life and Culture*, I-II (trans. A. Moller and A.I. Fausbell; London: Oxford University Press, 1926).

Petersen, John, *Reading Women's Stories: Female Characters in the Hebrew Bible* (Minneapolis, MN: Augsburg Fortress, 2004).

Polzin, Robert, *Moses and the Deuteronomist: A Literary Study of the Deuteronomic History* (New York: Seabury Press, 1980).

Pressler, Carolyn, *Joshua, Judges and Ruth* (Louisville, KY: Westminster John Knox Press, 2002).

Ryan, Roger, 'Letter 7: Samson to Delilah (Judges 13-16)', in *Yours Faithfully: Virtual Letters from the Bible* (ed. Philip R. Davies; London: Equinox, 2004), pp. 45-49.

Sandars, N.K., *The Epic of Gilgamesh: An English Version with an Introduction* (Penguin Classics; London: Penguin, 1960).

Schneider, Tammi, *Judges* (Collegeville, MN: Liturgical Press, 2000).

Slotki, Judah J., 'Judges: Introduction and Commentary', in *Joshua and Judges: Hebrew Text and English Translation with Introduction and Commentary* (ed. A. Cohen; SBB; London: Soncino Press, 1982), pp. 152-318.

Smith, Daniel L., *The Religion of the Landless: The Social Context of the Babylonian Exile* (Bloomington, IN: Meyer Stone, 1989).

Smith-Christopher, Daniel L., 'Reassessing the Historical and Sociological Impact of the Babylonian Exile (597/598-539 BCE)', in *Exile: Old Testament, Jewish and Christian Concepts* (ed. James M. Scott; JSJSup, 56; Leiden: Brill, 1997), pp. 7-36.

—, *A Biblical Theology of Exile* (Minneapolis, MN: Fortress Press, 2002).

Smith, Rupert, *The Utility of Force: The Art of War in the Modern World* (London: Penguin, 2006).

Soggin, J., Alberto, *When the Judges Ruled* (London: Lutterworth, 1965).

—, *Judges: A Commentary* (OTL; London: SCM, 1987).

Stuart, Douglas, *Old Testament Exegesis: A Handbook for Students and Pastors* (Louisville, KY: Westminster John Knox Press, 2001).

Sumner, William Graham, *Folkways* (Boston, MA: Ginn, 1907).

Tanner, J., Paul, 'The Gideon Narrative as the Focal Point of Judges', *BSac* 149 (1992): 146-61.

Thomas, D., Winton, 'The Sixth Century BC: A Creative Epoch in the History of Israel', *JSS* 6 (1961): 33-46.

Thompson, Geoff, and Susan Hunston, 'Evaluation: An Introduction', in *Evaluation in Text: Authorial Stance and the Construction of Discourse* (eds. Susan Hunston and Geoff Thompson; Oxford: Oxford University Press, 2000), pp. 1-27.

Trible, Phyllis, *Texts of Terror: Literary-Feminist Readings of Biblical Narratives* (Philadelphia, PA: Fortress Press, 1984).

von Rad, Gerhard, *Old Testament Theology* (trans. D.M.G Stalker; 2 vols., Edinburgh: Oliver & Boyd, 1962).

—, *God at Work in Israel* (trans. John H. Marks; Nashville, TN: Abingdon, 1980).

Webb, Barry G., *The Book of the Judges: An Integrated Reading* (JSOT-Sup, 46; Sheffield: Sheffield Academic Press, 1987).

—, 'Judges', in *New Bible Commentary 21st Century Edition* (eds D.A. Carson *et al.*; Leicester: Inter-Varsity press, 1994), pp. 261-86.

—, 'A Serious Reading of the Samson Story', *RTR* 54 (1995): 110-20.

Weber, Max, *Ancient Judaism* (trans. Hans H. Gerth and Don Martindale; New York: Macmillian, 1952).

—, *Economy and Society: An Outline of Interpretive Sociology* (trans. Ephraim Fischott *et al.*; eds. Guenther Roth and Claus Wittich; Berkeley, CA: University of California Press, 1978).

Wellhausen, Julius, *Prolegomena to the History of Israel* (trans. J. Sutherland Black and Allan Menzies; Edinburgh: A. & C. Black, 1885).

Wenham, Gordon J., *Story as Torah: Reading the Old Testament Ethically* (Edinburgh: T. & T. Clark, 2000).

Wilcock, Michael, *The Message of Judges* (Leicester: Inter-Varsity Press, 1992).

Wildavsky, Aaron, *Assimilation versus Separation: Joseph the Administrator and the Politics of Religion in Biblical Israel* (New Brunswick, NJ: Transaction, 2002).

Wolff, Hans Walter, 'The Kerygma of the Deuteronomic Historical Work', in Walter Brueggemann and Hans Walter Wolff, *The Vitality of Old Testament Traditions* (trans. Frederick C. Prussner; Louisville, KY: John Knox Press, 1975), pp. 83-100.

Wood, Leon, *Distressing Days of the Judges* (Grand Rapids, MI: Zondervan, 1975).

Yadin, Yigael, *The Art of Warfare in Biblical Lands in the Light of Archaeological Discovery* (London: Weidenfeld & Nicolson, 1963).

Younger, K. Lawson, *Judges/Ruth* (NIVAC; Grand Rapids, MI: Zondervan, 2002).

Zenger, Erich, *A God of Vengeance? Understanding the Psalms of Divine Wrath* (trans. Linda M. Maloney; Louisville, KY: Westminster/John Knox Press, 1996).

A longer bibliography for *Judges* is to be found in my doctoral thesis in the Bodleian Library, Oxford entitled, 'A Positive Reading of Judge-Deliverers in the Book of Judges: Challenging the Consensus' (2005).

Index of Authors

Printed in the United Kingdom
by Lightning Source UK Ltd.
126140UK00001B/133-150/A